Learning

The Essentials for Getting Started with Computers

Taken from:

Learning Computer Concepts: A Fundamental Understanding of Technology, Computer Applications, and The Internet
by Shelley O'Hara

ACKNOWLEDGEMENTS

Thanks to Chris Katsaropoulos for inviting me to do this project and providing indispensable guidance in the conception, organization, and execution of this project. I appreciate the constructive input from the reviewer, Ana Solomon. Her comments and clarifications greatly improved the book. Working with Jennifer Frew as the project manager and main traffic controller for the manuscript is a dream. Thanks, Jen. Finally, a hearty thanks to Mr. John Visaggi, President of DDC, for selecting this book for and writing the entertaining brochure.

To St. Jude for prayers answered.

Shelley O'Hara

Managing Editor	**Acquisition Editor**	**Education Reviewer**	**English Editor**
Jennifer Frew	Chris Katsaropoulos	Ana Solomon	Kristen Cassereau

Contributing Authors	**Design & Layout**	**Illustrations**	**Simulation Designer**
Jason Helmick	Amy Capuano	Karl Schwartz	Jeff Grisenthwaite
Ana Solomon	Su Y Chen		
Gregg Tennefoss	Elsa Johannesson		

PEARSON EDUCATION
75 Arlington Street, Suite 300, Boston, MA 02116
A Pearson Education Company

Contents

INTRODUCTION

You may not think of it, but you are living during a time of revolution. Just like the Industrial Revolution changed how people worked and lived, the computer revolution is doing the same. Personal computers weren't even sold until the start of the 1980s. Now they are in businesses and homes across the world.

Computers affect every area of our lives, and they will continue to do so in existing and new ways. Computers have also changed how we work. This applies not just to the equipment we use (typewriters vs. computers, memos vs. e-mail), but also to work style. Consider these other elements:

- The introduction of the computer has made flexible work situations possible. More people can telecommute (work from home). Small businesses are booming.
- Workers have more ways to stay in touch: e-mail, pagers, cell phones, faxes.
- Portable computers, including notebooks or handheld (palm) devices, let you take your work with you.
- The Internet has opened an entire world of opportunity for promoting services and selling goods.

Computers and Work

No matter what industry you work in now or wish to work in sometime in the future, you can find some common tasks that are aided by computers. Here are some of the common tasks that a computer can help you manage:

- *Write.* You can jot notes about a project or idea. You can also use your computer to create documents—reports, term papers, manuscripts, letters, proposals, memos, outlines, and more.
- *Communicate.* You have several means of communicating with a computer, including via fax (if you have a fax modem) or through e-mail.
- *Manage contacts.* You can keep track of friends, clients, customers, and business associates using contact management software and your computer.
- *Manage money.* You can track expenses, tally income, plan for taxes, and more using your computer and a spreadsheet program or a specialized program like Quicken.
- *Plan and manage your schedule.* You can enter meetings, classes, and to-do items on a schedule, keeping track of not only the date and time, but also the results of activities.
- *Plan and manage a project with a variety of schedules and deadlines.* You can keep track of key project dates and plan the entire timeline for a project.

Having an understanding of computers, therefore, becomes imperative to most kinds of success. To start, you need to know what a computer is and the basics of how it operates. Then you need some background information about computer programs, what kinds there are, and what they are used for. Computers and the Internet are so intertwined that to use the Internet you need to understand not only the computer, but you also need to understand Internet concepts, such as Web browsing and electronic mail (e-mail). The goal of this book is to provide you with this information so that you are well versed in all the main computer concepts.

What This Book Contains

The book is divided into 3 parts, each devoted to a particular area of computing. You'll find these parts:

- **Part I,** *Hardware,* starts with an explanation of computers and how they are put to use. This part also includes lessons on the hardware, or physical, components of a computer, including the processor, memory, keyboard, mouse, printer, modem, and drives.
- **Part II,** *Software,* focuses on the programs you use on the computer. These programs are what make the computer such a versatile tool. Starting with the system software (called operating system), this part also covers word processing, spreadsheets, databases, graphics, presentations and publishing, and programming.
- **Part III,** *Communication,* explains how you can expand a single PC to a world of PCs and covers both Internet basics and networking.

How This Book Helps You

This book contains several features to help you master the key concepts of computing. In particular, you'll find these elements:

- *Short, concise lessons.* Each lesson has several clearly defined objectives and focuses on a single topic. Figures illustrate key concepts, and the ending summary helps you to review what you've learned.
- *Up-to-date content.* The book covers the latest technology and programs so that you are well prepared as you further your education or get ready for the job market.
- *Web sites.* The Internet has expanded the ways we get information. To provide additional resources, you can visit any of the highlighted Web sites.
- *Helpful tips.* Each lesson also includes tips, how-to advice, troubleshooting information, or interesting asides that add another layer of knowledge.

LESSON 1: DEFINING A COMPUTER

Objectives

➢ **Review the history of computing**

➢ **Define a computer**

➢ **Describe the parts of a computer**

➢ **Understand the differences among computers**

➢ **List the types of computers**

The Evolution of a Personal Computer

A hobbyist named Edward Roberts built the first personal computer. A picture of his Altair homemade computer appeared on the cover of *Popular Mechanics* and excited budding computer enthusiasts everywhere. Roberts formed a company (MITS) and sold the first PC for $397. It came as a mail-order kit; you had to put it together. The system boasted 1K of memory, a processor with speed up to 2MHz, and didn't have a monitor or keyboard. You could flip switches and make lights blink. That was 1975, more than 30 years ago.

Figure 1.1. The Altair 8800 computer

When IBM entered the picture and started selling its first personal computer (1981), the personal computer became a little easier to use. A standard computer had 64K of RAM, two 5¼" floppy drives, a monitor (monochrome), and a keyboard. These computers cost anywhere from $3,000 and higher. Computers did not have sound cards or mice (at least not IBM PCs), and DOS was the main operating system. This was just 24 years ago.

Before hard disks: The hard disk was a novelty. Before hard disks, programs came on floppy disks, and you had to swap disks in and out to use the program and save your data. A hard disk was not standard equipment.

Let's jump ahead to the year 2004, where a typical computer system has 256M or more of RAM, a 40+G hard drive, 17" monitor, modem, sound card and speakers, and speeds up to 3GHz. And computer technology continues to evolve and at this quick speed. New technology is constantly being introduced to the market to make computers faster, more reliable, more affordable, and more user-friendly. Let's take a look at the components that make up a typical computer.

What is a Computer?

A computer is an appliance. What makes it different than other appliances, say like a refrigerator, is that there's not one single use for a computer. It's a versatile tool that can be used for many tasks.

WHAT CAN YOU DO WITH A COMPUTER?

Consider just some of the things you can do with a computer:

- *Create documents.* You can use your computer to create any number of documents: letters, memos, newsletters, brochures, presentations, budgets, income and profit statements, invitations, greeting cards, stationery, invoices, order forms, recipes, term papers, grading lists, phone lists, grocery lists, reports, manuscripts, illustrations, photographs, blueprints, design plans, advertisements, and many, many other types of documents. Document creation is probably the most common use for a computer. Creating documents is covered in Lesson 6 of this book.

- *Manage data.* Computers simplify the entry, update, and maintenance of data. This may be anything from a simple address book to a complex data order system including products, inventory, orders, and customers. Any collection of information (class schedule, student list, product inventory, video collection, etc.) can best be managed with a computer. Chapter 8 covers using this type of program.

- *Connect to the Internet.* The Internet is a network of networks, and you can connect to this resource and send electronic message (e-mail), chat with other people, display Web sites (information presented in a graphic format so that it is inviting, easy to browse, and linked to related information), participate in discussions, and more. For more information on connecting to the Internet, see Lesson 12.

- *Play games.* You can use computers to have fun, whether that be playing an arcade game like pinball or a card game like Solitaire. You might enjoy role-playing games, or you might fancy flight simulators. You can find games for just about any activity.

- *Get information.* The computer can also be a resource for information. You might use a computer encyclopedia to research data or look up articles and maps in an atlas. In addition to resources in programs or CDs, you can also find a wealth of information on the Internet, including current news, stock prices, articles, tips and advice, job hunting resources, homework help, and more.

- *Learn a new skill.* You can use a computer to learn how to type or learn a foreign language. You can find educational software geared toward children, teaching a child to read, for instance, as well as software geared for adults.

- *Shopping.* Use of the Internet for commerce and shopping is changing the retail sales marketplace. You can search for any type of item, purchase it, and have it delivered to your home. You can comparison shop and make sure you get the best deal.

WHAT BENEFITS DO YOU GET FROM COMPUTERS?

Computers can be used for many types of tasks, and they offer some specific benefits over the paper method for accomplishing these tasks. In general, a computer offers these benefits:

- *Error-free calculations.* A computer has incredible computing power. Not only can it quickly compute calculations, but it will not make a mistake when doing so. Whether calculating the total of a company's sales or computing precise measurements for an entire building, a computer simplifies any type of calculation.

- *Speed.* Not only does the computer not make mistakes, but it can perform computations in milliseconds, much quicker than a blink of an eye. It can also perform several tasks at once.

- *Flexibility.* A computer is flexible because it can be used for a variety of tasks. And a computer provides you a great deal of flexibility in working with the data you enter. As an example, consider an address list. With a computer, you can easily sort the list in any order. You can delete entries you no longer need and add new entries. You can quickly find a particular entry, and you can update an entry to keep the information current. The computer provides flexibility and versatility in working with the data you enter.

- *Expandability.* A computer also enables you to expand its current components by adding new features such as better sound, TV reception, a network, and more.

- *Storage.* A computer can store information digitally. One computer can store entire filing systems of paper data. Saving space is one benefit, but you can also find and retrieve data quickly from a computer.

- *Consistency and repetition.* A computer can handle repetitive tasks easily, accurately, and quickly. It won't get bored or distracted. It will provide the same quality on the first task as on the ten thousandth.

How a Computer Works

The great thing about a computer is that you don't really have to know how it works to use a computer. You don't know what makes a car work, do you? Many beginning users are intimidated by computers because they don't know how it works, and they think they will break it. Not true.

You don't need to know complex programming information to use a computer. You do not need mechanical information about how the components inside work. You simply have to understand a few key concepts of computing.

Two things work together to make a computer: the hardware and the software, as described in this section.

 Understand binary information. A computer is basically a collection of electronic circuits, and these circuits can be on or off (open or closed). The two states of the circuit are represented by two digits, 0 and 1. Hence you may hear the term binary system when referring to a computer. It may seem impossible to take two states and use it to effect, but by combining bits (0 or 1), you can represent any character or number.

HARDWARE

Hardware consists of the physical components that make up a computer. Most common systems have a monitor (the TV-like thing), a keyboard (which you type on), a mouse (for selecting items), and a system unit (see Figure 1.1). The system unit is the box, and inside this box is where you find the electronic wizardry like the CPU and memory. You'll read more about the system unit and other hardware components later in this chapter.

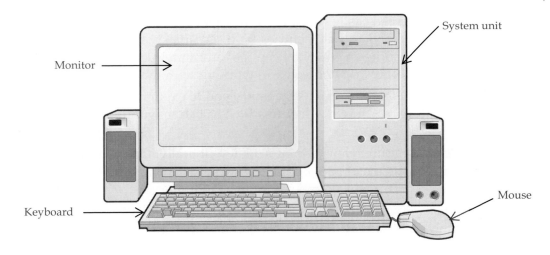

Figure 1.1. A computer system consists of a system unit, monitor, keyboard, and mouse.

SOFTWARE

The hardware can't do much without software. Software is a set of programming instructions that you use to accomplish a certain task. When referring to software, you may hear the terms program, application, software, or any combination of these terms (software application, for instance). They all mean the same thing.

Programs are designed for different purposes. For example, a word processing program is designed to facilitate creating documents (letters, memos, reports, and so on). A spreadsheet program used to create worksheets, such as budgets, expense records, and other documents dealing mostly with some type of numeric value. A database program is used to store, edit, and manipulate data, such as an address list or a schedule of classes. There are many other types of software for different functions as well. For instance, system software runs the computer, and antivirus software guards against virus contamination.

When dealing with software, keep these main concepts in mind:

- All computers come with an operating system, a special type of software described in the next section.
- New computers may also come bundled with application software. The programs that are provided will vary from system to system.
- You can purchase new programs and install them onto your computer. When you install a program, you copy the necessary program files from the program disks (from a CD) to your hard drive. You also set up access to these programs. For Windows systems, you add the program to your Start menu and/or create a shortcut icon to the program.
- Just as you can install programs, you can also delete them. When you do so, you remove the program files, and you will then not be able to run this program from your computer.
- Programs vary in price from free (called freeware) to expensive. You might spend thousands of dollars on a custom program. Most retail programs range in price from $25 up to several hundred dollars. The more sophisticated the program, the higher the price.
- Periodically new versions of programs are offered with new features. When you have an older version of a program, you may upgrade to the newer version. Usually an upgrade is not as expensive as buying the program new.
- A common practice now is to bundle commonly used programs together into a suite of programs. As an example, you can purchase Microsoft Office, which includes the most commonly used programs (a word processing program, spreadsheet program, presentation program, database, and mail program).
- For more information on the specific types of programs, refer to Lessons 6 through 11 of this book. These lessons each deal with the most common types of programs.

OPERATING SYSTEM

All computers require an operating system to work. New computers come with an operating system. You can also upgrade the operating system on your computer.

The operating system handles common tasks of using a computer, including starting the computer, starting a program, printing a document, and storing a file. The operating system takes your commands and translates them into language that the hardware can understand. As an example, you select the Save command to save a document; the operating system then handles the process of actually writing the document to a disk and also keeping track of where it is stored.

The most popular operating system is Microsoft Windows. Windows XP Home is the most common computer for home-computers. Windows XP also has a Professional edition that provides features for businesses and other more advanced users.

If you have a Macintosh computer, your computer will use the Macintosh operating system; the most current edition is called Mac OS X Panther.

 WEB: Get information on the latest versions of Microsoft Windows at www.microsoft.com/windows. For information on Macintosh products and its operating system, see www.apple.com.

You can read more about Windows and other popular operating systems in Lesson 5.

Hardware Defined

As mentioned, most computer systems consist of these key hardware components:

- The system unit
- The monitor
- The keyboard
- The mouse

This section briefly describes each of these elements. The next several lessons go into more detail on each of these components.

OUTSIDE THE SYSTEM UNIT: POWER BUTTONS AND DRIVE ACCESS

The system unit is the box-like item that usually sits on your desktop or stands on the floor. All of the other components are connected to the system unit via cables. Also, the system unit has a power plug, which you plug into an electrical outlet.

If you take a look at the outside of the system unit, you see buttons for turning on and resetting the computer as well as slots. These slots provide access to the drives on your system; you can access your floppy drive, CD or DVD drive, and any other drives you may have, such as a ZIP drive or tape backup drive (see Figure 1.2).

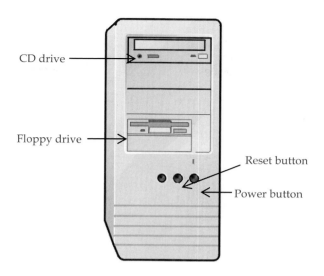

Figure 1.2. The front of the system unit has access to your floppy drive and CD drive.

In addition to these drives, most computers have at least one hard drive inside the system unit. (The next section describes this drive.) Drives provide a place to store programs and data. The floppy drives are used mostly to transport and backup files. For instance, you can copy a document onto a floppy disk from work to take home. Newer computers do not come with a floppy drive, but instead use CD discs for storing data. (You learn more about different drive types in Lesson 3.) You can select a floppy drive as part of a computer, and you might do this if you often share files or have used floppy disks to store information.

CD and DVD drives are used to store programs and collections of information. Most programs are distributed on a CD disc. You can also find collections of information (such as an encyclopedia or collection of clip art) on CDs. You can insert the CD into the drive, and then run the programs on the CD, access the information, and copy files from the CD, as needed.

 Read and write: Initially most CD-ROM drives were for reading information only; they could be used to access information and copy that information, but you could not write information to them (save a document to a CD for instance). Now most CDs allow both reading and writing. You can read more about different CDs in Lesson 4.

INSIDE THE SYSTEM UNIT: CPU, MEMORY, AND DRIVES

Inside the system unit is where the most important components of a computer are stored. These are stored in a case because they are sensitive electrical components that you don't need to handle. You'll find the CPU or central processing unit, memory, drives, and other electronic components inside the system unit (see Figure 1.3).

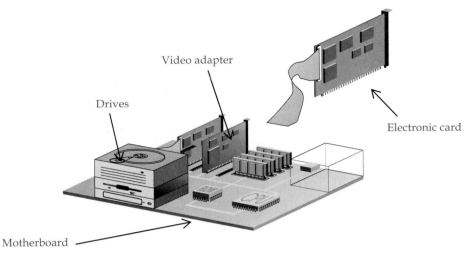

Figure 1.3. The inside of the system unit stores the motherboard, drives, and other electronic cards.

The brain of a computer is called the CPU or central processing unit or simply processor. This is a small wafer-size chip; you've probably heard of the most common chip maker (Intel). You can learn all about the different processor types in the next lesson. For now, just understand that the processor is stored on the motherboard inside the system unit, and the processor determines the speed and power of your computer. Figure 1.4 shows an illustration of a motherboard.

 WEB: Visit the site for Intel (www.intel.com) to get the latest information on Intel's processors. Another popular company that makes processors is AMD. You can visit their site at www.amd.com.

Figure 1.4. The motherboard houses the processor and memory; other components are connected to the motherboard via cables.

The motherboard is the main electronic board inside the system unit, and all the devices for a computer are connected to this motherboard (see Figure 1.4). In addition to the processor, the motherboard also houses the memory. These are also electronic chips. Lesson 2 covers memory in more detail. Memory is the temporary storage place for programs and documents that are open, that is, those you are currently working on. Systems vary in the type and amount of memory.

 Add memory: A common system upgrade is to add more memory. You can find more information on types of memory and how it affects system performance in Lesson 2.

You gain access to some drives from the front of the PC, but the drives themselves are housed inside the system unit. In addition to a floppy drive and CD or DVD drive, most computers have at least one hard drive. This is the primary storage space for programs and data. Some systems have more than one hard drive. All drives are connected to the motherboard via a cable.

The motherboard includes slots into which you insert electronic cards (also called add-on card, expansion card or board, adapter card, or interface card). These cards expand the capabilities of your system. Here are some examples of expansion cards:

- *Video card.* For your PC computer to display programs and data, you need a monitor (for the actual display) and a video card. The video card handles the communication from the processor to the monitor. This card is plugged into the motherboard and has a port, which you can access from the back of the system unit. You connect the card to the monitor via a cable.

- *Modem card.* Modems are used to communicate via the telephone with other computers (most commonly, the Internet). While you can purchase external modems, most modems are internal devices, electronic cards inserted into an expansion slot in your computer. Part of the card is accessible from the back of the system unit. You can plug your phone line into the phone jack on this accessible part of the card.

- *Sound card and speakers.* To play sound on a PC, you need a sound card and speakers. A sound card is plugged into an expansion slot. Speakers are hooked up through the part of the card that fits through the back of the system unit.

The system unit also includes a power supply, which provides the power to these electronic components. You don't have to mess too much with a power supply, but one thing you should do is be sure you have some type of power protector to handle electrical spikes or power surges. To protect your PC from these, consider using a surge protector to protect against power spikes. Businesses may take this protection one step further and use an uninterruptible power supply (UPS). A UPS runs your PC from a battery, which is continually recharged by the electrical outlet. This type of power supply protects against power outages. A UPS is often used with a network server.

INPUT: KEYBOARD AND MOUSE

You need a way to communicate with your computer and you usually do that with two input devices: a keyboard and a mouse. A keyboard is pretty simple to understand (see Figure 1.5). You press the letters or numbers on the keyboard. You type not only to enter text but also to select commands, such as Save, Print, or Exit. There are other input devices, such as a light pen.

Figure 1.5. A keyboard includes numbers, letters, symbols, and other special keys.

When computers were initially introduced, the interface (what you saw and how you used them) was text- or command-based. You had to type commands to get the computer to do what you wanted. The operating system Microsoft Windows changed all that. Windows and Windows programs use a graphical user interface (called a GUI and pronounced "gooey"). Instead of typing commands, you can point to what you want. To enable pointing, a mouse was established as a standard component on a computer. A mouse is a pointing device, and you use it to select commands and data, start programs, and perform other tasks. Figure 1.6 shows an illustration of a mouse. Lesson 3 covers keyboards and mice in more detail.

 Macintosh sets standard: Macintosh computers have always had a graphical user interface and included a mouse. Windows, in fact, imitated the Macintosh.

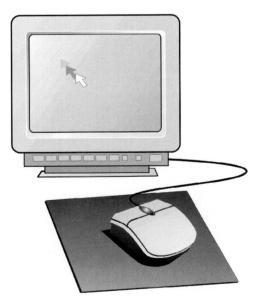

Figure 1.6. You use the mouse as a pointing device to select commands and text.

OUTPUT: MONITORS AND PRINTERS

Believe it or not, the first computer did not have a display. It was a box with a series of lights and switches on the front. You programmed the computer by flipping switches, and you could tell what was happening by the flashing of the lights. Of course, a display or monitor was soon added and is now an integral part of a computer. The monitor screen displays programs, error messages, and results of your input from the keyboard and/or mouse.

A monitor is actually two components: the TV-like thing and the electronic card housed inside the system unit. You may hear this card referred to as a graphics adapter or video adapter. You can find out all the important details of a monitor in Lesson 2.

To make paper copies of the documents you create, you need a printer. The printer is connected to the PC via a cable. You can read more about printers in Lesson 3.

What Makes a Computer Different

Now that you know what pieces and parts make up a computer, you may wonder how can they be so different? Why does one computer cost $500 and another $3,000? This section describes some of the ways that computers differ.

SYSTEM TYPE

The two most common types of computers are IBM and compatibles (often referred to generically as PCs) and Macintosh computers. The first mainstream PC was created by IBM, but other companies immediately began making the same computer. These were called clones or IBM-compatibles. While IBM may have initially dominated the personal computing market, it no longer does. Now the market is shared by companies such as Dell, Hewlett-Packard, Gateway, and others. Most computers sold today are PCs.

 WEB: Visit some computer sites such as Dell (www.dell.com) or Gateway (www.gateway.com). Look at the resources they provide for computer buyers as well as current computer users.

At the dawn of the computing era, another company offered a different type of computer, one that did not look like the original PCs and did not have any clones. This type of computer is called Macintosh and was created by a company called Apple. Macintosh computers still have a small share of the entire personal computing market. These computers are especially popular in graphics-intensive fields such as desktop publishing, illustrations, and other publishing fields. (Apple has become the big player in the field of digital music; you can find out more about this topic in Lesson 11.)

PCs and Macs don't differ in how they work or what you can do with them. They differ in the operating system. PCs, as mentioned, most often run Microsoft Windows. Macs use an operating system called System. It used to be that you could not open PC files on a Macintosh and vice versa, but the two have become more compatible and some systems may be able to read both Mac or PC disks.

POWER AND SPEED

If you price new computers, you'll find they vary in price even though two models may look exactly the same. Why? Because computers can vary in their processing power and speed.

Speed is determined by several factors including the type of processor, amount of memory, and other technical elements. Power is also determined by the processor. You can get a better understanding of speed and power by reading the next lesson on processors and memory.

ADD-ONS

Computers also vary in the other types of components they include. For instance, a computer may include a modem (for connecting to the Internet), sound card and speakers, and special drives such as CD or DVD drives. As a component becomes popular, it usually becomes a standard part of a PC. For instance, initially computers were not sold with modems, CD drives, or sound cards. You could purchase and add these components. Because a modem, sound card, and CD or DVD drive are so integral to computer use now, most new computers are sold with them as part of the standard package.

Newer add-ons include a digital camera, video or cable connections, scanners, and special game ports and devices (joystick or flight yoke for instance). You can learn more about these features in later lessons in this book.

SIZE

Another way computers differ is in size. Desktop computers fit on your desktop and are the most common system type sold. For portable computers, you can purchase notebook or palmtop computers. You can read more about the different types of systems in the next section.

Types of Computers

One way computers vary, as mentioned, is size, and you will encounter many different types of computers, as described in this section.

PERSONAL OR MICROCOMPUTERS

Most homes and businesses have personal computers, also called PCs or microcomputers. In this category, you may find models that sit on your desktop and are oriented horizontally (see Figure 1.7). Or you can find tower models that sit on the floor and are oriented upright (or vertically).

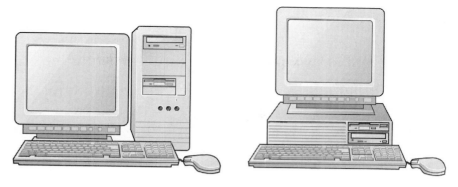

Figure 1.7. Desktop and tower PCs are the most popular today.

PORTABLE COMPUTERS

Many people travel or work outside an office. For these people, portable computers are very popular. This type of computer runs on batteries and can be carried with you. Portable computers encompass a variety of computer types, which vary by size. Here are the most common types:

- *Notebook.* As its name implies, notebook computers are roughly the size of a notebook. They differ in size and weight. The keyboard and display are connected, the keyboard is smaller, and the notebook may use a special pointing device such as trackball. This type of computer may also be called a laptop (see Figure 1.8).

- *PowerBook and iBook.* This are the names of the most popular Macintosh portables.

Figure 1.8. Notebook PCs are portable, weighing anywhere from 5 to 10 pounds.

 Smaller is not cheaper: Just because a notebook computer is smaller does not mean it is less expensive. In fact, this type of computer costs more than a comparable desktop model. Why? The components used are more expensive.

- *PDAs (personal digital assistants)*. This type of computer is a handheld device and is often used in conjunction with a desktop or other PC. For instance, you might use a PDA to keep track of appointments and notes. You can then download (copy) the information from your PDA to your desktop or notebook computer. This device may have a special keyboard; some use a pen or stylus for entering data. You may also hear this type of computer called a palmtop. Figure 1.9 shows a PDA.

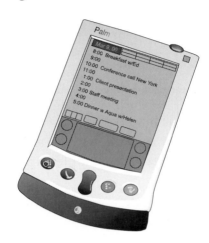

Figure 1.9. PDAs are useful for special-purpose applications, such as for keeping track of appointments or notes.

 Phone, e-mail, and fax: Many PDAs include capabilities that let it function as a cell phone, pager, fax, or even scanner. You may also be able to send and receive e-mail. This type of PDA uses infrared light to communicate with other computer systems.

 Cell phones. Many cell phones are also integrating other features such as the ability to take pictures, download weather or other information from the Internet, and store information.

NETWORKS

To share information and programs, computers can be linked together into a network. Networks that are housed in a small geographic area (such as within one office) are called LANs (local area networks). These may be connected via cabling or telephone wires. Networks that span a wide geographic area (perhaps across several sites, even states) are called WANs (wide area networks). Wireless networking has also become very popular. Rather than connect the computer via cabling, you can set up a wireless hub that can communicate without being physically connected, but instead through wireless transmission. You can find more about the different types of networks in Lesson 15.

The main computer of a network is called the server. This computer is the most powerful, houses common programs and data files, and may provide access to shared devices, such as a network printer. The server also stores the network operating system that controls access to the programs, files, and devices on the network. Computers connected to the server are called clients.

WORKSTATIONS

A more powerful type of desktop or PC may be referred to as a workstation. Popular workstation manufacturers include Sun, IBM, Silicon Graphics, and Hewlett-Packard. These computers are a step up from a microcomputer but not quite as powerful as a minicomputer. They are commonly used by professionals whose jobs require a lot of computation power, including engineers, scientists, and graphic artists.

MINI AND MAINFRAMES

A mainframe is a large computer that is capable of processing large amounts of data very quickly. A minicomputer is similar to a mainframe, only it cannot handle as much data. Both provide data capabilities for storage and handling beyond those of a desktop PC.

You can find mini and mainframe computers in government and business. For instance, the IRS has a mainframe for tax information. Your state driver's license branch houses its information on a mainframe. University computers are often mainframes. Banks, science labs, insurance companies, and other large businesses use mainframes.

Other computers, called terminals, are networked to the mainframe or minicomputer. You can gain access to the information on the mainframe or minicomputer through these terminals.

SUPERCOMPUTERS

The biggest and most expensive computer is called a supercomputer, and it exponentially expands the speed, power, and storage capacity of even mainframe computers. You'll find these computers in high-tech areas, such as the military, nuclear weapons, space programs, weather forecasting, and similar fields.

Buying a Computer

If you are thinking of buying a computer, you need to do a little preparatory work to ensure you get a computer that best matches your needs and at the best deal.

Follow these steps to research buying a computer:

1   Make a list of what tasks you want to do with your computer. The biggest mistake when purchasing a computer is buying a computer for price. The first factor has to be your needs. You should have a clear idea of what you want to use the computer for.

2   Make a list of the features you need. You can use the list of uses to help determine the features. Do you need a sound card? Modem? Special monitor? What kind of printer? What applications do you need?

3   Investigate places that sell computers. You can purchase computers through computer or electronic superstores, online, or even through office supply stores and discount retailers such as SAMS club. Visit some stores. Collect product information sheets. If you have access to the Internet, visit some of the big computer makers, including Gateway (www.gateway.com), Dell (www.dell.com), HP (www.hp.com), or Sony (www.sony.com). Print product information sheets. Purchase a computer magazine; most include numerous ads for systems, plus articles.

4   Make sure you understand all the technical terms, in the product sheets. You'll find lots of acronyms and technical terms, such as Intel Pentium 4 Processor, 2.8GHz, and USB ports. You should understand what each of these means. Use this book if you need help decoding the list. If you aren't sure about a particular item in a product spec sheet, ask.

5   Comparison shop. Once you collect all this information, you should be able to define the system you want. You can then compare prices. Another factor to consider is service, support, and reliability of the computer. You can research these factors in computer magazines or online at popular computer resources (such as www.cnet.com, which enables you to compare PCs).

Summary

- A computer is a tool you can use for a variety of tasks including creating documents, storing information, playing games, learning a new skill, and connecting to the Internet.

- Computers are accurate, flexible, reliable, and quick. They help automate routine tasks and facilitate data storage.

- The physical components of a computer are the hardware. Most systems consist of a monitor, keyboard, mouse, and system unit. You may also have a printer.

- The system unit houses the electronic components of your computer including the motherboard (holds the processor and memory), video adapter, drives, power supply, and slots for adding components.

- Software are the programming instructions that enable you to use your computer to perform a specific task. Word processing programs, for instance, enable you to create documents. Database programs simplify the management of data.

- All systems need a special type of software called an operating system. The most commonly used operating system is Microsoft Windows.

- Input devices enable you to enter information, select commands, and type text. You use keyboards for entering text. A mouse is used to select commands, start programs, and select text and objects.

- Output devices enable you to see or print the data you enter. A monitor displays programs as well as text or data you enter. A printer prints hard-copy versions of your documents.

- Computers vary in price, size, power, speed, and system type.

  The most common type of computer is a microcomputer. This type of computer is most often referred to as a PC or personal computer. In addition to this type of computer, you may encounter minicomputers, mainframes, workstations, or portable computers.

LESSON 2: CPUS, MEMORY, AND MONITORS

Objectives

> **Define computer processors**
> **Explain types of memory**
> **Define types of monitors**
> **Add to your computer**

What is a Processor?

A processor is the main electronic chip in a computer. The processor determines the speed and power of a PC. It is, in effect, the computer's "brain." This chip is part of the motherboard, the main circuit board inside the system unit. For all the pertinent facts about processors, read this section.

HOW PROCESSORS WORK

A processor is a set of transistors, several millions of transistors, etched onto a computer chip. The processor determines how the computer processes data and handles instructions (see Figure 2.1). Computers recognize the state of each transistor as on or off. This system is called binary because it uses two digits to represent the two states: 0 for off and 1 for on. One switch is called a bit (binary digit) and is the smallest unit of data.

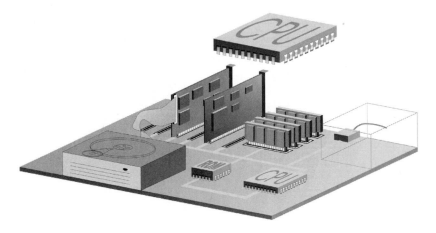

Figure 2.1. A computer processor.

 Base 2: Computers use a Base 2 number system, combining digits to represent numbers greater than 2. People use a Base 10 numbering system (1-10). When a number is greater than 10, we use more than one digit to represent that number.

To represent data, such as a letter, the computer groups together bits. A group of 8 bits is called a byte. You can arrange these 8 bits (one byte) into 256 possible combinations. This is important because each character in the alphabet (upper- and lowercase), number, and symbol on the keyboard (!, #, @, and so on) can be represented with one byte.

To standardize referencing characters, the ASCII character set was introduced. (ASCII stands for American Standard Code for Information Interchange.) Basically, each byte represents one character or symbol. For instance, here are some bytes, with the character they represent in ASCII:

0100 1101	M
0100 1001	I
0100 1011	K
0100 0101	E

TYPES OF PROCESSORS

The first computers used processors manufactured by Intel; Intel is still the dominant processor manufacturer in the industry. Intel initially used a numbering scheme to name its processors; the higher the number, the more powerful the processor. Numbers were used until recently, when Intel started using a name. Learning the different types will help you determine the age and speed of any PCs you use. You can also use this information if you are thinking of purchasing a new or used PC.

Here's a brief rundown of the history of processor development:

Processor	Description
8086	Introduced in 1978 and used in the first PCs.
8088	Introduced in 1979 and used in the first IBM PCs.
80286	Introduced in 1985. Called the "286." Obsolete now.
80386	Introduced in 1985. Called the "386." Also obsolete.
80486	Introduced in 1989. Called the "486." You may find some 486 systems still in use today. Added a math coprocessor and memory controller to the main processor chip.
Pentium	Introduced in 1993. This is where the numbering scheme was changed to a name. The Pentium is effectively an 80586 or 586 chip. This chip is five times faster than a 486.
Pentium Pro	Introduced in 1995. Increased the speed of the Pentium.

Pentium with MMX	Increased the multimedia capabilities of the Pentium.
Pentium II	Introduced in 1997. Increased the speed and added MMX technology to the Pentium.
Pentium III	This chip offers speeds up to 1.4 GHz. (See the section on speed.)
Pentium 4	The most current version of Intel's processors. You'll find that there are a variety of categories within the Pentium that detail technical information about the chipset, speed, and other elements, indicated with a complex numbering system. (Visit www.intel.com if you want complete information on all the various processors and technical details.) Just keep in mind that the higher performance of the processor, the higher the price of the computer.
Celeron	Provides features of the Pentium 4, but at a little slower speed. This chip is most affordable and less powerful.

 WEB: New processors are introduced periodically. For all the latest information, you can visit Intel's Web site at www.intel.com.

Intel used to be practically the only processor supplier, but now it's not uncommon to find computers that use processors (equally as good as the Pentium) from other companies (in particular AMD with its Athlon processor).

SPEED OF PROCESSORS

Older processors were measured in megahertz (millions of cycles per second) . This speed is abbreviated MHz. Computers now are much faster and are measured in gigahertz GHz (billions of cycles per second). Just keep in mind the higher the number, the faster the clock speed (and the more expensive the computer). One of the ways that processors differ is in the maximum speed you can achieve. Here's a breakdown of clock speeds by processors:

Processor	Speeds
Pentium II	233 MHz to 450 MHz
Celeron	950 MHz to 2.8 GHz
Pentium III	450 MHz to 1.4 GHz
Pentium 4	From 1.3 GHz up to roughly 3.6 GHz. Expect this speed to keep increasing and for new Pentium chips to have even higher speeds.

Moore's Law: The evolution of processors is summed up by Moore's Law. Basically, the CPU power doubles every 18 months. This fact was observed by Intel founder Gordon Moore.

You'll see this speed and other processor features advertised in brochures, Web sites, and print ads for new computers. Just keep this in mind (from Intel's Web site): "A higher number within a processor family can indicate more processor features, more of a specific processor feature, or a change in architecture."

 Clock speed doesn't keep time: A system clock is not used to keep time, but is a crystal that pulsates at a fixed interval. These digital pulses time and synchronize the tasks performed by the processor.

OTHER WAYS PROCESSORS DIFFER

Speed is probably the most hyped feature of a processor, and the one consumers focus on, but processors differ in other ways, as listed here:

- *Design or architecture of the chip.* The design of the chip is called the architecture and at its most basic is a measure of the number of transistors on the chip. To compare, the 386 computers had 320,000 transistors, and the 486 included 1.2 million. The Pentium has 3.1 million, and Pentium II includes 7.5 million! The more transistors, the faster the processing.

- *Cache.* A temporary storage area for frequently accessed or recently accessed data. Cache size is measured in megabytes (MB) or kilobytes (KB), and the bigger the cache side the better the performance/speed of the computer.

- *Front side bus.* The processor is connected via a set of wires (called the address bus) to the memory and other key components in your system. This speed is measured in GHz or MHz.

- *Chipset.* Intel defines the chipset in this way: "The chipset is the heart of the PC. It connects the processor, memory and other components, and moves data throughout the system, directly affecting overall system performance." The chipset includes lots of technical details about the system bus, for instance. Again, keep in mind that the more complex the chipset, the better the performance (and the more expensive the computer).

OTHER CHIP MAKERS

Intel is the most popular processor manufacturer, but it has gotten competition in recent years. You can also find systems with processors from AMD (Advanced Micro Devices) and other companies. These companies offer processors similar in speed and features to those of Intel.

As mentioned in Lesson 1, Macintosh computers use a different type of processor, initially made by Motorola. Motorola used a different numbering scheme, but the basic measurements of speed and registers apply. The first chips were named 68000, 68010, and 68030 and were introduced in 1979, 1983, and 1984s, respectively. These chips had a

32-bit register size. In the early 1990s more features were added, speed was increased, and the register size was increased to 64-bit. Models 68040 and 68060 were introduced at this time. Then came models MPC 740 and MPC 860 with a 128-bit register size.

Current Mac systems use a PowerPC G5 processor with speeds up to 4 GHz and built-in graphic enhancements.

 WEB: For information on chips used in Macintosh systems, visit www.apple.com.

Memory

Next to processors, the most important component of a computer is memory. Memory is another determining factor in speed and performance. The more memory, the faster the computer (and the more expensive). This section explains the different types of memory and how it works.

HOW MEMORY WORKS

The processor stores basic instructions, but it cannot store programs or data. To store this information, the processor needs a working area; this working area is the computer's memory, called RAM. Memory are chips on the motherboard or on a small circuit board that is plugged into the motherboard (see Figure 2.2).

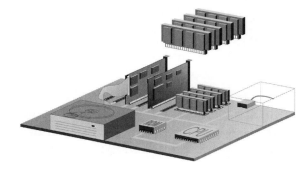

Figure 2.2. Memory is housed on the motherboard as chips or as a separate circuit board connected to the motherboard.

Data and information are stored in memory at specific locations, identified by a memory address. Using the address, the processor can store, retrieve, and release data from the different memory addresses. The amount of data that can be stored at one address varies, but you can generally estimate the storage to be one byte (about one character).

The processor sends requests for data (the memory address) along the address bus to memory. Data is then sent back to the processor through the data bus (see Figure 2.3). As a simple example, here's how this request works: the processor says; "Send me what's in mailbox 2," and then memory sends back the contents of that mailbox.

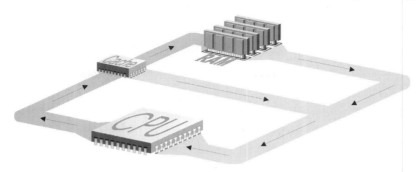

Figure 2.3. Memory requests travel back and forth from the processor to memory via the address and data buses.

TYPES OF MEMORY

A computer can have two main types of memory: ROM and RAM. ROM stands for Read-Only memory. These chips cannot be changed and contain data and instructions that have been burned in. ROM chips contain instructions for starting a computer, checking for hardware devices, and starting the operating system. This basic set of instructions is called the BIOS (basic input and output system).

RAM stands for Random Access Memory, and is the main working area for the processor. Instructions and data are stored (temporarily) in RAM while they are in use. Random refers to the fact that the processor can access each byte of data using the memory address, not necessarily in order.

 Why you need to save: Data in memory is stored only temporarily. If you lose power, all that data will be lost. That's why it's important to save your work. When you save, you copy the information from memory to disk or hard drive.

RAM SIZE AND SPEED

New computers come with a set amount of RAM, which is measured in megabytes (M or MB). (Remember that one megabyte equals approximately one million bytes and one gigabyte equals approximately one billion bytes.) In addition to the RAM that comes with a system, you can always add more memory. Most new computers have memory in the range from 256M to 1024M.

The speed of this type of memory is measured in nanoseconds (ns). The smaller the number, the faster the speed. You can expect to find speeds ranging from 60 to 100 ns.

A common mistake is to confuse memory size with hard disk size. Both are measured in megabytes and gigabytes. Remember that memory is only temporary storage. You will have much less memory on your system than hard drive capacity. As an example, a system may have 256M (256 million bytes) RAM and 4G (4 billion bytes) of hard disk space.

23

TYPES OF RAM

All computers use RAM, but the type of RAM they have can vary. RAM types vary in the technology they utilize (how efficiently the processor can access the RAM) and also the speed.

- *SDRAM.* Stands for Synchronous Dynamic RAM. It's one of the most popular type of RAM today and is found in most new systems. This type of memory provides data at fast speeds.

- *DDR-SDRAM.* Stands for Double Data Rate. This type of memory is an improvement over regular SDRAM and can increase the memory speed. One thing that makes this type of memory so popular is that memory makers are free to manufacture it because it is an open standard.

- *RDRAM.* Stands for Rambus Dynamic RAM. It improves performance by allocating memory in a new way.

- *RAMBus DRAM* (RDRAM). This memory was developed by Rambus, Inc. and like DDR-SDRAM increase the memory bus and the speed. Despite the speed, RDRAM hasn't been very popular because of price, as well as compatibility and other problem issues (heat).

MORE MEMORY TERMS AND CONCEPTS

You know the basics of how memory operates, but when reading system reviews or checking out new systems, you can also find other terms that relate to memory (and hence performance). Here are some other concepts you should understand:

- *Flash memory.* If you lose power, anything stored in RAM is lost. Flash memory stores data even when the PC is off. ROM, for instance, is a form of flash memory. Digital cameras also use flash memory.

- *Cache.* The processor and memory are constantly moving instructions and data back and forth. To help speed this process, processors include cache (pronounced "cash") memory. This memory is much faster than RAM and is used to store frequently used instructions and data. Rather than send requests via the address and data bus, the processor checks its cache first. The size of the processor cache is measured in kilobytes (K or KB).

 Clear Internet cache: The Internet can use a lot of cache space. You can clear this space by deleting temporary Internet files.

- *Video memory.* You'll learn more about video cards and monitors later in this lesson. To speed the display of images, most video cards also come with special video memory.

Getting System Information

When you purchase a new computer, you can review the specs to see the exact processor, memory, and other factors. If you don't remember or if you are using a PC that you did not purchase, you can get detailed system information using Microsoft Windows.

Follow these steps to get system information on a PC:

1 Right-click the My Computer icon and then select Properties. You see the System Properties dialog box (see Figure 2.4).

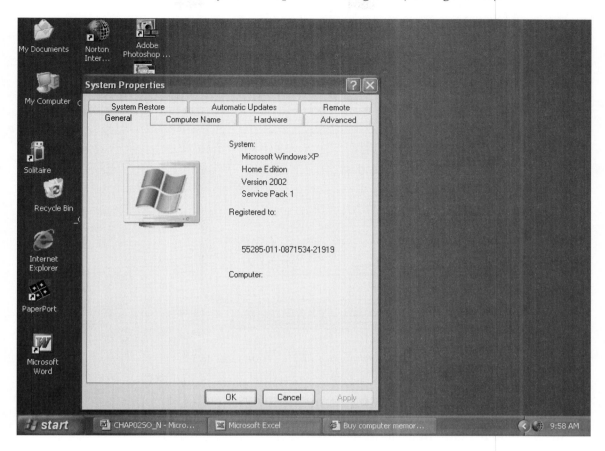

Figure 2.4. You can use this dialog box to get detailed system information.

2 On the General tab, review the information about the current operating system version, computer type, and amount of memory.

3 Click OK to close the dialog box.

Making Sense of Monitors

The other largest piece of equipment beyond the system unit is the monitor. To display programs and see data, your system has a monitor. The monitor is actually two components: the TV-like thing that sits on your desktop and an electronic card housed in your system unit (see Figure 2.5). (This card is sometimes called the video adapter or video card.) This section will explain the important concepts about a monitor and adapter.

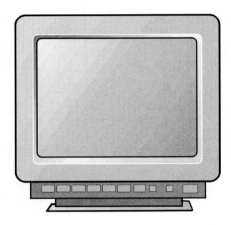

Figure 2.5. The monitor displays programs and data.

HOW MONITORS VARY

Monitors differ in image quality, size, and performance. Here are just a few of the factors to consider when evaluating monitors:

- *Size.* Monitors, like TVs, are measured diagonally. Common monitor sizes include 15" up to 21". The bigger the monitor, the larger the working area or display.

   Graphics work: People who work with graphics or detailed CAD programs often benefit from a bigger monitor. You can also purchase side-by-side monitors for displaying two pages at once.

- *Resolution.* Resolution is a measure of the number of pixels (picture elements) that can be displayed. The higher the number, the more detailed the image. Most monitors let you select from several resolutions. Common resolutions include 800 x 600 (800 pixels by 600 pixels) and 1024 x 768. To understand the difference, compare Figure 2.6, which shows 800 x 600, and Figure 2.7, which shows 1024 x 768.

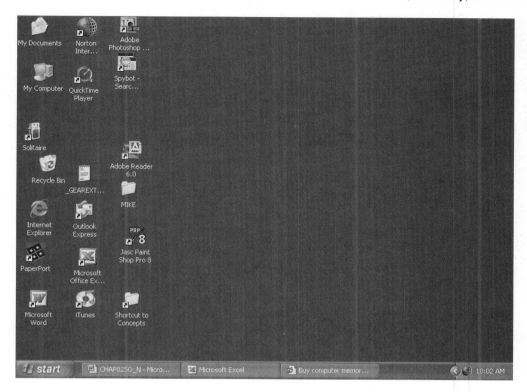

Figure 2.6. In 640 x 480 resolution, the image is bigger, and the image details are not as fine.

Figure 2.7. In 800 x 600 resolution, the image is smaller, but the quality is better.

Select your resolution: You can change the resolution of your monitor. To do so, right-click a blank part of the Windows desktop and then select Properties. Click the Settings tab and then select the resolution by dragging the Screen resolution slider bar.

- *Colors.* Monitors also differ in the number of colors they can display. Like resolution, you can usually switch among different color settings.

- *Display standard.* Older monitors may use a different standard for the display such as VESA. You don't have to worry about this standards since they are not relevant.

- *Footprint size.* Monitors tend to be big and bulky and take quite a bit of desk space (footprint). Some newer monitors use a flat-panel display, like those used for notebooks.

 Monitors and TV. You can also get monitors with special features for displaying HDTV on your comptuer monitor. You can find more about the entertainment features of a computer in Lesson 11.

GRAPHICS CARD

The quality of your image is determined in part by the actual monitor, but also by the video card. The video card is housed inside your system unit; your monitor is connected to the card via a cable. The monitor and the video card are a set. That is, when you purchase a new computer, it comes with a graphics card. If you purchase a new monitor, you can use the existing graphics card (if you buy compatible monitor) or get a new graphics card. As another combination, you can purchase a new graphics card that extends the capabilities of your current monitor. The graphics card must support the type of monitor you own.

Most graphics cards include memory to help speed the processing of the data image. This memory is called video RAM, or VRAM. The more memory, the faster your computer can process and display the image. You can also find special graphics accelerator cards, which greatly enhance your graphics capabilities. The average user doesn't need a speedier card. If you use your computer for extensive multimedia (creating videos, playing graphics-intensive games, creating multimedia), you may want to consider a graphics accelerator card.

LAPTOP MONITORS

Laptops (notebooks) use a different type of monitor. The regular monitor type is too bulky, so laptops use a flat-panel monitor that's usually about 1" thick. Most laptops use a liquid crystal display (LCD). Calculators use the same type of display. You can find two types of LCDs: active matrix and passive matrix. These differ in the technical details of how the transistors and pixels are aligned. Basically, active matrix displays are better quality, but more expensive.

Purchasing a laptop? Monitors for a laptop can vary greatly and may be the most important consideration when purchasing this type of computer. What's the best way to evaluate them? Look at the display yourself. You can see which laptop has the crisper display.

Adding Components to Your Computer

As your needs expand, you may want to consider upgrading your computer. You can upgrade just about every major component. But first consider the benefits you will get from that upgrade. Some upgrades will extend the life of your computer, making its speed and power acceptable for a longer timeframe. Others may not be worth the cost and effort. You may be better off purchasing a new PC. Review this list of upgrading tips:

- *Upgrade the processor.* You can upgrade the processor, but keep in mind that it's not the only thing that determines performance. If the other components cannot take advantage of the speed and features of this processor, you may not gain anything. It's similar to putting a racing engine into a Volkswagen. You'll only get so much performance gain. Also, your system must offer a processor that can be upgraded.

- *Add more memory.* Memory is a fairly straightforward upgrade, easy to do and offering a pretty good performance gain. This type of upgrade is especially useful if you use more than one application at a time.

     WEB: You can get upgrade information for memory at Buy Computer Memory (www.buycomputermemory.com).

- *Add more disk space.* Programs and data files quickly consume your hard drive. You can gain more storage space by adding another disk drive. You may also want to add other drives, such as a tape backup for making backups or a ZIP drive (higher-capacity floppy drive). For more information on disk drives, see Lesson 4.

- *Upgrade your monitor.* You can purchase a newer (bigger, better) monitor for your PC. Or you might add a graphics card to speed performance. A newer graphics card is most useful for game fanatics. A bigger monitor might be suited for those in any type of graphics or desktop publishing field.

Summary

- A processor is the brain of a computer and determines its speed and power.

- A processor consists of millions of transistors etched on a chip. The transistors are either on or off and represent 0 or 1. This numbering system is called binary, and one switch is a bit, the smallest unit of data. Eight bits equal one byte.

- Intel is the most popular manufacturer of computer processors. Initially processors were named with numbers, but Intel changed that with the introduction of the Pentium. The most recent chip is the Pentium 4.

- The clock speed of a processor is measured in gigahertz (GHz) or megahertz MHz for older computers. The higher the number, the faster the computer. Top speeds are in the range of 3-4 GHz.

- Processors also differ in the architecture of the chip, the chipset, and the cache.

- A computer has two types of memory: ROM and RAM. ROM stands for Read-Only Memory; this memory stores unchanging data such as the BIOS.

- RAM stands for Random Access Memory and is the computer's working area, a place to temporarily store program instructions and data.

- RAM is measured in megabytes. Most new systems have at least 256M of RAM.

- To display programs and data, you need a monitor. A monitor is the display and requires the video card (housed inside the system unit) to work.

- Monitors vary in the size (measured diagonally), resolution or image quality, and number of colors that can be displayed.

- Laptops use a special type of monitor; most are LCDs, or liquid crystal displays. You can buy flat-panel monitors for your computer that take up less space; this type of monitor costs more.

- To extend the life of a computer, you may consider upgrading some of the components. Before you upgrade, be sure the performance gain will be worth the price and effort. Sometimes it's better simply to purchase a new computer.

LESSON 3: ENTERING DATA AND PRINTING

Objectives

➢ **Use the keyboard**

➢ **Use a mouse**

➢ **Use other input devices**

➢ **Use a printer**

Using Your Keyboard

Your computer has a keyboard, which you use to enter data, select commands, and move around in a document. In addition to the alphanumeric keys, the keyboard has other special keys. This section describes the typical keyboard.

TYPICAL KEYBOARD LAYOUTS

Most keyboards use a layout called QWERTY, named for the keys in the first 6 characters in the first row of alphabetical characters. Figure 3.1 shows a typical keyboard layout. The letter and number keys are easy to recognize. You also have keys for special characters such as ! or @. In addition, a keyboard includes these special keys:

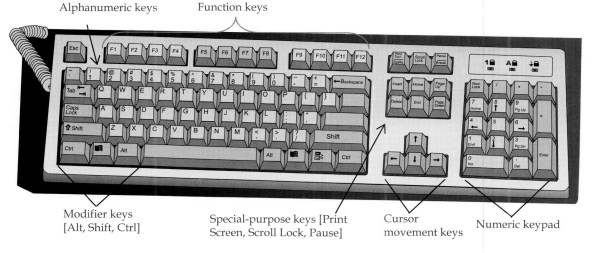

Figure 3.1. A typical keyboard includes alphanumeric keys, a numeric keypad, and function keys.

• *Function keys.* The function keys are labeled F1 through F12 and usually appear on the top row of the keyboard. Some keyboards include two sets of function keys at the top and left. Before the popularity of Windows and a graphical interface, function keys provided access to program features. For instance, you may press F1 to get help or F5 to start the speller. Function keys are still used as keyboard shortcuts.

31

- *Movement keys.* To move around a document, you can use the movement keys. (See the next section on movement keys.)

- *Modifier keys.* You can use the Shift, Alt, and Ctrl keys in conjunction with other keys to perform a different task. As a simple example, press the Shift key to type a capital letter. Alt and Ctrl are usually used for keyboard shortcuts. For instance, in Windows press Ctrl+X as a shortcut for selecting the Edit, Cut command.

- *Numeric keypad.* To simplify the entry of numbers, most keyboards include a numeric keypad. You can press the Num Lock key and use this keypad to enter numbers. If Num Lock is not pressed, you can use these keys for cursor movement.

 Turn Num Lock on: To turn Num Lock on, press the Num Lock key. Press the key again to turn it off. You can tell when Num Lock is on because you should see an indicator light on the keyboard.

- *Special-purpose keys.* Your keyboard also includes some special-purpose keys including Print Screen (used for printing the current screen), Scroll Lock (used for special cursor movements in different programs), and Pause (used for pausing a program, usually some type of batch program).

MOVING AROUND A DOCUMENT

The movement keys enable you to move around in a document. This set of keys also includes two editing keys (Insert and Delete). Here's a common list of movement keys and their associated action.

Key	Description
Up ↑	Move up one line
Down ↓	Move down one line
Left ←	Move left one character
Right →	Move right one character
Page Up	Display the previous page or screen
Page Down	Display the next page or screen
Home	Move to the beginning of the line or document
End	Move to the end of the line or document
Insert Ins	Change editing modes from Insert to Typeover
Delete Del	Delete the selected item

Backspace vs. Delete: You can use either Backspace or Delete to delete selected text or graphics. You can also delete individual characters. Backspace deletes characters to the left of the insertion point. Delete removes characters to the right of the insertion point.

AVOIDING INJURY

While it may seem ridiculous that you can get injured typing, you can. Repetitive movements, such as typing on a keyboard, can cause repetitive stress injuries (RSI), such as carpal tunnel syndrome. To protect yourself, consider these tips:

- *Type with your hands in the proper position.* Your hands should be parallel to the floor when typing. That is, you shouldn't have to bend your wrists up or down to type.

- *Use a wrist rest.* You can purchase a wrist rest to support your wrists when typing. You can also purchase bracelets to wear as a support.

- *Purchase a special keyboard.* Companies have created new ergonomic keyboards to prevent injury. For instance, Microsoft sells a special keyboard with a layout more suited for typing (see Figure 3.2). This keyboard is contoured, allowing a more natural movement for typing.

Figure 3.2. You can purchase ergonomic keyboards.

 WEB: Visit http://www.microsoft.com/hardware/mouseandkeyboard to get information about the keyboards (and mice) Microsoft offers.

- *Take breaks and do stretching exercises.* You can also avoid injury by doing exercises to stretch and relax your wrists and fingers. Also, take a break if you have long spells of typing.

Using a Mouse

Initially all a computer had for input was a keyboard, which was fine because all computing was command-based. You had to type a command to get the computer to do anything. Macintosh and Windows programs changed all that. Windows changed from a command-based computing system to a graphical user interface. That is, instead of typing a command to start a program, you could use an icon. You can double-click a program shortcut icon to start the program or use the Start menu. Both require the use of a mouse.

 Macs and mice: Macintosh computers always used a graphical interface and included a mouse. In fact, Windows (some say) was modeled on the Macintosh or at least on technology employed by the Mac.

Now a mouse is standard equipment on a computer, and you use a mouse to perform these common tasks:

- *Start programs.* As mentioned, you use a mouse to start a program. You can double-click a program icon or click the commands in the Start menu.

- *Select text.* When you want to modify text, you start by selecting the text you want to edit, format, or otherwise change. You can select text with a mouse by dragging across it. You can also use the mouse to select data in other programs, for instance, a range in a worksheet or entries in a database.

- *Move and resize items.* You can use the mouse to resize a window or to move a window around on the desktop. You can also use a mouse to move and resize graphics. Figure 3.3, for instance, shows a picture selected. Note the selection handles around the picture. You can use these to move and resize this picture.

Figure 3.3. You can use a mouse to select and move or resize a graphic object.

TYPES OF MICE

When you purchase a new computer, it comes with a mouse. Different manufacturers offer different mice, but most look similar to one illustrated in Figure 3.4. The mouse may be shaped differently (to best suit your hand); it may come in designer colors. Most mice include at least two buttons (a right and a left button). Some may offer a third button. The new IntelliMouse mouse by Microsoft includes a scrolling button in the middle of the mouse. You can use this to scroll through a document. Macintosh mice may have only one button.

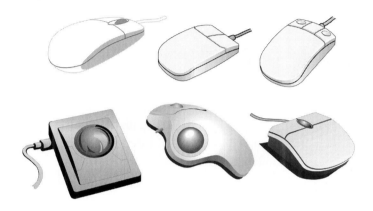

Figure 3.4. Most mice include at least two buttons.

Newer systems may have an optical mouse. Introduced in 1999, optical mice have a light emitting device (LED); this displays a red light that bounces light off the surface and then sends information to the computer telling it where to move. The cursor appears to move very smoothly, one reason for its popularity. Also, because it doesn't have any moving parts, the mouse is less likely to develop problems, including dirt getting inside the mouse and affecting its tracking sensors. Finally, this type of mouse does not require a mouse pad.

 WEB: Visit www.logitech.com, a popular mouse maker. Take a look at the different types of mice and keyboards offered. Note the other products this company makes.

Regular mice connect via a cable to the system unit. Newer optical mice use infrared technology, and they are not connected with a cable. You also have a special file on your system called a mouse driver. This file tells your operating system the type of mouse and how to work with the mouse.

 Change mouse drivers: If you are having problems with your mouse or get a new driver or new mouse, you can update the mouse information. In Windows, right-click My Computer and select Properties. Click the Hardware tab and then click the Device Manager button. Then expand the listing for Mice and other pointing devices so that you can see your mouse listed. Click your mouse and then click Properties. Click the Driver tab. You can use the options in this dialog box (including other tabs) to review driver information and update the driver.

COMMON MOUSE ACTIONS

To use a mouse, you need to learn these common mouse actions:

- *Point*. To point with the mouse, you move the mouse on the desktop until the corresponding pointer on-screen points to the item you want.

- *Click*. To click, you press the mouse button once. Most often you click the left mouse button. For shortcuts, you may be instructed to click the right mouse button. This is called right-clicking.

- *Double-click*. To double-click, you press the left mouse button twice in rapid succession.

- *Drag*. Hold down the mouse button and drag the item on-screen. When the item is where you want, release the mouse button. Dragging is used to move windows, icons, and objects. You can also drag and drop text when editing a document or copying or moving files.

 Practice. Some users, especially beginners, have problems with double-click. They click, move the mouse slightly, and then click again. This won't work. You have to double-click without moving the mouse on the desktop. A good way to practice mouse tasks is playing Solitaire on the computer.

 Trouble with double-click? Also, if the double-click speed is too fast or too slow, you can change it. To do so, click Start and then Control Panel. Open the Mouse Properties Control Panel. (In Classic view, double-click the Mouse icon. In Category view, click on Printers and Other Hardware and then click on Mouse in the lower half of the window.) Adjust the double-click speed as needed.

Using Other Input Devices

Mice and keyboards aren't the only type of input devices. (Devices used to enter data are often called input devices.) You can also find trackballs, joysticks, game pads, and others, as covered here.

TRACKBALLS

A trackball looks like an upside-down mouse. On a mouse, you'll find a little ball underneath that rolls along the desktop. In a trackball, this ball is on top, and you move the pointer by rolling the ball. Because it takes less space, a trackball is often found on notebook computers.

 Giving presentations: You can purchase a special kind of trackball useful for presentations. Rather than stand at the computer to display the presentation, the presenter can move around the room and move from slide to slide with the remote-control trackball.

Other notebook computers use a trackpad for moving the mouse. For instance, IBM's popular notebook ThinkPad uses a trackpad (see Figure 3.5). You move the mouse by moving your finger around on the pad. To click, use the left button beneath the trackpad. To right-click, click the right-button. Other manufacturers call this a touchpad.

Figure 3.5. As another alternative, a notebook computer may include a trackpad, used for moving the mouse pointer.

JOYSTICKS AND OTHER GAME DEVICES

If you play a lot of games, you may want a more arcade-like control. In this case, you can use a joystick, flight yoke, or other game device (like a steering wheel). The joystick includes a lever for moving around as well as buttons (see Figure 3.6).

Figure 3.6. For games, you might use a joysticks, which connects to a special game port on the back of the computer.

PENS

If you've ever signed for a package electronically, you've used a type of electronic pen. Some computers provide this type of input device. You can use the pen not only to write notes but also to select commands. Many PDAs (personal digital assistants) include an electronic pen. Because handwriting varies so much, a pen isn't that useful for typing data. It's appropriate for notes and signatures, but not for longer documents.

Graphic artists and engineers often use a special type of light pen with a drawing or digitizing table for drawing or creating blueprints. With a graphics tablet, for instance, an artist can sketch, trace, or work with existing drawings by using a light pen to draw on the tablet.

TOUCH SCREENS

Another popular type of input device is a touch screen. Every time you take money out of an ATM, you use this type of entry. You touch the screen to select commands and enter data. Many libraries include this type of entry system because it is easy to use. As another example, you may come across an information kiosk at the shopping mall that provides access to information via a touch screen.

VOICE RECOGNITION

Typing and entering data are the most repetitive, error-prone, and tedious tasks for using a computer. New ways of getting data onto the computer are introduced, perfected, and adapted all the time. For instance, voice recognition is another way to enter data. Currently, this type of input isn't mainstream; you may find it in some programs, but it's probably not accurate enough to use it for entering lots of data.

This type of input device works by translating spoken words into text, using a sound card, a microphone, and voice recognition software. You can use this setup not only to enter text, but also to select commands. Most programs come with commands they recognize. Because voices differ, you must speak clearly and spend some time training the software to recognize your unique pronunciation.

 Cameras and scanners: Cameras and scanners are also considered input devices. These hardware components are covered in Lesson 11.

Printing

Keyboards and mice help you enter data. On the other end, you have output, and the printer is the most common output device. (A monitor may also be considered an output device since it displays characters, but most people think of printers when they think of output.)

Printers let you print hard-copy versions of these documents. Printers vary in cost, quality, speed, and special features. Cost is directly related to the quality and speed. You can find printers starting at under $100 and costing up to several thousand dollars. Quality is a measure of the resolution similar to a monitor's quality, only printer resolution is a measure of the number of dots per inch (dpi). Speed is measured by the number of pages printed per minute (ppm). Slow printers print around 2 pages per minute. Speedier (and more expensive printers) may be able to print 20 pages or more. Printers may also have extra memory to speed processing of pages.

Printers also vary in how the image is created on the page. You can find three basic types of printers: dot-matrix, inkjet, and laser.

DOT-MATRIX PRINTERS

Dot-matrix printers were once a popular choice because they were inexpensive. These printers work by firing a series of pins against a ribbon to create dots. Think about an impressionist painting, composed all of dots. A printout from a dot-matrix printer is the same. Each character, number, or illustration is composed of lots of little dots. The quality of the printout ranges from OK to pretty bad. This type of printer is pretty much obsolete, although you will find it in companies that need to print multipart forms. For example, car service stations often print their receipts (multipart forms) on a dot-matrix printer.

INKJET PRINTERS

Inkjets are probably the most common type of printer today. They offer a good mix of quality and affordability. This type of printer includes of cartridges that squirt ink onto the page (see Figure 3.7). Most inkjet printers print in color as well as black and white. (Inkjets offer the most affordable way to have a color printer. See the section on color printers later in this lesson.) Prices range from entry-level inkjet printers at less then $100 up to $800 or more.

Figure 3.7. An inkjet printer is a popular model, especially for low-cost color printing.

LASER PRINTERS

Laser printers create an image using technology similar to a copy machine. The paper is rolled around a drum, and toner is applied from the drum to the paper. This type of printer may be more expensive than a comparable inkjet, but it is reliable, durable, and provides great quality. Laser printers are especially useful as network printers. You can expect speeds ranging from 10 to 20 pages per minute for black and white. Prices begin around $200. Figure 3.8 shows an illustration of a laser printer.

Figure 3.8. A laser printer provides great quality and good printing speed.

COLOR PRINTERS

It used to be that you could purchase only high-end (expensive) color printers, but the introduction of color inkjet printers changed all that. This type of printer offers color at an affordable price. (Expect to pay a little more for a color inkjet vs. the same quality black-and-white printer.) You can find color inkjet printers as cheap as $70 or so.

If you purchase a color printer, the specifications may include two speeds: one for printing in black and white and one for printing in color. (Color takes more time, as do documents with lots of graphics.)

You can also purchase color laser printers, but these are more expensive than their black-and-white counterparts and much more expensive than inkjet color printers.

COMBINATION PRINTERS/FAXES/COPY MACHINES

You can also find printers that combine several features. Designed for small businesses and home offices, this printer type can functions as a printer, a fax, and a copy machine. Inexpensive models of this type of printer cost around $130. You can also find printers with more features and better quality in the higher price range.

 WEB: Visit www.hp.com. Use the links to view the various types of printerse that his popular printer manufacturer sells as well as the pricing and various technical differences among the different printers.

PHOTO PRINTERS

As digital cameras have become more popular, special photo printers were introduced to the market. You can find small photo printers that print on traditional size and quality photo paper. You can also print from other printers to special printer paper. If you plan to print photos, check out the photo features of a general purpose printer (if that's your choice) or a special photo printer. The best way to evaluate them is to visit a retail store and view actual photos printed from the various printers. You can also find photo printer reviews which include pictures printed from various printers to get a good idea of each printer's quality. (You can learn more about digital cameras in Lesson 11.)

PRINTING SUPPLIES

To use a printer, you need supplies, including paper and ink. The ink will depend on the type of printer and specific model. Some may use a ribbon, similar to a typewriter ribbon. Others use cartridges. For instance, most laser printers use toner cartridges. The price of the ink can get expensive. You may pay as much as $80 for a toner cartridge for a laser printer. (How long these supplies last depends on how much and what you print. If you print a lot of graphics, for instance, the toner will run out sooner. If you print mostly text, your toner will last longer.)

If you have a color printer—for instance, an inkjet color printer—you'll have at least two cartridges: one for black and one or more for color.

PRINTER PORTS

A printer is connected to your system unit via a cable. One end of the cable plugs into the printer and one into the back of the system unit. Most printers connect to the LPT port (often called the printer port or parallel). You may find some printers that connect to the serial port or the USB port. Figure 3.9 shows an example of a parallel port.

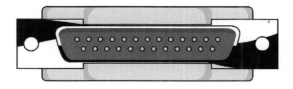

Figure 3.9. This is called a parallel port because communications go both ways along the cable.

Printing A Document

Printing a document in most applications is similar.

Follow these basic steps:

1 Open the document you want to print.

2 Select the Print command. Usually, you select File, Print. You can also look for a Print button in the toolbar or in Windows use the keyboard shortcut (Ctrl+P). You see the Print dialog box (see Figure 3.10).

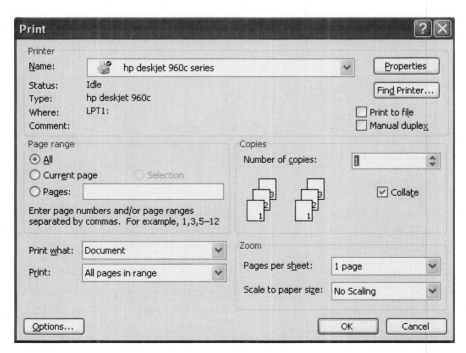

Figure 3.10. Select options for printing this document.

3   Make any changes to the options for printing the document, including the number of copies, pages printed, and so on.

4   Click OK. The document is printed.

 Save time and paper: You can save time and paper by previewing your document before printing. Look for a Print Preview command in the File menu.

Summary

- To enter data into the computer, you need input devices. Common input devices include keyboards, mice, trackballs, and pens. Newer technology includes voice recognition capabilities.

- Most keyboards use the QWERTY layout. In addition to alphanumeric keys, you'll find function keys, movement keys, numeric keypad, and other special-purpose keys.

- A mouse is a pointing device used for selecting commands, starting programs, and selecting text and objects. Mouse actions include point, click, double-click, and drag.

- The newest type of mouse is an optical mouse which doesn't have any moving parts and uses a LED to position the mouse cursor on the screen.

- To print hard-copy versions of your documents, you need a printer. The two most popular printer types are inkjet and laser printers. These printers vary in cost, quality of image, and speed (measured in pages printed per minute).

- Printers connect to your computer via a port, usually the LPT or parallel port (sometimes called the printer port). You can also find printers that connect to a serial or USB port.

- To print a document, use the File, Print command.

LESSON 4: STORING DATA

Objectives

> **Define hard drives**
> **Use a floppy drive**
> **Learn about CD and DVD drives**
> **Familiarize yourself with other storage devices**

Defining Hard Drives

To use a computer effectively, you need a permanent place to store your data and programs. This storage space is provided by a hard disk, a magnetic storage device inside your system unit. This section explains how hard disks vary, how they work, and how you use them to keep data and programs organized.

HOW HARD DRIVES VARY

Hard disks vary in three main ways: capacity (size), speed, and drive standard. The capacity of a drive is measured in megabytes (M or MB), and more commonly gigabytes (G or GB). A megabyte would be equal to about 1 to 1½ floppy disks. A few years ago a 500M drive was considered big. Now most new computers come with drives that start at 40G and go up from there to several hundred gigabyte drives. The bigger the drive, the more data and programs you can store. You'll be surprised how quickly a hard drive fills up, with your data and with programs.

M/MB and G/GB: M stands for megabyte and is roughly 1 million bytes. You may also see this measurement abbreviated MB. G or GB stands for gigabyte and is roughly one billion bytes.

Check drive size: If you aren't sure how big your drive is in Windows, double-click My Computer and then right-click your hard drive and select Properties. You can see the capacity as well as the used and free space on your drive.

The second way that hard disks vary is speed, and you'll find two measurements of speed: seek time and transfer time. The seek time is the amount of time starting from the time the computer requests the file up to the second that the drive delivers the first byte of the file. Seek time is measured in milliseconds (ms); most hard drives have average access times in the range of 8.5 to 12 milliseconds.

The transfer time (also called data rate), the other indicator of hard drive performance, is how quickly the drive can transfer the data, that is, read or write data to the disk. This speed is measured in megabytes per second (MBps) or kilobytes per second (KBps). You can find speeds from 50MBps up to 100MBps. The higher the number, the faster the drive.

To communicate with the processor, a hard drive uses a controller, which is connected to the motherboard either as a built-in part of the motherboard or as an expansion card (see Figure 4.1). Controllers follow different standards, and you'll also see the standard as a way to distinguish drives.

Figure 4.1. The hard drive is housed inside the system unit and is connected to the processor via a controller.

HOW A HARD DRIVE WORKS

A hard disk is sealed in a vacuum chamber and consists of several aluminum platters coated with a magnetically sensitive material (usually iron oxide). This coating enables the data to be polarized by an electromagnet. Like processor data, the magnetic bit can be on or off, but unlike a processor, it does not require electricity to maintain its current state (on/off). Drives have read/write heads that move over the disk surface and change the polarity of the magnet (see Figure 4.2). That's how data is written and read from the disk. Read heads relay the information from disk; write heads record the information to disk.

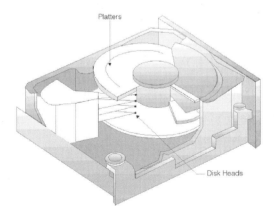

Figure 4.2. A drive stores data by charging magnetic particles.

To prepare a disk for use, you need to format it. Formatting a disk writes a series of concentric circles around each platter (like a phonograph, but each circle is separate rather than continuous). These tracks are numbered, and the number of tracks on a disk depends on the drive type.

Tracks are then divided into pie-like sections called sectors (see Figure 4.3). Sectors are also numbered. So now the drive is divided into little areas, each with a unique number. (Think about a running track, divided into lanes. Each lane may have dividers to indicate the distance or the starting place for runners. These lanes are similar to the tracks on the disk. If the running track was divided into equal segments, these are similar to sectors.)

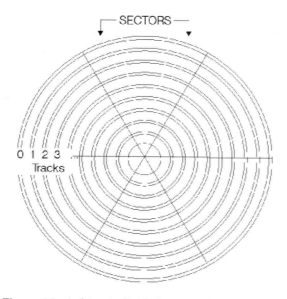

Figure 4.3. A drive is divided into tracks and sectors.

Depending on the drive type, the size of the sector can vary. Also, you'll find that the number of sectors per track varies. As an end user, you don't need to worry about the number of sectors and tracks. However, this information is useful if you ever hear or read about this specification; you'll understand what they refer to. Also, you need a basic understanding of how data is stored so you can grasp drive performance issues, such as defragmenting (covered later).

The hard disk, remember, consists of several platters, stacked on top of each other and each with its own read and write head. The drive can usually read and write to both sides of the platter. Usually one side of one platter is not used.

HOW A DRIVE STORES DATA

You now know how the data physically is written and read from the disk, but how does it work mechanically? How does the drive know where to find data and where to write new data?

As mentioned, each track and sector is numbered. The operating system uses this numbering scheme to find areas that are not used for writing or saving data and also to find data to retrieve (reading data). The operating system stores this information in a table. In previous versions of Windows, this was called the file allocation table (FAT or FAT32. Newer versions use NTFS, which provides more reliability, better performance, more security, and other advanced features.

When you save a file, the operating system finds space that is available. The drive goes to the first area (called cluster) and fills it up. If the file is too big to fit in one cluster, the operating system goes to the next available cluster and writes data to that area. This continues until the entire file is stored. Note that the file may be stored in several clusters and that the clusters may not be next to each other.

When you want to open a file, the operating system finds the various sectors that store that file. Then the drive goes to the first cluster to retrieve the first part of the file, goes to the next cluster, and so on until the entire file is retrieved.

Initially, on a new drive, the open clusters are contiguous, but over time as you add and delete files, the file areas may be noncontiguous. Files may be fragmented (stored in clusters all around the disk). You won't lose data because they are fragmented, but it does slow performance. To improve performance, you can defragment the drive, basically rearranging the stored clusters and putting all full clusters at the start of the drive and all open clusters together after the full ones. There are programs that automatically perform this function for you.

ORGANIZING A HARD DRIVE

The drive and operating system take care of storing and retrieving data. You only need to keep track of file names and locations. Each time you save a new file, you assign a name and a location or folder. You can think of your hard drive as one big filing cabinet. If all the files were stored in one cabinet, finding a particular file would be cumbersome. Instead, a cabinet is divided into folders. Likewise, your hard drive is divided into folders, including folders created by programs and folders you create. To keep your data organized, you need to give some thought to your folder structure. Keep these pointers in mind:

- Each drive has a name, which consists of the drive letter and a colon. If you have a floppy drive, it is named drive A:. The first hard drive is drive C:. If you have more than one hard drive, they are named D:, E:, and so on. The CD or DVD drive, if you have one, uses the next free letter. If you have only one hard drive, the hard drive is drive C: and the CD drive would then be named D:. If you have two hard drives (C: and D:), then the CD drive would be drive E:.

- In a Windows environment the main folder on each drive is called the root. This folder contains all the other folders on your computer. This folder does not have a name, but is indicated with the backslash key (\).

- You can have folders within folders. These nested folders are sometimes called subfolders.

- Windows sets up several folders. The tools and programs needed to use Windows are stored within a main folder called Windows. This folder contains several folders within the main Windows folder.

- Windows also sets up a special My Documents folder. It's a good idea to include all of your data within this folder because it's easy to access this folder and with all of your data within one main folder, backing up your data is also quicker.

- Within the My Documents folder, you'll find folders for My Pictures, My Music, and My Videos. These help store these special file types together in one location.

- In addition to the folders Windows sets up, you can create your own folders. You should spend some time thinking of an organizational strategy for your work. You might include folders for each type of document (artwork, letters, databases, and so on). You might set up folders by project. If several people use the computer, you might set up folders for each person.

- When you install a new program, the installation program will set up a separate folder for its files. This folder may also contain subfolders (folders within folders). Most applications have a built-in installation program that leads you through the installation process.

 Access My Documents folder: You can quickly access the My Documents folder by clicking Start and then clicking My Documents. You may also add a shortcut icon to this folder to your desktop.

- When you save a file, you assign a file name and a folder. The combination of folder and name is called the path. For instance, if you save a file named CHAP01.DOC on drive C: in a folder named CONCEPTS, the path to this file would be C:\CONCEPTS\CHAP01.DOC. Note that the drive, folder, and file name are separated by backslashes. With Windows, you don't need to type the path. Instead, you can browse through the folder structure to have Windows supply the path name for you.

DISPLAYING THE CONTENTS OF YOUR HARD DRIVE

To see the contents of your drives in Windows, you use the My Computer icon. You can then open any of the drives and then open any of the folders.

Follow these steps:

1 Click Start and then click My Computer. Or if you have a desktop shortcut to My Computer, double-click this icon. You see drive icons for each drive on your system (see Figure 4.4).

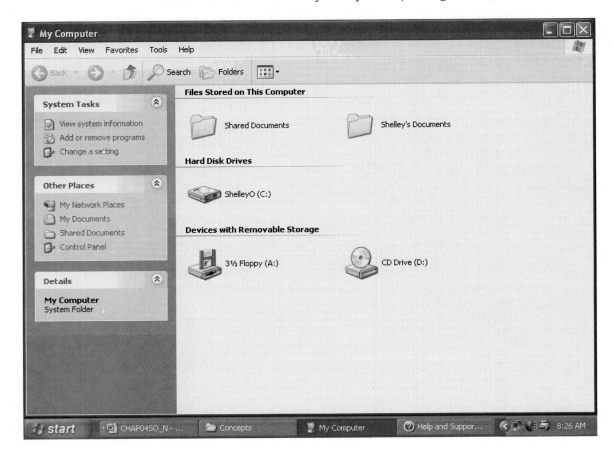

Figure 4.4. My Computer displays icons for each drive on your system.

2 Double-click the drive you want to open. For instance, double-click drive C:. You see the contents of that drive. Notice that folders are indicated with a folder icon (see Figure 4.5). Windows also uses different data icons for different file types as well as programs.

Figure 4.5. You can display the contents of the drives on your system.

3   Continue opening folders until you find the file or folder you are looking for.

4   When you are done browsing your system, click the Close (X) button to close the folder window.

CHECKING, BACKING UP, AND OPTIMIZING YOUR DRIVES

To keep your drive performing in top shape, you should perform some routine maintenance. Windows includes tools for checking your disk for errors. You can also use special tools to defragment the files (reorganize them so that opening and accessing files is quicker) and improve performance. Keep the following guidelines in mind:

- Clean out unneeded files. One way to improve performance is to get rid of unnecessary files. You can delete files manually or use the Disk Cleanup feature of Windows (see Figure 4.6). To access this tool, open My Computer and then right-click the disk you want to tidy up. Select Properties. Click the Disk Cleanup button to start the wizard. From here, you can check for unnecessary files and then select/confirm which of these targeted files are deleted.

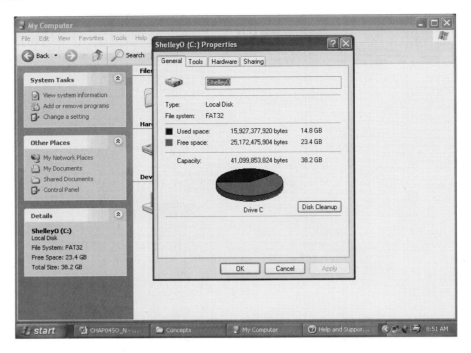

Figure 4.6. You can clean up (delete) unnecessary files on your system.

- Check the drive for errors. You should also periodically scan your drive for errors using the program included with Windows. Open My Computer and then right-click the drive you want to check. Click Properties. From this dialog box, click the Tools tab and then click the Check Now button (see Figure 4.7).

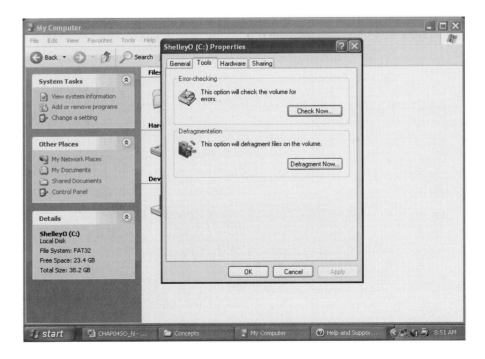

Figure 4.7. You can scan a disk for errors.

- Over time, all drives become fragmented. If your drive has become fragmented, you can use the Disk Defragmenter included with Windows to defragment the drive. You can access this from the Tools tab (see the preceding bullet item). Click the Defragment Now button to start the process. (Note that defragmenting can take a while.)

- Back up your work. Hard drives and computers develop problems. To safeguard your data, you should periodically make a spare or backup copy of your files. You can do so manually by copying files from your hard drive to a CD, for instance. Or you can use special backup software and special storage devices for your back up needs. (Other backup options are covered later in this lesson.)

- Protect your computer. If you have an Internet connection or share files with others, your system needs to be safeguarded against viruses. You should install an antivirus application to check your system for viruses. (This type of software is covered in Lesson 13.)

Using Your Floppy Drive

Hard drives are the primary storage of a computer. Hard drives store your data files and your program files, as well as important information about your computer setup (information about your printer, mouse, display, and so on). Your computer may also have another type of drive: a floppy drive.

What use does a floppy drive have? A floppy drive is used to get information onto your hard drive. For instance, you might store a file on a floppy disk. You can open the file from the floppy disk and save it to your hard disk. A floppy drive also does the reverse: enables you to get information off your hard drive so that you can take that information with you. For instance, you might work on a document at home and then want to take the document to work. You can copy the document from your home system to a floppy. From the floppy you can then copy the document to your office computer.

 Back up important files: You can also use floppy disks to make extra backup copies of important documents. Backing up your work is very important. You'll be best off if you learn this *before* you lose your work.

FLOPPY DRIVES VS. HARD DRIVES

A floppy drive works similar to a hard drive, with these key differences:

- To use a floppy drive, you have the drive itself (accessed via a slot on the front of the system unit) and a disk. You insert the disk into the slot so that the drive can then read and write information to the disk.

- Hard drives store much more data than a floppy drive and are also faster. Most floppy disks can store a maximum of 1.44M of data. Compare that to hard drives that can store 40+G of data.

- A hard drive comes formatted, and you usually never, ever want to reformat a hard drive. You do this only in the most extreme circumstances. Most floppy disks come preformatted. If not, you need to format them to prepare them for use. You can reformat a floppy disk, but doing so erases all the data on that disk.

 Floppy is not floppy: Many beginning users are confused when they hear the term "floppy" disk because the disk is not floppy. But it used to be! Older systems used a different disk type, which was floppy. These disks measured 5¼" in size (compared to the 3½" size of common floppy disks now) and could not store as much data.

FLOPPY DISK CARE AND MAINTENANCE

Because you can physically handle a floppy disk, you need to take some precaution in handling this type of disk. Here are some points to keep in mind:

- As mentioned, before you can use a floppy disk, it must be formatted. Some disks are sold preformatted or you can use your system to format the disk. If you format a disk that contains data, all that data will be erased.

- If you don't want someone to be able to save data to a disk or format a disk, you can write-protect it. To do so, slide the write-protect tab up. Figure 4.8 shows the anatomy of a floppy disk, including the write-protect tab.

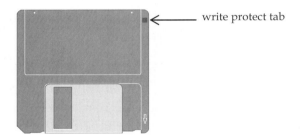
write protect tab

Figure 4.8. A floppy disk is 3½" in size and includes a tab for protecting the disk.

- To keep your disks organized, put labels on them and write the contents of each disk on the label. You might also include the date. Store the disks in a safe place.

- Keep your floppy disk out of extreme heat or cold.

FLOPPY DRIVE REPLACED WITH CD/DVD DRIVES

Floppy disks used to be the only way to easily transport data, and floppy drivers were standard equipment on computers. With the advent of CD and DVD drives that enable you to both read and write data, floppy disks are not always needed. (CD and DVD drives are covered next.) If you purchase a new computer, you may not have a floppy drive. Instead, you can use your CD or DVD drive to copy, share, and back up files.

Using CD and DVD Drives

A floppy disk is limited in the amount of data it can store. As programs got larger and multimedia became so popular, a new type of storage device was introduced: the CD drive (see Figure 4.9). This drive uses a different method for storing data; lasers are used to read and write data. These discs can store much more data than a floppy drive. Typically, a CD can store 700M of data. Compare that to 1.44M of data on a floppy disk. A CD is the equivalent of approximately 450 floppy disks.

Figure 4.9. A CD can store much more data than a floppy disk.

Most programs come on CDs. You install them from the CD to your hard drive. You can also find collections of information on CDs, such as encyclopedias, clip art, fonts, and other information. You can also play audio CDs on your computer, and you can use your computer to create audio CDs. (Digital music is covered in Lesson 11.)

 Play your music CDs: You can play music CDs on your computer, although the sound quality will only be as good as your computer speakers allow. To do so, use Windows MediaPlayer (included with Windows) or any of the other popular music players.

DRIVE SPEED

CD drives differ in speed and type. Speed is measured in kilobytes per second (KBps), and the read and write speeds of a CD are slower than those of a hard drive. Speed is indicated as a measure of how much faster the CD is than the original speed of the CD drive. 8X means 8 times faster. 24X means 24 times faster. 48X means 48 times faster. These measurements can be deceiving, though, because you aren't sure what X indicates. The X roughly equals 150 kilobytes per second, but this isn't standardized. If purchasing a new system, get the exact CD access and transfer times.

TYPES OF CD DRIVES

Initially, only CD-ROM drives were available. With these drives, you could only read data from the disc. (ROM stands for Read Only Memory.) Newer drives enable you to read and write data. Here's a breakdown of the various drive types:

- *CD-ROM.* The original CD drive. With this drive, you can only read information.
- *CD-R.* Stands for CD Recordable. With this type of drive, you can read information and also record your own CD-ROM discs. The information that is written to disc cannot be changed.
- *CD-RW.* Stands for CD Rewritable. You can not only read and write data to disc, but you can also rewrite and erase data on the disc. The speed for rewriting data is slower than reading or recording.

DVD

In addition to CD drives, DVD (digital versatile disc) drives have also become common on computers. You are probably familiar with DVD discs and drives for viewing movies. You can also find this type of drive on newer PCs.

DVD uses a different technique for storing data on the disc and can store a lot more data in the same amount of space as a CD, up to 7 times more data than a CD. This type of disc can store from 4.3G up to 17G of data. Speed is measured the same as CD drives; common speeds include 4X and higher. DVD drives are slower at reading and writing data than CD drives. Also DVD drives can read CD discs.

Like CD drives, you'll find different types of DVD drives:

- *DVD-R.* With this type of drive, you can read information and also record data to the DVD once. The information that is written to disc cannot be changed.
- *DVD-RW.* DVD Rewritable. You can not only read and write data to disc, but you can also rewrite and erase data on the disc. The speed for rewriting data is slower than reading or recording.
- *DVD+R.* New in 2002, you can write once with this type of drive which offers enhanced compatibility and performance.
- *DVD+RW.* Includes added technical advantages to the traditional DVD-RW drive.

Other Storage Options

You can find still more storage options. You are likely to see these in use with networks or businesses that require frequent backups. If you need to store and move large amounts of data, you may need a larger-capacity portable drive. For instance, artists or multimedia creators often create files that are huge. If they need to send these files to someone else, they may use a higher-capacity drive, such as a Zip drive or a Jaz drive. Another popular drive type is flash memory drives,

ZIP DRIVES

One type of drive that provides more storage capacity is magnetic disk cartridge drives. These drives use cartridges that can store up to 150M of data. The Bernoulli box was a popular type of this drive. Next came the SyQuest drive, and in 1995, the Iomega Zip drive was introduced. This drive can store 100M, 250M, or 750M, depending on the drive. Zip drives can be internal or external. The internal drives will operate faster. The disk is about the same size and looks like a floppy disk, but you cannot use floppy disks in the Zip drive or vice versa.

These drives vary in how data is stored and the medium used to store the data (disk, cartridges, etc.). You can use only the medium designed for that drive and you cannot mix media. That is, you cannot, for instance, use a floppy disk in a Zip drive. The person to whom you are sending the data must have the same drive type. For instance, if you store a presentation on a Zip drive and send it to a client, that client must also have a Zip drive in order to access the information on the drive.

Iomega also offers a REV drive designed as a replacement for tape backup drives (covered next). These drives, which can also be used as removable storage, are faster than tape and can store up to 35G (or up to 90G if you compress the data).

 WEB: Visit Iomega (www.iomega.com) to get information on the different storage devices they offer.

TAPE DRIVES

You may find another type of drive used mainly for backups. This type of drive stores the information sequentially on a tape (like a cassette tape). Because of the sequential storage method, these drives are not useful for storing data you need to retrieve quickly. They do provide an inexpensive and quick method of making a copy of all the data on your system for backup and can be set to automatically back up at a given time. This drive is often used to back up network servers.

Tape drives differ in the type of tape cartridge they use and the amount of data that can be stored on a tape. The highest capacity use digital audiotape (DAT).

 Size doesn't matter: The size of the cartridge is no indication of the capacity.

You must use the type of medium designed for your particular tape drive. Also, you cannot use that medium on tape drives not designed for your medium. That means a tape drive is usually used for one system, to store and if needed restore data from that system onto tapes. This type of drive is not used to transport data, for instance, from one computer system to another.

USB FLASH MEMORY DRIVES

This new type of portable device is about the size of a car key and connects to your computer's USB port. You can use it to share your data by saving the files (photos, music, documents) to the device and then plugging it into another computer. Drives vary depending on capacity (amount the device can store); you can find 128M, 256M, 512M, and 1G mini drives. This type of drive also differs in physical size. For instance, Iomega offers a mini and micro drive; the micro drive is about the size of a thumbnail!

Summary

- To store data permanently, your system includes a hard drive. Hard drives vary in size or capacity, speed, and standard.

- Hard drive size is measured in gigabytes (G or GB).

- To use a disk, it must be formatted. Formatting divides the disk into tracks and sectors, each area with a unique number. The operating system uses this number to keep track of where data is stored.

- Windows sets up a My Documents folder with subfolders to encourage you to keep your documents organized. In addition to using these folders, you need to create new folders for storing your data.

- A floppy drive provides a way to take data and documents with you from one computer to another.

- For more data storage, most new systems include a CD drive that you can both record (and possibly rewrite) data to. These drives vary in speed and type. CDs can store as much as 700M of data.

- DVD stands for digital versatile disc and was originally designed to distribute films. DVD drives are also found on newer systems and these drives can read DVDs as well as CDs.

- If you need a higher-capacity portable drive, you can purchase one of several, including a Zip drive.

- Tape backup drives are useful for backing up data. These drives store data sequentially like a tape cassette.

- If you need a small portable device, you may consider one of the new flash memory drives that connect to your computer via a USB port.

LESSON 5: USING YOUR COMPUTER (OPERATING SYSTEMS)

Objectives

- ➤ **Define an operating system**
- ➤ **Distinguish between DOS and Windows**
- ➤ **Identify high-end operating systems**
- ➤ **Work with windows**
- ➤ **Work with applications**

What is an Operating System?

The operating system is a special kind of software that all systems must have to operate. The operating system handles and manages all system operations including booting up the system, displaying information on your monitor, starting programs, printing files, storing files, opening files, managing keyboard and mouse input, and more. The operating system takes these common user actions (such as double-clicking the mouse) and communicates that action to the appropriate hardware component, getting that component to do the requested action (for instance, start a program).

The most common operating system, especially for consumers, is Microsoft Windows. You will also find other operating systems for Macintosh and high-end systems, such as workstations. This lesson explains the key concepts dealing with this critical system software.

DOS and Windows

People who have used computers for a long time remember DOS. (DOS stands for "disk operating system" and was developed by Microsoft for IBM for use on the first PCs. This particular brand of DOS was called MS-DOS.) This operating system was command-based. To get the computer to do anything, you had to type a command. And the interface—what you saw when you used your computer—had a black screen and a C:\ prompt. Figure 5.1 shows a DOS window.

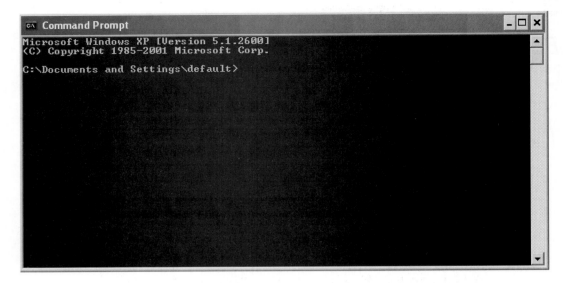

Figure 5.1. To make the computer perform a task, you had to type
commands in the proper format (called syntax).

To copy files, start a program, do anything, you had to type commands in the proper
format, as in this example:

COPY *.DOC C:\MEMO\

This command would copy all of the document files (*.DOC) in the current folder to the
folder MEMO on drive C. Using DOS was not easy.

MORE DOS DIFFICULTIES

DOS programs, which are now virtually obsolete, were a little easier to use than DOS
itself because most provided menus, which you could use to select commands. DOS
programs also often used function keys. The disadvantage is that each DOS program
looked and worked differently. Just because you could use one DOS program didn't
mean those skills would work in another program. Using DOS and DOS programs was
like trying to communicate with people from France, Italy, Germany, and Spain, each
with its own language, customs, standards, and so on.

Also, DOS did not centralize key system information, such as the printer or the mouse.
You had to use batch files to set up the mouse (special mini-programs) and in some
cases you had to set up the printer to work with each program you used.

Here were some other disadvantages of DOS:

- You could run only one program at a time.
- Your system could handle only 640K of RAM. To use RAM beyond that
  point, you had to use special memory software.
- File names were limited to 8 characters.
- Using the operating system was not intuitive.

INTRODUCING WINDOWS

Windows changed the PC computing world by providing a different operating system with a more user-friendly interface. Introduced in the mid-1980s, Windows used a graphical user interface (GUI, pronounced "gooey") that imitated the Macintosh. Rather than type commands, you could point to little pictures called icons. Figure 5.2 shows the desktop of a current version of Windows.

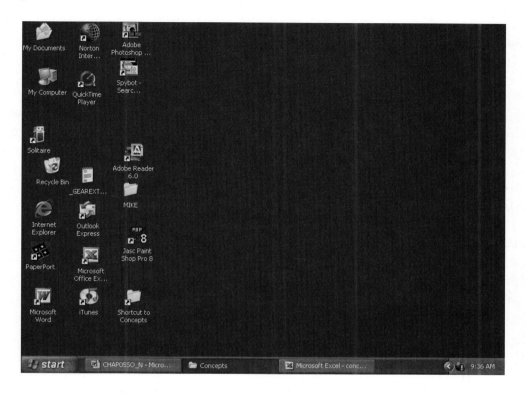

Figure 5.2. Windows uses a graphical user interface.

Windows (all versions considered here) provided these benefits:

- **Better interface.** The graphical user interface made using a computer much easier, especially for beginners.

- **Consistent program design.** Windows programs must follow a standard design. Most programs look and operate in a similar fashion. For instance, selecting a menu command is the same throughout most Windows programs. Getting help in programs works the same way. This change benefited the user. Once you learn one Windows program, you can use the same basic skills in other Windows programs.

- **Multitasking.** With Windows, you can open and work with more than one program at a time.

- **Shared system resources and information.** This operating system not only shares resources, such as the printer, but also stores this key information in one location. Once you set up your printer in Windows, you can use that same printer in any Windows program without modification.

- *Simplified program setup.* Installing and starting programs are easier.
- *Customized desktop.* You can customize the desktop (what you see when you start Windows), plus many other features of Windows.

WINDOWS VERSIONS

The first version of Windows was introduced in 1985 and was not successful. Newer versions were subsequently introduced, and with Windows 3.0, Windows became a success. In 1995, Microsoft released Windows 95, which was a complete overhaul of Windows, dramatically improving the user interface as well as technical details that helped optimize the performance of Windows.

Windows 98 was introduced in 1998. A newer version of Windows, Windows Millennium edition, was released in September of 2000. Some of the new features of Windows Me include advanced digital media functions. With these tools you can create, edit, and share digital pictures, movie clips, and audio files. Using these new features, users can create a video, including animated graphics, edit the video, and then post it to the Internet. Also, in response to the number of homes that have multiple computers, Windows Me includes home-networking capabilities.

In addition to these consumer-oriented Windows versions, Microsoft also developed an operating system for higher-end systems and especially for networks. The first network version was called Windows for Workgroups. Then came Windows NT. (You can find different versions of Windows NT, as this product has evolved.) In 2000, Windows released Windows 2000, an operating system in between NT and regular Windows designed for businesses.

The most current version of Windows is Windows XP. This version of Windows included a big change to the look of Windows, aimed at making it even easier to use. Windows XP also added features that provided more reliability, higher performance, and greater customization.

Windows XP comes in Home and Professional editions. Most new computers come with Windows XP Home. If you are hooked up to a network or are a small business, you may want to use Windows Professional.

WINDOWS UPDATES

Microsoft is working on yet another upgrade to Windows, which will probably be introduced in 2005 or 2006. In the meantime, Microsoft periodically adds small updates to Windows to improve features and fix problems (such as holes in security). You can download and install these updates at www.microsoft.com. After awhile, Windows makes available a complete set of these updates as a service pack. You can download and install these service packs to update your version of Windows. At the time of this book's writing (Fall 2004), Service Pack 2 for Windows XP was just introduced.

Other Operating Systems

While Windows is the most common operating system, it isn't the only operating system available. You can find other operating systems, especially on special system types. For instance, the Macintosh uses a different operating system. Workstations often use a different operating system, and networks may also employ something other than Windows. This section discusses some of the other common operating systems.

MACINTOSH SYSTEM

Macintosh computers have always had a graphical user interface. In fact, much of Windows was copied (or imitated) from the Macintosh operating system. This operating system is called "System," and the current version is System OS X Panther.

If you've used Windows, you won't have any trouble using a Macintosh because tasks and features are similar. Both use a mouse to point to and open icons. Both enable you to set up your desktop with features you most often use. Menus and program windows look similar. The Macintosh includes a group of programs called the Control Panel for managing components such as the keyboard and mouse. Given these (and other) similarities, most of the contents of the section "Working with Windows" will apply to the Mac as well.

 WEB: Visit www.apple.com to get information about the latest Mac operating system.

UNIX

Unix is the granddad of all operating systems and was initially popular in university settings. This operating system is most often found on high-end systems and workstations, and it has features that are uniquely suited to this environment. Unix can run on many different types of computers, including mainframe and minicomputers. It is a multitasking, multiprocessing operating system.

The downside? Unix is command-driven like DOS. (DOS was somewhat based on Unix, so you'll find that some DOS commands are pulled directly from Unix.)

LINUX

Linux is another popular operating system. It is like Unix in many ways: it can run on almost any computer and it has Unix-like commands. The difference is that Linux is free and therefore has been successful in the computer industry and mainstream media.

 Finland student: Linux was developed in 1991 by a 21-year-old college student named Linus Torvalds from Finland. Torvalds did not like DOS, so he decided to write his own operating system.

PALMTOP OPERATING SYSTEMS

Because palmtop and other handheld computers are limited in size, they cannot store a complete operating system. Therefore, they need a simpler version of system software. Windows developed an operating system for these types of devices. Called Windows CE, this operating system can be found in palmtop computers, handheld computers, and household devices. In addition to Windows CE, you can find other popular operating systems including the Palm operating system by Palm Pilot.

Working with Windows

To get an idea of what you can do (and how to do it), you can review this primer on key Windows tasks, including displaying files, starting programs, and more.

UNDERSTANDING THE DESKTOP

When you start a Windows computer, you see the Windows desktop (see Figure 5.3). Like your physical desktop, the Windows desktop includes tools to get you started using your computer. Here are the key elements usually found on the desktop:

Customize: Keep in mind that you can customize your desktop, adding program icons, changing the background image or color, and arranging the icons. Your desktop, then, probably looks different than the ones shown in this book's figures. You will find, though, that many of the icons (such as the Recycle Bin) are almost always displayed on the desktop.

Figure 5.3. The Windows desktop is your starting point for all PC tasks.

- *Start button.* You use this button to start programs, but also to access other commands for using Windows, including getting help and accessing the Control Panel.

- *Taskbar.* The Start button is displayed on the taskbar. This taskbar also displays buttons for all open programs and windows, providing you an easy method for switching between programs. The taskbar also includes icons for tasks. As an example, if you are printing, you will see a printer icon on the taskbar (far right part of the taskbar).

- *Icons.* The little pictures on the desktop are called icons. You'll have some special Windows icons (covered in this list), plus any icons you have added. You can add icons for programs, files, folders, or devices so that you have fast access to them.

- *My Computer.* This is a special Windows icon. You can open this icon to view the drives on your system and their contents. If you don't have a shortcut icon to My Computer on the desktop, you can access this icon from the Start menu.

- *Recycle Bin.* Another special Windows icon, this system folder contains all the files you have deleted. When you delete a file, it is not deleted, but moved to this special folder. You can retrieve the file if needed or delete it from the bin permanently.

- *My Documents.* Yet another Windows icon, this is a folder that is often used to store all your documents. You can add a shortcut icon to the desktop as well as access this folder from the Start menu.

- *Program icons.* You may also see program icons on your desktop. You can double-click the program icon to start the program.

DISPLAYING MY COMPUTER

When you need to find a particular file or folder, you can use the My Computer icon. It displays icons for each of the drives on your system as well as special system folders (see Figure 5.4). To open the icon and display the contents of your system, click Start and then click My Computer. If you have a desktop shortcut icon for My Computer, you can also double-click the icon to display its contents. Once opened, you can do any of the following:

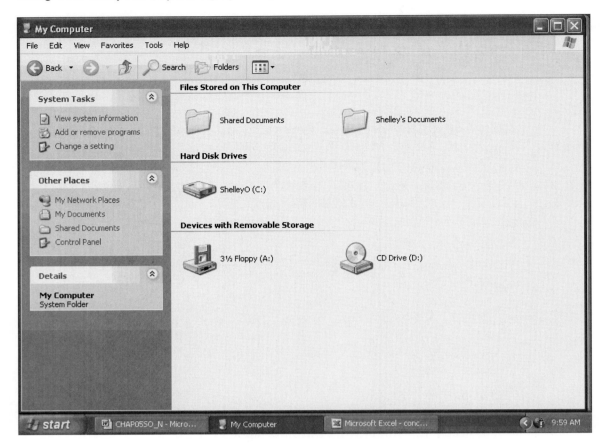

Figure 5.4. Use My Computer to display the drives on your computer.

- You can double-click a drive icon to open the drive. You may be looking for a folder or file to copy, move, or delete. Or you might be looking for a program file so that you can create a shortcut to the program. The section "Managing Files" covers these tasks in more detail.

- Select common tasks from the task pane (the left part of the window). For instance, you can view system information or change system settings.

- You can get information about the drives. For instance, you might want to see the amount of free space on your hard drive. Right-click the drive and select Properties.

- You can access system tools, such as commands, to scan a disk for errors, format a floppy disk, or start a backup program. To display a list of commands and tools for drives, right-click the drive. Then select the command you want.

RESIZING, MOVING, AND CLOSING WINDOWS

Everything in Windows is displayed in a window on the screen. That window may contain a program or content (list of files or folders). When you open an icon, you see the contents. As an example, when you open My Computer, you see the drives on your system. If you start a program, that program is opened in a window. All windows have the same set of controls which you can use to move and resize the window. Figure 5.5

identifies these controls. You can move and resize the windows as needed (similar to rearranging papers on your physical desktop). You can do any of the following:

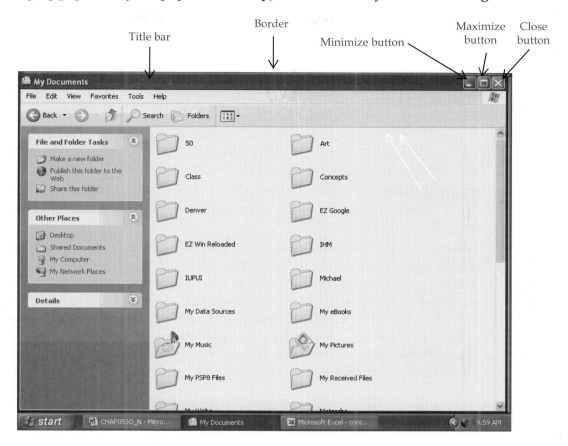

Figure 5.5. You can use the window controls to change the size and shape of the window as well as close the window.

- To close the window, click its Close button or choose Close from the File menu.

- To minimize a window (keep it open, but shrink it to a button on the taskbar), click the Minimize button.

- To expand a window to fill the entire screen, click the Maximize button. When a window is maximized, you cannot resize or move it. Also, the Maximize button changes to a Restore button. Click this button to restore the window to its previous size and location.

- To move a window, drag the title bar.

- To resize a window, put the pointer on any of the window borders or corners and drag the border.

- To scroll through a window, click the scroll bars. You can find scroll bars along the right or bottom of the window (if not all of the contents of the window can be displayed within the window).

- All open windows have a taskbar button for the window. To change to another window, click its button in the taskbar.

MANAGING FILES

As mentioned, one of the main tasks of an operating system is file management. The operating system will handle the storing and opening of files. You also will need to do some file maintenance, and to do so, you can use Windows. Most common tasks are listed in the task pane; you can use these commands to copy, rename, delete, and perform other file maintenance tasks. Keep these guidelines in mind:

- The first step is to select the item you want to work with. If you want to copy a file, for instance, select that file by clicking it. You can select a single file, a group of files in a row, a set of files that are not in a row, or all files (click Edit, Select All). You can also select a folder by clicking it. The commands in the task pane vary depending on what you have selected.

- If you don't like the original name you used for the file, you can rename it, using a more descriptive name. Select the file, click **Rename this file**, type a new name, and press Enter.

- You can move or copy files as needed. You might move a file if you want to store it on a different drive or in a different folder. You can copy files if you want to keep an extra copy or perhaps you want to keep the original, but modify the copy. Use the **Move this file** and **Copy this file** commands to move or copy files. Windows displays a dialog box that lists the drives and folders on your computer. You can select the appropriate folder from this list. (Click the plus sign next to a folder to display subfolders within.) Figure 5.6, for instance, displays the Move Items dialog box.

Figure 5.6. You can select the folder to which to move (or copy) the selected items.

- You should delete files you no longer need so that you can free up that disk space. To do so, select the file(s) and then click Delete this file or Delete the selected items. Note that deleted files are not really deleted, but moved to the Recycle Bin.

- You can open the Recycle Bin (double-click it) and retrieve any of the items. You can also use the Empty Recycle Bin command to permanently get rid of all the items in the Recycle Bin.

- You also use Windows to create new folders to keep your files organized. To do so, open the folder in which you want to place the new folder. Then click Make a new folder, type a folder name, and press Enter.

- The toolbar buttons and task pane also enable you to navigate to other drives and folders on your computer. You can click any of the folders or drives listed under Other Places. You can also use the Up One Level button in the toolbar to move up through the folder structure.

 Can't find a file? If you cannot find a file by browsing, search for it using the Search command. Click the Start button and then select Search. Follow the prompts in the task pane to select the type of file you want to search for, enter the search criteria (you can search by name, date, content, and other file features), and start the search.

 Back up work: Your documents are the most valuable item on your computer. You may have some documents that you are unable to re-create. Therefore, it's important that you save your work while you create documents. It's also critical that you keep an extra copy (backup) of your data files. You can copy files manually to a CD. Or you can use a backup program. You should backup often!

USING THE ACCESSORY PROGRAMS

Windows includes some accessory programs (mostly stored in the Accessories folder. Click Start, then All Programs, then Accessories to view these programs.) Here are just a few highlights of these accessory programs and program folders:

- *Solitaire* (see Figure 5.7). Solitaire is a good way to relax or pass the time. Solitaire is also any excellent way for new users to master the mouse (learn to click, drag, double-click, etc.). Note that Solitaire is an accessory program, but may not be listed in the Accessories folder. If you don't see it listed, click Start, All Programs, and then Games.

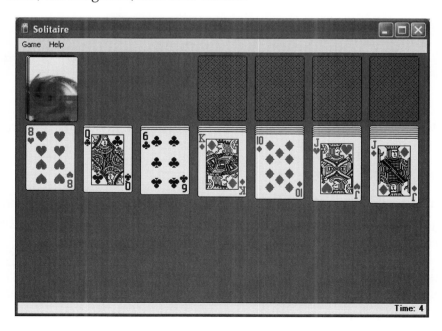

Figure 5.7. Be careful! You can get addicted to playing the computer version of Solitaire.

- *Calculator.* Use this simple program to perform calculations.

- *Entertainment programs.* In the Entertainment folder, you can find programs for playing sounds, media files, and audio CDs. You can also control the volume. Lesson 11 covers entertainment features in more detail.

- *System tools.* For access to system tools, check out this folder. You can also scan a disk for errors, defragment a disk, and schedule maintenance tasks using the programs in this folder.

- *Paint.* You can create simple illustrations with this paint program, shown in Figure 5.8.

Figure 5.8. Express your creativity with this paint program.

- *WordPad.* You can use this simple word processing program to create documents.

RESTARTING AND SHUTTING DOWN

You shouldn't just turn off your computer. Instead, you need to use a command. First, exit all programs, saving any documents that are open. Then click Start and then Turn Off Computer. Click Turn Off.

If your computer gets stuck (won't respond), you can restart. You may also need to restart if you make a change to the setup of the computer (add a new hardware component, for instance, or make a change). Click Start and then Turn Off Computer. Click the Restart button.

If you are unable to display the Start menu (the computer isn't responding at all), you may have to reset the computer by turning it off and then back on using the Power or Reset button.

 Stuck? If your computer gets stuck (won't respond), you can sometimes close the problem program. Press Ctrl+Alt+Delete to display the Task Manager which lists all open programs. Select the program you want to exit and click End Task.

If you are connected to a network, you may perform a different procedure for logging off and shutting down the PC. Check with the system administrator or class instructor.

Using Programs

Most of your time spent using a computer will be spent within a program, such as a word processing program or a game. (Part II covers programs in more detail.) This section covers key information on installing, starting, and exiting Windows programs.

One of the great advantages that Windows brought to computing was program consistency. Most programs look and operate similarly. Skills you learn in one program are transferable to other programs. As an example, you select a menu command the same way in most Windows programs: click the menu name and then click the menu command. Many programs include the same menus (File, Edit, View, Help) and same commands in those menus (Save, Open, Copy, Paste).

INSTALLING NEW PROGRAMS

Most programs come with an automated installation program. Usually you insert the program CD and the installation will start automatically. If this doesn't work, you can use the Add or Remove Programs feature to add new programs or uninstall programs. Click Start and then click Control Panel. In Category view, click the Add or Remove Programs link. (In Classic view, double-click the Add or Remove Programs icon.)

When you install a new program, the installation program should add a program icon to the Start menu. (It may also add a program shortcut to your desktop.) The next section explains how to start programs from the Start menu.

STARTING AND EXITING PROGRAMS

Windows provides several ways to start a program:

- To view a list of all your programs, click Start and then All Programs (see Figure 5.9). Some programs are listed on the menu; click the program name to start the program. Some programs, like the accessory programs, are stored within folders on the Start menu. Click or point to the folder name until you see the program. Then click the program name to start it.

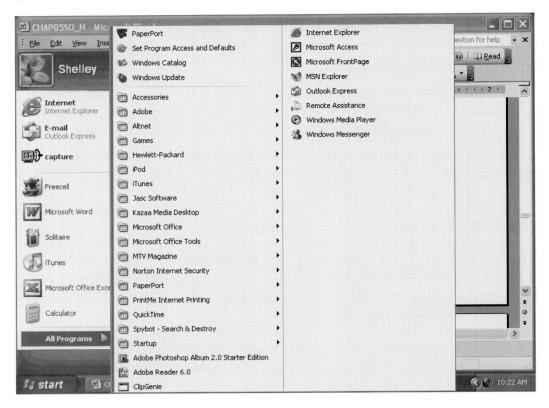

Figure 5.9. You can start programs from the Start menu.

- The most often used programs are listed on the opening Start menu (as well as programs for accessing the Internet and email). If your program is listed here, you can click Start and then click the program name without having to display and select from the complete list.

- You can add desktop shortcuts to commonly used programs. You can then double-click the program icon to start the program.

- You can double-click a file to open that file in that file's associated program. For instance, if you double-click a Word document, Windows will start Word and open that document. (If Windows doesn't know which program to use to open the file, you'll be prompted to select one.)

When you are done working in a program, exit the program. Doing so frees up system resources. You can exit by selecting the File, Exit command, by clicking the Close button, or by pressing the keyboard shortcut key (Alt+F4). Before exiting, be sure to save any documents you have created. Saving a document is covered next.

SAVING A DOCUMENT

As you know, when you type or enter data, it is stored in memory, which is not permanent. If you exit the program or turn off the computer, all that data is lost. To make a permanent copy of the data, you save it to your hard drive or floppy disk. Doing so copies the data from memory to the disk. All of the information is saved as one file.

The first time you save a document, you assign a file name and a location (folder and drive). You usually see the Save As dialog box, which enables you to type a name, select a drive, and/or select a folder (see Figure 5.10).

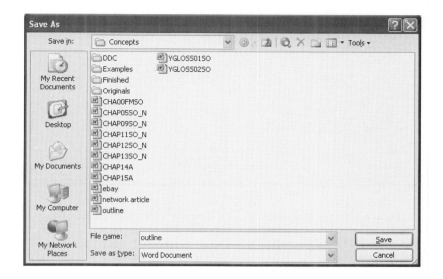

Figure 5.9. Use this dialog box to save a document.

You shouldn't just save once, but instead save periodically as you make changes to the file. The disk version includes only the additions you have made up to saving the file. Any changes or additions after you saved are not saved until you save again. To save a file again, use the File, Save command, press Ctrl+S, or click the Save toolbar button. When you save again, you do not have to type the name and select the location. When you select File, Save, you save the file with the same file name and location as before.

 Save to new location: If you want to save a document to another location or with a different name, you can use the File, Save As command. Type a new name or select a new location. The original remains intact.

OPENING A DOCUMENT

When you save a document, it is then available for you to open and work on again. Most work is an ongoing process, so you may need to refer to the document, make changes to the document, print the document, or change the appearance of the document. To open a document, use the File, Open command. You can then select the file you want to open, usually from a dialog box similar to the Open dialog box shown in Figure 5.11. Double-click the file you want to open. If the file is not listed, you can change to another drive or folder using the Look in drop-down list.

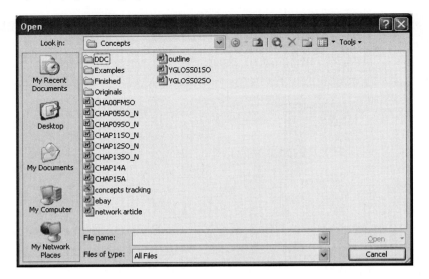

Figure 5.10. Open documents you have saved from this dialog box.

Customizing Windows

One of the other benefits of Windows is that you can customize it to work and look just the way you want. The following, for instance, provides just a few of the features you can change:

- You can change the image that is displayed on your desktop (see Figure 5.12), use a screen saver, change the colors used, and make other changes to the appearance of Windows. You make most of these changes in the Display Properties dialog box. Right-click a blank area of the desktop and then click Properties. Use the various tabs to make changes.

Figure 5.12. You can display a background image on your desktop.

- Change what items appear on the desktop. For instance, you can add shortcut icons to programs, files, or folders.

- You can also change the look of the Start menu and the taskbar. For instance, you may want to hide the taskbar so that you have a little more room to display your programs. To make these changes, right-click the Start menu and then click Properties. Use the tabs here to make changes to both the Start menu and the taskbar.

- If you are left-handed or if you have trouble with using your mouse, you can customize the mouse. You can switch the right and left button purposes, and you can adjust the double-click speed. To make these changes, open the Mouse properties in the Control Panel. Click Start and then Control Panel. In Category view, click Printers and Other Hardware and then click Mouse in the lower half.

These are just a few of the many, many ways you can adapt Windows so that it suits your preferences.

Summary

- All computer systems require an operating system to work. This special system software handles common tasks, such as starting programs, saving files, displaying things on the monitor, and more.

- The most popular operating system is Microsoft Windows. You can find several Windows products, each designed for a specific market (consumers, businesses, networks). Windows XP is the current version.

- Other popular operating systems include the Macintosh Operating System, Unix (used on high-end computers and workstations), and Linux (a free version of a high-end operating system similar to Unix).

- Windows uses a graphical user interface which enables users to point to what they want. Most Windows programs follow a standard design so that once you learn one Windows programs you can transfer these skills (selecting a menu command, saving a document, copying text, for instance) to other Windows programs.

- When you start Windows you see the Windows desktop, which includes the Start menu, taskbar, and icons.

- Everything in Windows is displayed in a window. You can move, resize, open, and close windows as needed.

- You can use Windows to perform common file maintenance tasks, such as copying a file, creating a new folder, deleting files, and renaming a file.

- To start a program, use the Start menu. You can also start programs from shortcut icons on the desktop.

- When you create a new document, you must save it to keep a permanent copy. The first time you save a file, you assign a file name and location. Once a file is saved, you can open the file to review, make changes, print, or change the appearance of the document.

LESSON 6: CREATING DOCUMENTS (WORD PROCESSING PROGRAMS)

Objectives:

➤ **Define word processing**

➤ **Identify the main word processing programs and features**

➤ **Type and edit text**

➤ **Format text**

➤ **Format paragraphs**

➤ **Format pages**

➤ **Use special word processing features**

What is Word Processing?

The most common type of computer program and the program used in most homes and offices is a word processing program. With a word processing program, you create documents and much more. In this section you will learn what you can do with a word processing program and where you might expect to put this program to use.

TYPES OF DOCUMENTS

You can use a word processing program to create any type of text-based documents, including letters, memos, faxes, reports, manuscripts, newsletters, brochures, contracts, resumes, and manuals. Figure 6.1 shows a document created with a word processing program.

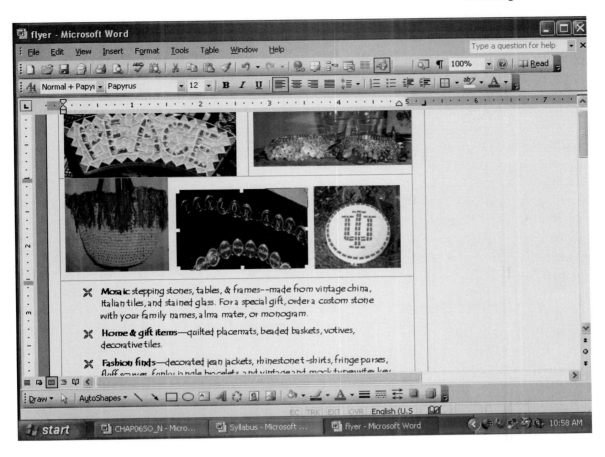

Figure 6.1. You can use a word processing program to
create any type of document, including a flyer.

A word processing document is often the basic building block for complex documents—documents that contain different types of data. For instance, you can insert a chart, text, and illustrations in a word processing document. For documents from different programs, you most often combine them in a word processing document.

When are you likely to use a word processing program? And what types of documents are you likely to create? What features? Here are some examples:

- *Resumes.* If you are looking for a job, you can create a resume listing your education, job skills, and personal information. You can use formatting features such as a bigger font for your name and address and bullets for key points to make the document attractive.

- *Letters.* If you type letters to business associates, colleagues, friends, or relatives, use a word processing program instead of writing the letter. Not only is it faster, but you can enliven your letter, perhaps with photographs or other illustrations.

- *Invitations/flyers.* Having a party? Helping with a car wash? You can create invitations and flyers, using clip art and fonts, to create eye-catching results.

WHO USES THIS KIND OF PROGRAM

Most office workers use this type of program. Administrative assistants typing correspondence, managers creating reports, department heads typing memos. You'll also find this type of program in school: teachers creating assignments and students.

If you are a writer, you can use a word processing program to compose your documents. A word processing program enables you to type, edit, format, print, and distribute any type of written publication—book, manual, term paper, newsletter, poem, song, brochure, advertisement, flyer, invitation, menu, article, magazine, booklet, etc.

Journalists write and submit stories in electronic format, and may also do research using any of the various resources found on CDs, microfiche, or the Internet. The paper or magazine may be both printed and published online. Even if the publication is just printed, the layout was most likely done on a computer.

 WEB: Many newspapers are distributed via the Internet, including *USA Today* (www.usatoday.com), the *Chicago Tribune* (www.chicagotribune.com), and *The New York Times* (www.nytimes.com).

 TRY IT: See if your local paper is published on the Internet. If so, visit that site. Does it have an unique features in the online version?

If the job somehow involves words, you'll likely use a word processing program.

BENEFITS OF WORD PROCESSING

A word processing program offers many benefits. First, you can see the words on-screen as you type, so you can easily correct errors. You can backspace to delete and retype an incorrect word. Second, you can easily add text to any part of the document. Simply click where you want the new text and type. The new text is inserted, and the existing text moves over. And finally, you can delete text easily. You can select the text and press a key to delete it. The existing text moves up to fill in the gap.

FEATURES OF WORD PROCESSING PROGRAMS

In addition to making typing and correcting text easier, a word processing program offers many features to simplify document creation. The following lists the basic features of word processing programs:

- *Editing features.* In addition to being able to insert and delete text, you can also copy and move text. You can copy and move within a document or from one document to another. You can even copy and move text from one program to another program. This copy and paste makes editing easier and also saves time so that you don't have to retype text. To move text, you cut the text and then paste it in the new location.
- *Checking features.* Most word processing programs have a spelling program. You can use this feature to check your document for errors. Some programs

have a grammar checker for checking grammar and a thesaurus for looking up synonyms.

- *Formatting features*. Word processing programs offer many features for enhancing the look of the text. You can use a different typeface, make headings larger, change the text color, set tabs, and more. (You can find more on formatting later in this lesson.)

- *Special features*. Programs also offer special features, such as tables, graphics, Web publishing tools, and more. You can use these special features to create complex documents.

Word Processing Programs

Now that you know what this program is used for, you can learn about the different programs available. You might already be using this type of program. Or you may have a word processing program and not even know about it! And if you are shopping for new software, you can pick out the program best suited for your needs.

POPULAR PROGRAMS

The two main word processing programs are Microsoft Word and Corel WordPerfect. The popularity of these programs has evolved, mirroring changes to the operating systems. At first, DOS-based word-processing programs were the most popular, and the king of the DOS word processing world was WordPerfect. WordPerfect was especially popular with lawyers.

When Windows gained popularity, so did Windows programs, and the most popular word processing program for Windows is Microsoft Word. This is now the most popular and commonly used word processing program.

 WEB: For information on Word for Windows, visit Microsoft's Office page at office.microsoft.com. For information on WordPerect, visit Corel's Web site at www.corel.com and then look for links for information on WordPerfect.

Both Word and WordPerfect are top-of-the line, full-powered word processing programs and have comparable features. In addition to these programs, you can find simple versions of word processing programs. Windows, for instance, includes a word processing accessory called WordPad. Figure 6.2 shows the WordPad screen. Microsoft Works also includes a simpler version of a word processing program. If you use a Macintosh, you can use AppleWorks.

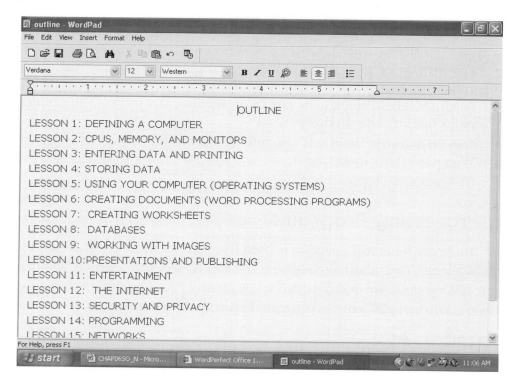

Figure 6.2. You can use WordPad to create simple documents.

STARTING A PROGRAM

To start a word processing program in Windows, you open the Start menu, point to All Programs, point to a program folder (if necessary), and then click the icon for the program. If you have a shortcut to the icon on your desktop, you can double-click this icon to start the program.

To start a word processing program from another system, give the command to start the program.

 TIP: What program do you have? If you aren't sure which program you have, click Start and then click All Programs. Look for icons for Microsoft Works, Microsoft Word, or WordPerfect. To use the WordPad program, click Start, select All Programs, and then click Accessories. Click WordPad to start this program.

BUYING A PROGRAM

If you do not have a word processing program but would like to purchase one, you can expect to pay $100 to $300. The range in price varies depending on the program and whether you are upgrading from an existing version to a new version. You can purchase this type of program at computer stores, through online storefronts, or by calling any of the mail-order software companies.

When purchasing a program, be sure to get the most current version. Also, if you require more than a word processing program, consider a suite, such as Microsoft

Office. This package bundles together several popular programs. The programs included vary depending on the version. Also, some computer manufacturers include bundles that include different programs. All bundles include Microsoft Word, Microsoft Excel, and Microsoft Outlook. Other versions may include Micrsoft PowerPoint and/or Microsoft Access. Check out the bundle deals if you are shopping for new programs.

Finally, make sure your computer can run the software. You can find a list of requirements—the required disk space, processor type, memory, and so on—on the package or in the program description.

Typing and Editing Text

The easiest part of using a word processing program is typing and editing text.

 TIP: Not a good typist? Typing is more important now than ever. If you aren't a great typist, work on your typing skills. Included on the CD that comes with this text is a complete typing course and Windows-based typing tests.

UNDERSTANDING THE PROGRAM TOOLS

Most word processing programs look similar (especially Windows programs). Figure 6.3 shows a blank document in Microsoft Word. You can expect to find these key elements in most programs:

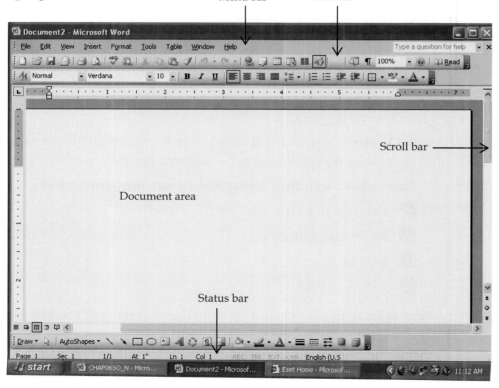

Figure 6.3. A word processing program has tools to help you use the program features.

- *Menu bar*. The menu bar lists the names of the menu. To open a menu, click its name. You see a list of commands. To select a command, click that command.

- *Toolbars*. Toolbars are rows of buttons; each button is a shortcut to a frequently used command. For instance, click the Bold button (the one with a B) to make text bold.

- *Document area*. The area where your text will appear when you type is the big blank area.

- *Status bar*. For information about the current document, such as the current page, check the status bar.

- *Window controls*. You also have control buttons for opening and closing the document and program windows. If you see scroll bars along the right and bottom, you can use this to scroll through the document.

TYPING TEXT

To type text, you simply press the keys on the keyboard. As you type, the character appears on-screen, and the flashing vertical line (called the *insertion point*) moves right.

When you reach the end of the line, the program will wrap the word to the next line, so you do not have to press Enter. In fact, a common error for beginners is to press Enter at the end of each line. Don't. It *does* matter if you press Enter. Doing so inserts hard line breaks. If you add or delete text, the text will not adjust correctly. That's why you should just let the text break where it will. You can press Enter when you want to end one paragraph and again if you want to insert a blank line.

Another mistake beginners often make is pressing the spacebar twice at the end of each sentence. Just use one space. Also, don't use the spacebar to indent text. Use the Tab key instead or set indents (more on this later).

MOVING AROUND THE DOCUMENT

The insertion point indicates where text will appear when you type. You can move this pointer to another spot in the document using the keyboard or the mouse.

To use the keyboard, press the cursor movement keys:

⬅ Left one character

➡ Right one character

⬆ Up one line

⬇ Down one line

Most programs offer several other keyboard combinations for moving around. Learn these to save time. For instance, pressing Home usually moves the insertion point to the beginning of the line, whereas pressing End usually moves the insertion point to the end of the current line.

To use the mouse, move the mouse pointer (which looks like an I-beam) to the spot you want. Then click to place the insertion point.

MAKING SIMPLE CHANGES

You can easily correct simple mistakes as you type. Press Backspace to delete characters to the left of the insertion point. Press Delete to delete characters to the right of the insertion point. To add text, move to where you want to place new text and start typing.

MOVING AND COPYING TEXT

Word processing programs make rearranging a document easy. You can move text from one location to another. You might rearrange the sentences in a paragraph so that they flow better. You might move whole sections around in a document. You can even move text from one document to another.

Copying is also a part of editing. You might want to repeat the same text in another location in a document. Or sometimes you need to repeat the same idea, but worded differently. Don't retype. Copy the text instead and then modify the copy.

Copying and moving use a similar process and the same analogy: cut and paste. To move text, you cut it from its original location and then paste it in the new. To copy, you copy and then paste. When you cut and paste, the original text is deleted from that location and moved to the new location. When you copy and paste, the original and the copy appear in the document.

Look for Cut, Copy, and Paste commands in the Edit menu. Most programs also have keyboard shortcuts and toolbar buttons for these features.

The basic steps follow:

1   Select the text you want to copy or move.

2   Select the command (Edit, Cut to cut or Edit, Copy to copy).

3   Move to where you want to place the text. Be sure to click the mouse to place the insertion point.

4   Select the Edit, Paste command to paste the text.

SELECTING TEXT

To perform most editing and formatting tasks, you start by selecting text. If you are using most programs, you'll find that concept often: "Select the text and then… Select the file and then… Select the image you want and then…"

Selecting identifies the thing that you want to modify. In a word processing program, most often that is text. You can select text by dragging across it with the mouse button or by holding down the Shift key and highlighting the text using the arrow keys. Figure 6.4 shows text selected.

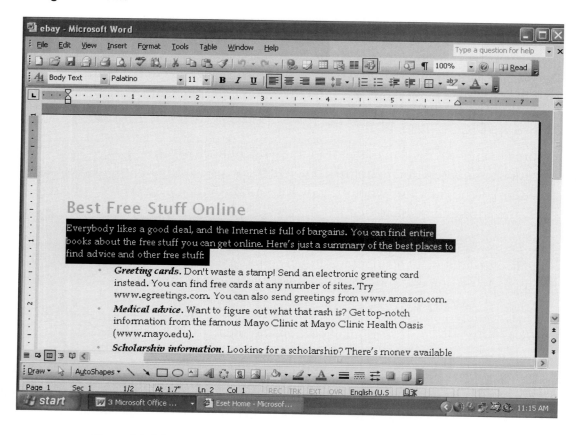

Figure 6.4. Most editing and formatting tasks start with selecting the text.

Formatting Text

The content of any document is the most important part of the document, but the content may be ignored if the document's appearance isn't presentable. To make sure your document is attractive and readable, you can make enhancements to the text. Changing the appearance of something is called *formatting*. This section discusses formatting text.

DEFINING FONTS

A typeface is a set of characters (letters and numbers) in a particular style. A font is a specific combination of the size, style, and weight of a particular typeface. That concept can be confusing. Times New Roman is a typeface. Times New Roman 12-Point Bold is a font. For the most part, the terms "typeface" and "font" are used interchangeably.

You can use any of the fonts on your system and printer. Each printer has its own set of internal fonts; these are indicated with a printer icon in the font list. Windows also can use TrueType fonts (fonts stored as files on your drive) and comes with several fonts. Your programs may also add new fonts to the Windows font folder. You can use any of these fonts.

Fonts are measured in points, with 72 points to an inch. To make text smaller, use a smaller point size. To make text larger, use a larger point size. The body text of a document is usually 10 to 12 points. For instance, this text is 11 points.

In addition to the typeface and size, you can also use styles. The three most common include bold, italic, and underline. Depending on the font and the program, you may also have special effects available, such as shadow and emboss.

CHANGING THE FONT

To change the font, you select the text you want to change. Then you can use one of two methods: the toolbar method or the command method.

Most programs provide toolbar buttons for changing the font. You can use these buttons to select a typeface, a point size, and a style. Figure 6.5 identifies the toolbar buttons for each of these changes. The document shows you some examples of changes.

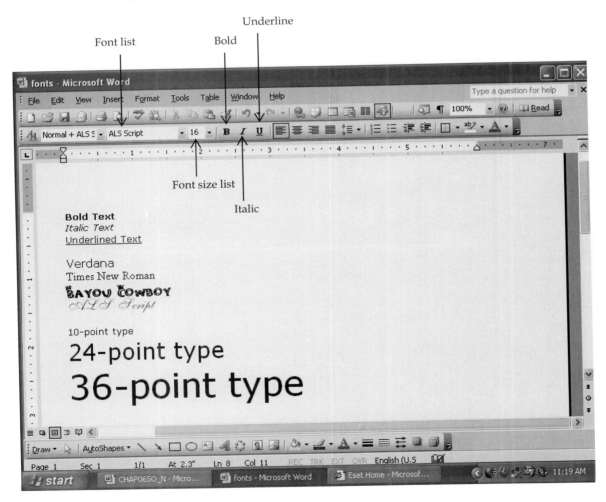

Figure 6.5. You can use the toolbar buttons to change the font.

The toolbar method is the fastest method, but if you have several changes to make at once or you want to try some special effects, use the command method. Look in the Format menu for a Font command. Select this command to display a dialog box of options. Figure 6.6 shows the dialog box for Word. Notice that you can not only select the font, size, and style, but also try some special effects, including changing the color of text. The preview shows a sample of the text with these formats.

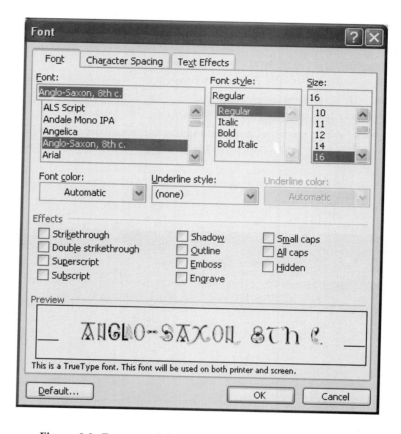

Figure 6.6. For several changes, use the dialog box method.

 TIP: Don't go overboard! Too many fonts, sizes, and styles are distracting. Keep your formatting simple.

Formatting text is especially important in "fun" documents, such as invitations to a party or a flyer describing a sale. You can experiment, mixing fonts and sizes, until the look of the document is perfect.

Formatting Paragraphs

In addition to changing the look of the text, you may also want to format the paragraphs. Common changes include changing the alignment, indenting text, double-spacing lines, and adding bullets or numbers. Most word processing programs provide these features.

ALIGNMENT

When you type text in most programs, it is left-aligned. That means the text aligns with the left margin. For document headings, you might prefer a different alignment—for instance, centering. You can center a line or an entire paragraph. You can also right-align a paragraph. Some programs offer another alignment choice: justified text. In justified text, the left and right margins are flush (even). Figure 6.7 shows an example of four alignments.

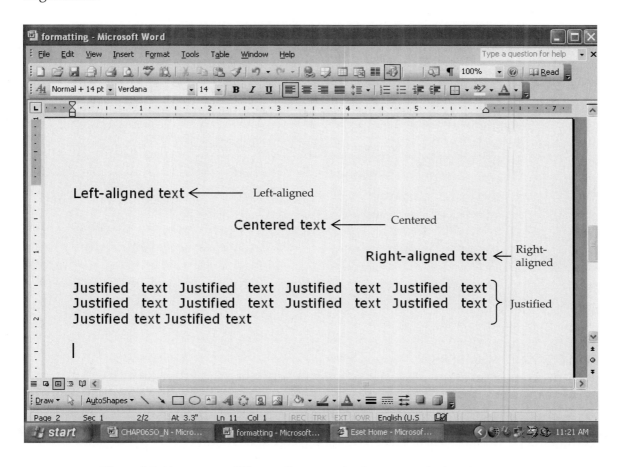

Figure 6.7. You can use different alignments for the paragraphs in a document.

To make a change, select the paragraphs you want to modify and then use the buttons on the toolbar or look for a Format, Paragraph command.

 TIP: Not sure what a particular toolbar button does? Try putting the pointer on the button. The name should pop up.

LINE SPACING

If you need to alter the spacing of the paragraph, don't manually insert blank lines. Instead, you can use the program to add space. Most term papers and other manuscripts are double-spaced. You may also be able to use other intervals (1.5 spacing, for instance) or add space above or below a paragraph. Look in the Format menu for a Paragraph command. Then use the dialog box that appears to make the changes.

 TIP: You can use keyboard shortcuts for line spacing. Press Ctrl+1 for single-spacing or Ctrl+2 for double-spacing.

INDENTS

To make the first line of a paragraph stand out, you can press Tab to indent the text. You can also use your program to indent the first line, to indent all lines (to set off text), or to create a hanging indent, where all lines but the first line is indented. As an example, in a report if you cite text that is longer than five lines, you usually indent this text from the left and right margin.

Many programs display a ruler at the top. You can use this ruler to set tabs and to make indenting changes. The ruler can be confusing because you have to drag just the right marker to make a change. Try it if you want. If you don't like the ruler, use the menu command.

Also, keep in mind that when you set indents, you do so for the selected paragraphs only. This does not change the margins. If you want to move all of the text over, you can change the margins of the page.

BULLETS AND NUMBERS

To set off ideas, you can use a bulleted list. Don't type an asterisk before each line. Instead, let your program add a bullet. Most programs, even the simple ones, have bullets. You may also be able to add numbers. Look for buttons in the toolbar or commands for bullets or numbering in the Format menu. Some word processing programs automatically start the numbering feature if it thinks you are creating a numbered list.

Formatting Pages

For one-page documents, you probably won't need to make changes to the page. For longer documents, use your program to make appropriate changes, such as changing the margins, adding page numbers, and more.

MARGINS

Most programs have default margins that work well. (They usually are set to 1" for the top and bottom margins and 1 ¼ " for the left and right margins.) To fit more on a page, you might want to make the margins smaller. To fit less on a page (and make the document fill more pages), use bigger margins. As another example, if you use letterhead, you may want to adjust the top margin to accommodate the letterhead.

To make these types of changes, use the File, Page Setup command. (This command can be hard to find because you would think the command would be within the Format menu. Look under File.) As you can see from Figure 6.8, most Page Setup dialog boxes have options for changing the margins. Make your selections and then click OK.

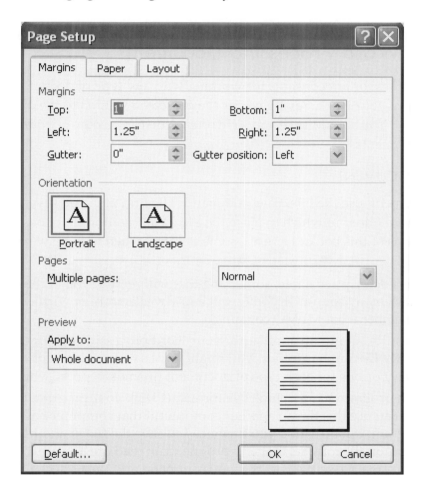

Figure 6.8. Make changes to the page formatting in the Page Setup dialog box.

PAGE NUMBERS

In a longer document, consider adding page numbers to keep the pages in order. Some programs may have commands for adding page numbers. Word, for instance, lets you set up a page number at the top or bottom of the page and then creates a header or footer depending on your choice. In others, you may have to set up the page numbers in a header or footer.

HEADERS AND FOOTERS

A header is text that repeats at the top of all pages in a document. A footer is text that repeats at the bottom of all pages. Most programs let you add text, such as page numbers or document names. You can also add graphics—for instance, a company logo—in a header or footer.

 TIP: Get fancy! Some programs let you turn off headers and footers on the first page or use different headers or footers in sections or for odd and even pages. Check your program documentation.

Handling Word Processing Documents

One of the most important concepts for working with any type of document is saving. You need to save your work. Saving copies the on-screen version to the disk, making a permanent copy. You should save and save often. You can also print your word processing documents.

SAVING A DOCUMENT

To save a document, use the File, Save command. The first time you save you type a file name and select a folder in which to place the file. (You can find more on files in the previous sections of this book.) Here are some pointers when naming word processing documents:

- Use a descriptive name, something that will remind you of the contents. MEMO may sound OK today, but a few weeks from now, you won't remember what MEMO contains.
- Consider setting up a folder for your word processing documents by using the My Documents folder. You might have several folders, one for each project or one for each type of document (memos, reports, letters).
- Each program has a default file format. (Check your program to find yours.) You can use this file on another computer if that computer has the same program. If it does not, you may need to save the file in another file format. Common file formats that any program can read are TXT (text) and RTF (rich text format). Use the File, Save As command and then select a file type from the dialog box.
- You should periodically get rid of documents you no longer need. First make a backup copy and then delete the files. Doing so will free up disk space and keep the files you do need less cluttered.
- You can also save a document to a floppy disk. To do so, select this drive when you save and name the document.

PRINTING A DOCUMENT

Word processing documents are for the most part intended to be printed, and all programs enable you to print. Most also include a preview feature. Check the preview first to make sure the document looks as you intended. Doing so can save paper and printing time. Make any changes and then print. The command to print is usually File, Print. You then select any printing options such as whether to print all pages or a range as well as the number of copies to print (see Figure 6.9). Your program may also have a toolbar button for printing and a keyboard shortcut (usually Ctrl+P).

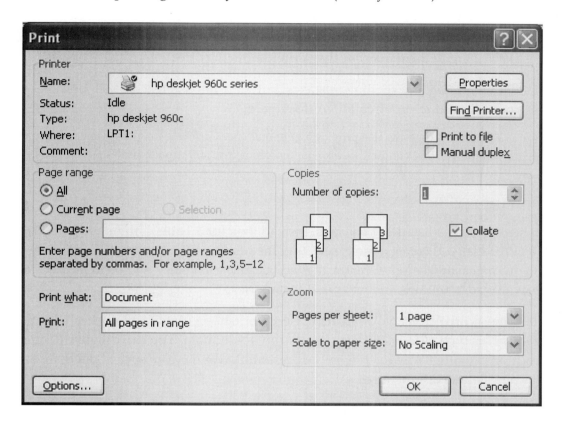

Figure 6.9. Select your printing options and then click Print.

Special Word Processing Features

Most programs, even the basic ones, will include the features already discussed. The more complex programs will offer additional features to make creating documents easier and to enable you to create more sophisticated documents. This section describes some of these other features you are likely to find.

CHECK YOUR SPELLING

Many programs include a spell checker. You should use this program to check the words in your document. Before you think you can quit worrying about spelling forever, understand how the speller works.

The speller works by comparing the words in your document to the words in its dictionary. It then flags any words it cannot find. That does not necessarily mean that the word is misspelled. Proper names or terms may not be found in the dictionary. For this type of flag, you can ignore the misspelling or add the word to your dictionary so that it is not flagged again.

If the speller finds the word in its dictionary, the word will not be flagged. That means words that are spelled correctly, but used incorrectly, will *not* be flagged. Consider this sentence:

Their going to the party, but they don't know the directions to *there* house.

The speller won't flag any spelling mistakes, but your English teacher will find the errors. You still need to proofread your document.

 TIP: Some programs also provide a grammar checker. These may flag some common errors, but they are also not foolproof. You still need to proofread.

ADD TABLES

If you have to type a list, don't use tabs. Instead look for a Table command. Programs such as Word let you create a table, selecting the number of columns. When you use a table, you can easily keep the entries aligned because each entry will be in its own cell. You can also add columns and rows and sort entries.

In Word and WordPerfect, you can also insert worksheets (data from a spreadsheet program). This type of format is also handy for tabular data. You can divide a document into columns, another way to enliven the presentation and create special documents, such as newsletters or brochures.

GRAPHICS

If you want to add illustrations, you may be able to use simple drawing tools included with your program. For instance, in Word, you can draw shapes, such as a circle, arrow, and square.

You also can insert graphics using the Insert command. You may insert predrawn images called *clip art*. The program may come with a set of clip-art images, which you can use freely. You can also find clip art on the Web or sold as collections in the software section of retail stores. You can use clip art to create your own special stationery.

As an alternative, you can scan in images using a scanner and insert these in a word processing document. Or you might have a digital camera and insert these photographs in a document (see Figure 6.10).

Figure 6.10. You can insert clipart, scanned images, or digital images from a camera into your document.

Be aware that adding graphics is a simple way to enliven a document, but keep these pointers in mind:

- The quality of the printout will depend on your printer. Also, the more complex the graphic, the longer the printing time.
- You may need to spend some time adjusting the graphic—getting the text and the graphic to flow just how you want and resizing or cropping the image.
- If you plan to publish the document on the Internet, use a file format that most browsers can display (JPEG and GIF are common Web graphic file formats).
- You cannot use copyrighted graphics without permission.

MAIL MERGE

You may not be familiar with the terms used to describe this type of document (form letter, mail merge, merge letter, etc.), but you most certainly have seen this type of letter. They start "Dear Fill-in-the-Blank" and your name has been inserted liberally throughout the document. This type of letter is useful when you want to send the same letter to a large group of people.

Most word processing programs help automate the process of creating this type of letter. Basically, you have two documents: the main document (the actual letter) and the list of names and address. The letter contains special codes that tell the program where to insert the variable information, such as your name.

 Use the list again: A common question with merges is whether you can use the same list again. Yes. You don't have to re-create the list. You can use it with another letter. You just need to make the associations for the mail merge. Check your specific program for help on associating mail merge documents.

If the program has this feature, it attempts to make the process easy, but it can be confusing. Take your time and work through it. If you need to create this type of letter, this feature is definitely worth learning.

PUBLISHING FEATURES

High-end word processing programs, such as Word and WordPerfect, also contain features that help you create a more complex document layout. You can set up sections, divide a document into columns, change the page orientation, and more. You can also use predefined document templates and styles to help in formatting.

With the popularity of the Internet, many programs also offer features to help you create a Web page using your word processing program. You can insert Web links and save your document as a Web file (an htm or html file). The program may offer additional Web publishing features.

Summary

- Word processing is the most commonly used productivity program. Microsoft Word is the best-selling program in this category.

- This type of program helps you to create any type of document. Features help edit, change the appearance, check, and print documents.

- You type text using the keyboard. As you type, the text appears on-screen. You can easily make corrections using the Backspace and Delete keys. Use the arrow or cursor movement keys to move around the document. You can also move the mouse pointer and click to place the insertion point within the document.

- Formatting means to change the appearance of a document. With word processing programs, you can format the text (change the font, make text bold, etc.), format paragraphs (use indents, add bullets, and so on), and format pages (change the margins, add headers and footers, etc.).

- When you create documents, remember to save your work. When you save a document the first time, you assign a file name and a folder. You can also print your work using the File, Print command.

- Inserting tables, adding graphics, and creating form letters are some special features of word processing programs.

LESSON 7: CREATING WORKSHEETS

Objectives

> Describe spreadsheet programs
> Identify spreadsheet programs and basic features
> Enter data
> Create formulas
> Format data
> Create charts
> Use your spreadsheet as a database
> Save your work

What is a Spreadsheet?

A spreadsheet is probably the most common application next to word processing. If you need to work with any kind of numbers (financial data or statistical information), you'll benefit from a spreadsheet program. In this section you will learn about the places you might use a spreadsheet program as well as review the most common programs available.

TYPES OF WORKSHEETS

Spreadsheet programs are used to create documents called worksheets, which are set up like accounting paper. You'll find rows and columns, used mostly for entering figures. Here are some examples of different worksheets you might create or work with:

- *Sales.* If you work in sales or perhaps sell some product yourself, you might use a worksheet to total sales. Businesses often use worksheets not only to total sales, but to forecast sales, to spot trends, to pinpoint sales problems, and to break down sales into meaningful categories. For instance, a company might total sales by division to see which division leads in sales. As another example, the same company might also total sales by quarter to see when sales peak (see Figure 7.1).

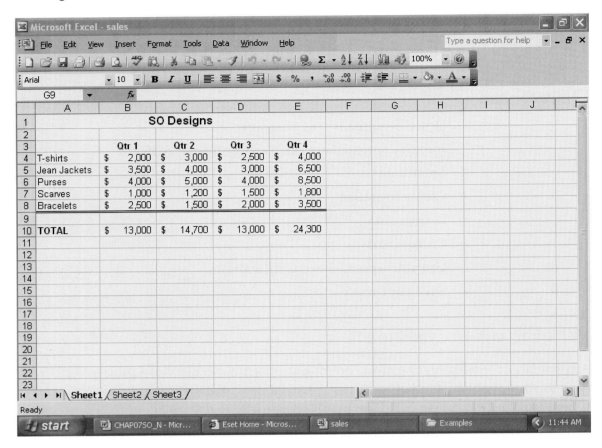

Figure 7.1. You can use a worksheet to total sales.

- *Budget.* You can list your expenses and create a budget. You can project what you think you'll spend, track what you actually spend, and compare the two.

- *Income.* If you have several sources of income, you can total your income with a worksheet. You might also use a worksheet to keep track of expenses and to prepare for tax time.

- *Invoice.* You can set up a worksheet to list and total services for an invoice.

- *Project management.* To keep track of projects, you can list goals or milestones and then track progress.

- *Data list.* Although a spreadsheet is not a full-featured database program, you can use it to keep track of simple lists, such as products, inventory, or collections.

- *Scientific data.* For certain science projects, you might use a worksheet to enter and evaluate data.

WHO USES THIS TYPE OF PROGRAM?

Although you may think strictly of accountants when you see a worksheet, you're likely to find this type of program in almost any type of office. All kinds of sales organizations use worksheets for keeping records not only of sales, but also of products and inventory. Sales managers may create a department budget and track expenses as they relate to that budget. The business manager may use a computer to pinpoint areas where a company can save money. The manager may plan for future purchases or expansion.

Small and large businesses use spreadsheet programs to prepare and analyze income and expense information. To manage the finances of a business, the company financial person may keep a list of vendors and pay bills (accounts payable), keep track of customers and what they owe (accounts receivable), send invoices, and create reports (for instance, create aging reports to see which accounts are past due and how far past due they are).

Contractors use worksheets to prepare bids. For instance, a roofing company might create a worksheet listing the work and materials and associated costs. A scientist might enter results of experiments and analyze data using some of the more sophisticated features of the program.

Accounting personnel keep track of money, and often use spreadsheets (or other financial programs) to manage invoices, track taxes paid, manage payroll, and so on.

You'll find that spreadsheets are a popular program for this type of professional, as well as special accounting programs and tax preparation programs.

 Personal accounting: Your personal finances can benefit from this same type of management. You can find check register programs that not only let you enter and balance your checking account, but also help you create and track a budget. You can use this same program to manage savings accounts, print checks, and more. Two popular programs are Quicken and Microsoft Money.

FEATURES AND BENEFiTS OF SPREADSHEET PROGRAMS

The benefits of a spreadsheet program are great. You start by entering the data into a worksheet; once it is entered, you can do a great deal with that information. The most common thing you will do is some type of calculation. As an example, you can sum all your expenses for the month. The differences between doing this manually with a calculator and with a spreadsheet program are these:

- *Error-free calculations.* It's easy to make a mistake when entering figures using a calculator. You might mistype or forget an entry. With a spreadsheet program, you don't have to worry about mistakes because the program will not make a mistake calculating. (You do have to be sure you've entered the correct values.)

- *Fast recalculations.* If you forget an entry, an entry changes, or an entry is no longer valid, you can make a change. You don't have to redo the calculation: the program does it for you. You can easily add new rows and columns within an existing worksheet if, for instance, you forget something.

- *Data entry shortcuts.* You can use shortcuts to enter data, especially formulas. You can create a formula and then copy it to other places in the worksheet. Because of how cells are referenced, the same formula will work in other places.

- *More analysis.* Once the data is entered, you can manipulate it. You might sort entries from largest to smallest. You might find the average of your monthly food expenses. You can use the data to make forecasts. For instance, what if you received a 6% raise? What would your yearly income be? Your monthly income?

- *Special functions.* In addition to common mathematical functions, such as addition, subtraction, multiplication, and division, you can use special formulas called *functions*. You can find functions for figuring a loan payment to calculating the return on an investment.

- *Charts.* You can chart the data. Sometimes a chart shows a relationship or trend that the values themselves don't readily show. For instance, if you chart your expenses in a pie chart, you might notice that the largest chunk of your income is spent on CDs.

Spreadsheet Programs

The most popular spreadsheet program is Microsoft Excel . This program is sold as a separate package and also as part of Microsoft Office (a bundle of common business applications). If you use a spreadsheet program, you will most likely be using Microsoft Excel.

If you have a home computer, you might have Microsoft Works. This program, often bundled with home computers, is an integrated program with a word processing, a spreadsheet, and a database module. Works and Excel are similar, although Excel includes many more features.

 Spreadsheet history: One of the first programs created for a computer was a spreadsheet program. Lotus created its spreadsheet program which it named 1-2-3. If you have used computers for a long time, you may remember this popular program.

 WEB: If you do not have a program but would like to purchase one, you can get information on Excel by visiting Microsoft's Office site at office.microsoft.com.

Entering Data

The hardest part of creating any document is entering the data. Once you've done this task, you'll find you have a great deal of flexibility in working with that data. In this section, take a look at the layout of a typical worksheet and also read about some shortcuts for entering data and formulas.

UNDERSTANDING THE PROGRAM TOOLS

You start a spreadsheet program in Windows the way you start most programs: click the Start button, select All Programs, point to a program folder (if necessary), and then click the icon for the program. You then see the program window.

 Create a shortcut icon: If you use a program often, create a shortcut to that icon on your Windows desktop. To do so, find the program file and then drag it from the file window to the desktop using the *right* mouse button. When you release the mouse button, select Create Shortcuts Here.

Most spreadsheet programs look similar, work similarly, and include similar features. Figure 7.2 shows the program window for Excel. If you use another program, your window will look different, but it probably contains the same features:

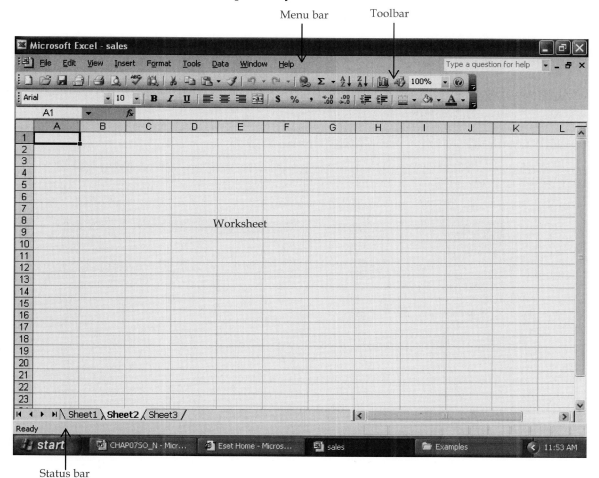

Figure 7.2. Like most programs, a spreadsheet program includes a menu bar and toolbars.

- *Menu bar.* The menu bar lists the names of the menu. To open a menu, click its name. You see a list of commands. To select a command, click that command.

- *Toolbars.* Most programs include toolbars with buttons for frequently used commands. In Excel, you'll find buttons for working with files (Open, Save, and Print, for instance), buttons for copying and pasting data, buttons for creating formulas, and buttons for sorting data. The second row in this program (called the Formatting toolbar) includes buttons for changing the appearance of the worksheet entries.

- *Worksheet*. The worksheet is the area where you enter data. A worksheet is a grid of columns and rows, and the intersection of a column and row is called a cell. Each cell has a reference or name, and the reference is composed of the row number and column letter. For instance, A1 is the first cell in the worksheet (column A, row 1).

- *Formula bar*. The formula bar contains the entry of the current cell and the cell reference. When you are creating or editing an entry, this formula bar also includes buttons for making or canceling the entry.

 Defining a range: If you want to work with more than one cell, you can select the cells by dragging across the range of cells and highlighting them. A group of cells is called a range and is referenced by the cell in the upper-left corner, a colon, and the cell in the lower-right corner.

- *Status bar*. The status bar displays handy information. For instance, in Excel if you select a range of numbers, you'll see the total in the AutoCalculate area of the status bar.

UNDERSTANDING A TYPICAL WORKSHEET LAYOUT

Most worksheets follow a simple table layout, shown in Figure 7.3. Note the key elements:

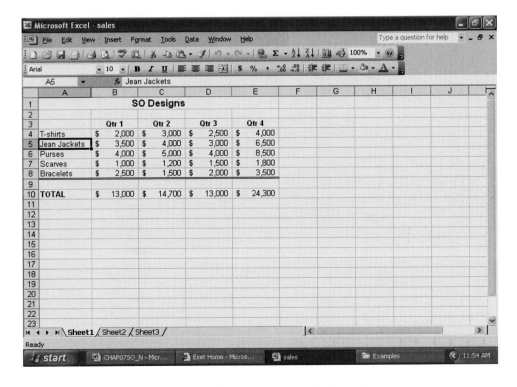

Figure 7.3. Most worksheets are set up in this table format.

- *Worksheet title*. To identify the contents of the worksheet, you might include a title at the top. You can also include other information, such as the date or the creator of the worksheet.
- *Column and row headings*. The column headings identify the contents of the columns and are usually categories (quarters, months, divisions, years, for instance). The row headings identify the contents of the rows and are usually specific items. For example, in this worksheet, the columns list the quarters, and the rows list the specific product.
- *Cell address.* The current cell is indicated with a black box. The address for this cell appears in the formula bar. The cell address consists of the column letter and row number.
- *Values*. The values are the numeric entries.
- *Formulas*. The last row of the above worksheet includes formulas. In this example, these formulas total the entries in that column using the SUM function.

Keep in mind that this is a typical layout, but you aren't limited to this structure. You can set up rows and columns and formulas in any pattern that suits your purpose.

ENTERING TEXT AND NUMBERS

To make an entry in a worksheet, you select the cell by clicking it. You then type the entry and press Enter. If the entry contains any letters, it is considered a text entry or label. If the entry is all numbers, it is treated as a number. To type a negative number, type a minus sign before the number or type the number in parentheses.

Some numbers are not really numbers; for instance, your Social Security number or address. When entering a number that is not a value, type an apostrophe before the entry to indicate it is a label.

Look for shortcuts: If you have to set up a worksheet, look for program shortcuts. For instance, in Excel you can use the fill feature to fill in data, such as the months of the year, days of the week, or some other sequence you set up. You can also copy cells.

You can move around the worksheet by using the cursor movement keys or by clicking the cell where you want to make an entry. To select several cells, click the first cell, hold down the mouse button, and drag across the other cells you want to select. The range appears highlighted.

Creating Formulas

When you create a worksheet, you usually have some purpose in mind, such as totaling sales. You have certain key values and then you want to find out some information about those values (such as what they total). To perform some calculation on the entries, you create a formula. You can type a formula yourself or use the predefined formulas, called functions.

HOW FORMULAS WORK

The reason it's important to know how formulas work is that they are the main benefit of a spreadsheet program. When you build a formula, you reference the cells that contain the values. For instance, consider this formula shown in Figure 7.4:

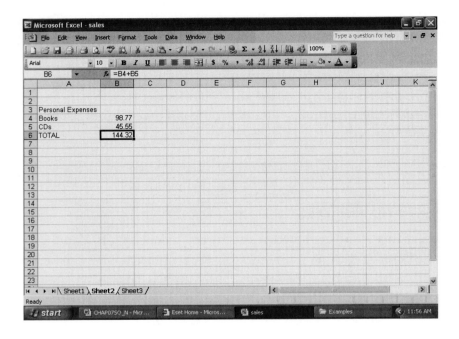

Figure 7.4. Most formulas reference cells.

= B4 + B5

This formula takes the value in B4 and adds it to B5. How is this different than simply adding these two values? It's different because you can change B4, B5, or both B4 and B5, and the formula will be recalculated automatically. This enables you to perform "what-if" analysis.

WHAT ARE FUNCTIONS?

You can type formulas, using any of the typical mathematical operators: + for addition, – for subtraction, * for multiplication, and / for division. You can also use predefined formulas called functions. These take some of the tedium out of building formulas. For instance, rather than use this formula:

=B1+B2+B3+B4+B5

You can use this one:

=SUM(B1:B5)

This function sums all the entries in the range B1:B5. Note the key components of a function: the equal sign, function name, and argument. All formulas start with an equal sign. This tells the program that the entry is a formula. The function name usually gives you a clue to the function purpose. SUM sums entries. SIN finds the sine of an angle. The arguments are what can be tricky. The arguments are what the function needs to perform the calculation. For instance, to find a sum, the function needs to know which cells to sum. Often you use cell references or a range, as in this example, for the argument.

Most programs include commands and features for using functions. For instance, in Excel, you can use the Insert Function command to view the arguments required for the function (see Figure 7.5).

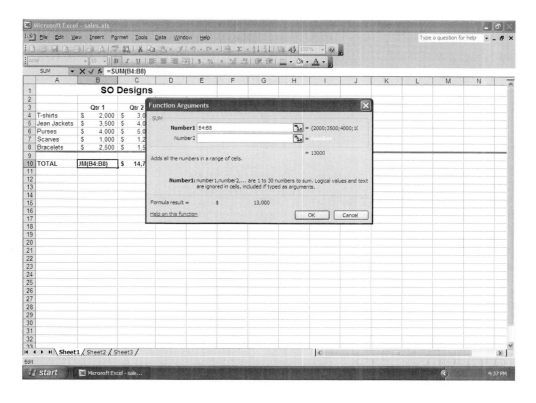

Figure 7.5. You can get help creating functions.

 Use AutoSum: In Excel, you can quickly sum a range using the AutoSum button. Click where you want the function, select what you want to add, and press Enter.

Making the Worksheet Look Nice

Like a word processing document, the content of any document is the most important part of the document. But is appearance important? Compare the two worksheets in Figures 7.6 and 7.7. Which is easier to understand? In Figure 7.6, you don't know if the numbers represent units or money amounts. Figure 7.7 makes this clear by formatting the numbers. Also, lines and boldface are added to make the column headings stand out and to emphasize the totals.

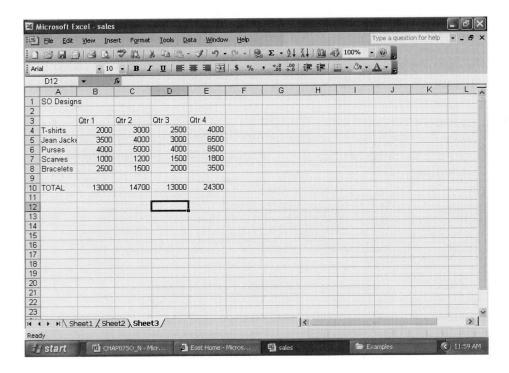

Figure 7.6. A worksheet before formatting.

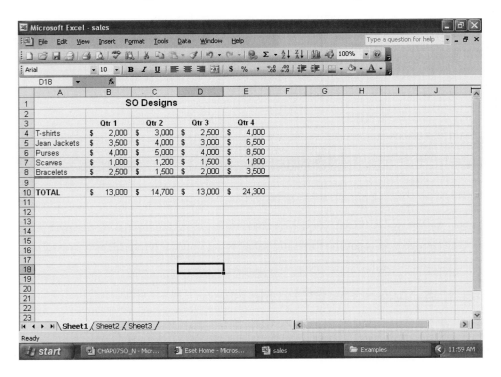

Figure 7.7. A worksheet after formatting.

Remember that changing the appearance of data is called formatting. The features you can use to format a worksheet are similar to those for formatting word processing documents. Here are some changes you might consider:

- *Change the font*. You might want to use a different font or font size. A common change is to make the worksheet title bigger or to use bold or underline for the column headings so that they stand out.

- *Change the look of the numbers*. Numbers can mean different things. For instance, 100% and $100 are not the same. To make the meaning clear, you can select an appropriate number format for your entries. You can select from several styles.

- *Change the alignment*. By default, text entries are aligned with the left edge of the cell and numeric entries with the right. To keep your data aligned, you can make changes, selecting left, center, or right alignment for entries.

- *Shade or add borders*. You can also shade a range to call attention to it. As another choice, you might add borders; for instance, a double underline below the totals.

- *Add headers and footers*. Like a word processing document, you can insert page numbers, the worksheet name, the worksheet date, or other information on each page. To do so, set up a header or footer.

   Date stamp: Worksheets are usually updated over a period of time. To keep track of when changes were made, add a date to the header or footer.

- *Change the page setup*. You can make changes to the margin of the page. Another common change is to use landscape orientation (rather than portrait). With this paper orientation, the text prints across the wide dimension of the page rather than down. Use this for a worksheet with lots of columns.

Creating Charts

Most spreadsheet programs enable you to chart the data. This charted data comes in handy for presentations or reports. Charts often visually summarize numbers at a glance. For instance, look at the pie chart in Figure 7.8. What can you quickly see from this chart? What is the best-selling product from this quarter?

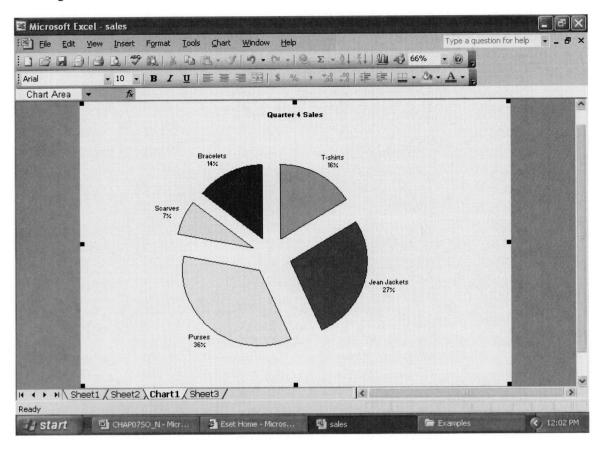

Figure 7.8. You can chart data from a worksheet.

You'll find lots of different chart types, including bar, line, column, pie, 3D charts, and others. Each chart is suited for a particular message. For instance, line charts often show changes over time. Pie charts show how the parts add up to the whole. You can use the charting features and online help to get charting advice.

The great thing about creating a chart is that if you change the data, the chart is updated automatically.

Using a Worksheet as a Database

As a last example of a spreadsheet's usefulness, consider using a worksheet as a simple database. Most programs include features for managing simple data lists. For instance, consider the worksheet in Figure 7.9. This worksheet keeps track of product inventory. You can perform lots of tasks with this list. You can sort in alphabetical order or by product number. You can sort by price. You can use a function to calculate the average price. You can create a function to return the highest (MAX) and lowest prices (MIN). You can filter the list to show just the top entries.

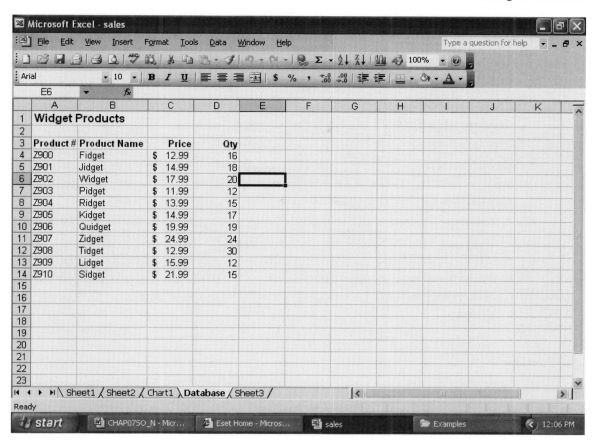

Figure 7.9. Set up a simple database as a worksheet.

When you use the worksheet to track data lists, note that the column headings identify the contents of that column or field. (Field is a database term used to define a single piece of data, such as a product name.) The rows contain the specific information or records. (Again, if you are not familiar with databases, a record is one set of data; for instance, the information about one product.)

Handling Spreadsheet Documents

Like word processing documents, you need to save your worksheets. When you save the first time, you assign a file name and a folder for your file.

In some programs, you may have several worksheets available in the same document. For instance, in Excel, you can have several worksheets, all saved together as one workbook file. Each page or sheet in the workbook can contain data, charts, any type of entry. You can also create formulas that refer to other cells on other pages in the workbook. All of the sheets are saved together with one name as a workbook file.

 Print your work: You can also print your worksheet or part of one using the File, Print command.

Other Financial Programs

In addition to spreadsheet programs, you can find other special-purpose programs for dealing with financial data. Here are some of the most common:

- *Checkbook manager.* You can buy programs to manage your checkbook. The most popular is Quicken. With this program, you can make entries in the register, print checks, balance your account, set up a budget, and more.

- *Tax preparation.* To help prepare your taxes, you can purchase tax programs, such as TurboTax. These programs, in addition to helping you complete your taxes, often enable you to submit the final tax file electronically.

- *Accounting software.* Big companies may use special accounting software to keep track of accounts payable, accounts receivable, and payroll.

- *Small business manager.* Smaller companies may use a small business manager program, such as QuickBooks. This program helps you create and track invoices as well as handle other aspects of owning or managing a small business.

Summary

- Spreadsheets are the second most commonly used productivity programs. Microsoft Excel is the best-selling program in this category.

- You use this type of program to create worksheets. Most worksheets consist of text entries, numeric entries, and formulas.

- A spreadsheet program not only performs calculations without error, but also enables you to make changes to entries and have the formulas that reference those entries be recalculated automatically.

- You can use predefined formulas called functions.

- You can change the appearance of the entries to make the worksheet easy for your audience to understand.

- Create charts to visually show data. You can select from several chart types.

- You can use a spreadsheet program to manage simple data lists.

LESSON 8: DATABASES

Objectives

> **Describe database programs**
> **Understand the structure of a database**
> **Enter data**
> **Update data**
> **View database information**
> **Query the database**
> **Create reports**

What is a Database?

A database program is used to keep track of information about people, products, events, transactions, or other items. Think about a simple Rolodex, which you use to keep name and address information organized. The list includes all the pertinent information (name, address, phone numbers, etc.) on one card, and the cards are organized alphabetically. That's the basic concept behind a database program; only a database program offers much more sophistication and flexibility than a Rolodex.

TYPES OF DATABASES

To understand the usefulness of a database program, let's take a look at some types of databases that are used:

- *Contacts.* At its simplest, a database can be used to track people. In addition to names, addresses, and phone information, you can also keep other dates, such as business information. Contact management is critical in business. You might need to keep track of clients, customers, vendors, competitors, members, or any other group of individuals. Figure 8.1 shows a contact screen for a popular database program called Access.

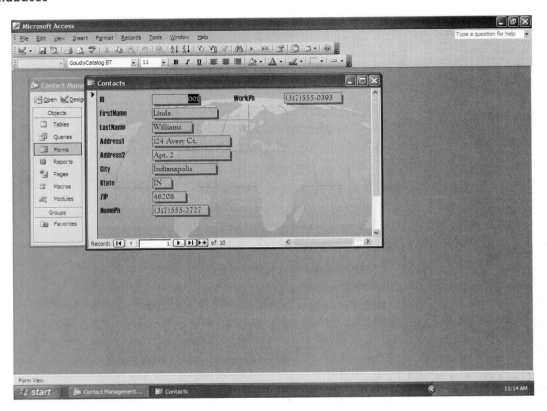

Figure 8.1. One of the most common applications of a database
program is to keep track of contacts.

- ***Products.*** If a company sells some type of product, a database is an ideal way
  to organize information about that product or to keep an inventory. This type
  of database might store the product number, description, number sold,
  number in inventory, and so on. With most programs, you can create several
  databases with multiple tables in each and link them. For example, you might
  have one database table that lists basic product information and then another
  that tracks sales and inventory.

- ***Transactions.*** Databases are often used to keep track of transactions — sales or
  rentals, for instance. Banks also use very large databases to keep track of
  transactions.

- ***Billing.*** Businesses use databases or accounting programs that function
  similar to a database program to keep track of various accounts, such as
  accounts payable and accounts receivable. Doing so makes it easy to generate
  invoices, track expenses, and total income.

- ***Personnel.*** To keep track of employees, businesses often use a database for
  personnel. This database can store not only information about that person,
  but also hiring, salary, and tax information. Schools and universities also use
  databases to keep track of student information.

- ***Schedules.*** Databases can be used to track schedules, but they also make
  planning a schedule easier. Think about a school or university and all its
  classes. Imagine planning not only when the classes were held, but also

where they were held, who was teaching them, and who was signed up—without the help of a computer. Databases simplify the scheduling of classes and other events.

- *Collections.* Similar to a product database, a collection database keeps track of the items in a collection. This might be a simple list of the CDs you own or a sophisticated and detailed list of the pieces in a museum with acquisition information, value, location, and other key data.

- *Scientific and other research data.* Scientists and other researchers use databases to store information about a particular project. As a simple example, think about a marketing company that has a database of current and potential customers with all the related information.

This list gives you just a few examples of the many types of databases. Anytime you come across a collection of facts or data pieces that need to be organized, think of a database. As a final example, think about renting a movie from your local video store. That store not only uses a database to track which movies it stocks, but also has a database for its customers. The store also has a database that keeps track of the rentals, who rented what, when it's due, who owes late fees, and so on. The store might also have a database of vendors from which they order videos. And it probably has a database to keep track of employees and payroll information. So a database allows you to search for information in a variety of ways.

PLACES YOU MIGHT FIND THIS PROGRAM

You're likely to encounter databases in many places. First, you are probably an entry in several databases. Again, think of the video example. If you have rented a movie, you are in that database. You are probably also listed in a database at your office or school. If you sign up for mailing lists or receive any catalogs, you're in those databases. The government has massive databases to keep track of you and especially your income. If you take money out of a bank machine, that's another database transaction. If you think about it, you encounter this type of program in lots of places in your everyday life.

Second, you may encounter a database at work. For work, you'll find two types of people using a database program. You have those that enter and work with the data and those that create the database systems. For instance, an assistant might log mail or project information in a database. If you work in a store and record the sale of a product, you are most likely using some type of database program. A video clerk who checks out a movie for a customer is using a database program to track that transaction.

You can find some common applications for databases, but most databases are customized to suit a particular customer. You'll find database designers that either create a program from scratch or use a popular program (like Access) to create a customized solution. That's the second type of user and also a point that can be confusing. Each database looks different and may provide different functions.

Underneath, however, the databases operate on the same principles and provide the same benefits, as covered next.

DBMS: When discussing databases, you might see the designation DBMS (database management system). You'll also hear terms such as database programmer, database engineer, and others used to refer to people who create customized databases.

FEATURES AND BENEFITS OF DATABASE PROGRAMS

The benefits of a database program are immense, especially if you consider the paper method of keeping track of data. Imagine keeping track of customers on paper. What if the information changed? What if a name was not filed or spelled correctly? Imagine again the nightmare of trying to arrange something as simple as a schedule of classes for a school on paper. Indeed, a database program provides many advantages, including the following:

- *Enter data simply*. Although the hardest part of a database program is actually getting the data entered, once it's entered you have so much control. Also, most programs provide shortcuts for entering data. With a standard form, you ensure you are keeping track of the same information. You can easily spot missing data.

- *Find data easily.* The paper method for finding a certain piece of information is tedious. With a database, you can quickly pull up the information you need, and you have a variety of methods for finding that information. For instance, suppose you can't remember a customer's name. You can look up the customer by the city or state. Or you might remember that the name starts with *Tr*. You can search for customers whose last names match this entry.

- *Keep data updated.* One look at anyone's address book will tell you how messy it is to keep track of data manually. People move. Numbers change. With a database, you can quickly and easily find and update any of the information.

- *Track more detailed information*. A database makes it easy to keep related information together. If you have to track data manually, you may not want to go to the effort to note someone's birthday or gift preference. With a database, you can easily track this information. Doing so provides you with the pertinent information you need.

- *Sort data.* You can rearrange the data in a database to suit your needs. For instance, for a mailing, you might want to sort by ZIP Code. You can sort names in alphabetical order. For a product database, you might organize the database by price to see how the products stack up price wise. Then you can re-sort by past sales to view which product has sold the most. Re-sort again to see which products are running low on inventory. With a few commands, you can change the order to view the data in the organization that makes most sense for your particular purpose.

- *Query data.* With a database program, you can also query or question the database. You might create a query that says, "Show me all customers in

South Carolina." In a product database, you might say, "Show me all products that have less than five items in stock. " In a video database, you might query, "Show me the most rented movie this week. " The possibilities are endless.

- *Create reports.* With sorting and querying, you can also create printed reports for analysis or distribution.

- *Transfer the information from a database into a spreadsheet.* This offers more ways to work with the database information.

POPULAR DATABASE PROGRAMS

The most popular full-featured database program is Microsoft Access. This program is sold as a separate package and also as part of Microsoft Office (a bundle of common business applications). Other popular programs include Corel's Paradox and Lotus Approach.

In addition to the full-featured programs, you can find special-purpose programs, especially for contact management. ACT! is a popular program for keeping track of contact information for businesses.

Also, keep in mind that you can find customized database programs. These might be unique programs, designed for a particular business or office. Or they might be customized versions of a popular database. For instance, a developer might use Access to create a program for sales or inventory for a particular company.

 WEB: Visit office.microsoft.com for product information on Access. For information on ACT!, go to www.act.com. For information on Approach, visit www.lotus.com and look for information on their SmartSuite package, which includes Approach.

Setting Up a Database

Before you can enter data, you first must set up or build a database. The information in this section will not only help you understand what you can include if building a new database, but also tell you what types of fields you can expect to find when entering data in an existing database.

UNDERSTANDING DATABASE STRUCTURE

When you work or read about databases, you often hear specific terms used to describe the structure or setup of a database. In particular, you need to understand the concept of fields, records, and tables.

A field is one particular piece of information. For example, in a simple address database, you have fields for first name, last name, address, city, state, and ZIP Code. Each field is separate and has its own field name, field type, format, and size.

A record is the collection of fields about a single item. For instance, in the same address database, a record would be the name, address, city, state, and ZIP Code for one person. In a typical database table, fields appear in the columns with the field name at the top, and individual records are listed in each of the rows (see Figure 8.2).

 Fields defined: The field is the holder for the data. Each field has a unique name and contains a specific piece of information. The data entered in the field is part of the record. One set of fields about a particular person or object makes up one record.

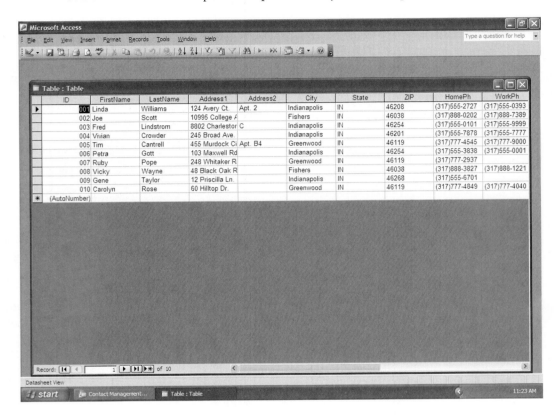

Figure 8.2. A database table consists of fields (columns) and records (rows).

In a flat-file database, the database consists of a single file and is basically a simple list of information. For more complex situations, the structure expands beyond a single file to several related files. In this type of database (called a relational database), a database is made up of several tables that can interact with each other. The tables are linked by a common field. For instance, think about a catalog mail-order company. You might have one database of customers, one of products, and one for orders. The customers might have a unique customer ID, used in the order to link the customer information with the order. This saves having to repeat all the pertinent customer information (name, address, and so on) with each order. Each of the products may include a unique product number. When an order is made, instead of including all that product information, the order references the product number, effectively linking the information in the order to the information in the product database.

CREATING A DATABASE

If you use a customized database, the fields and tables are already defined. You have the structure set up for your use. If you create a new database, you start by defining the fields you want to include. Most programs include some predefined templates you can use. For instance, in Access you can select from several predesigned databases, such as asset tracking, contact management, event management, expenses, inventory control, ledger, order entry, time and billing, and others (see Figure 8.3).

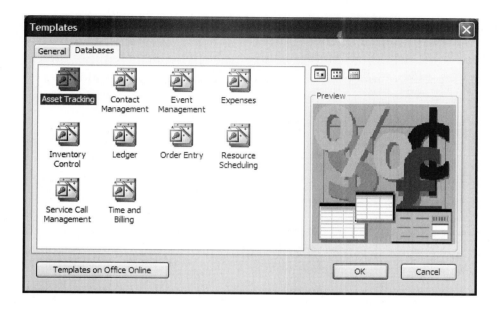

Figure 8.3. To create a new database, you can start with an existing template.

If you create a database from scratch, you define the fields you want to include. Most databases have set field types that you can include. The following lists the most common field types:

- *Text*. As the name implies, text fields include text and are used to store alphanumeric information. You may also hear this type of field called a character field.

   Numbers may be text: Just because a field includes numbers does not necessarily mean it's a numeric field. Numeric fields are used for values. Entries for Social Security and other ID numbers, phone numbers, addresses, and other seemingly numeric fields are really text fields.

- *Numeric*. This type of field is used to store purely numeric information. You'll find any type of numeric value, including money, units of measurement, statistics, percentages, and so on.

- *Date and time*. Dates and times are stored in a specific format. That way you can do things such as age an account or time an event.

- *Logical*. Logical fields can be one of two entries, basically Yes or No (or On or Off or True or False).

- *Memo*. For information that does not fit easily into a category, use a memo field. You can include notes or comments, for instance.

- *Object*. You'll find other media types in this field. This might include a picture of an employee or product, a sound file, a clip-art image, a video clip, or any other type of nontext entry.

In addition, many databases include a counter field that is used to identify each record uniquely. For instance, a counter field might be used to create a unique invoice number in an invoice database.

Databases also often have a key field (or primary key). Similar to a counter field (and sometimes the key field is the counter field), this key uniquely identifies each record. As an example, a product number might be the key field in a product database.

Entering Data

The hardest part of creating any document, including a database, is actually entering the data. Most programs provide shortcuts for entering data, as well as for checking or validating data.

When entering data, you can use a form to concentrate on one record at a time or you may enter data into the database table directly. Figure 8.4 shows an Access data form; Figure 8.5 shows an Access database table.

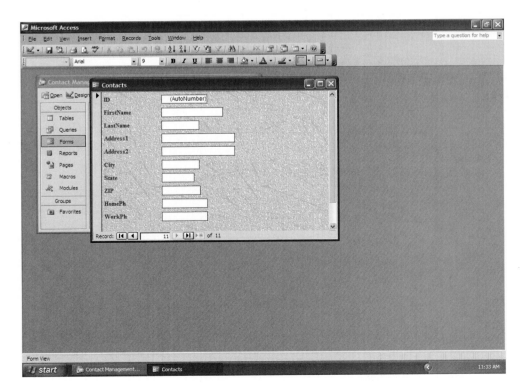

Figure 8.4. You can enter data in a data form.

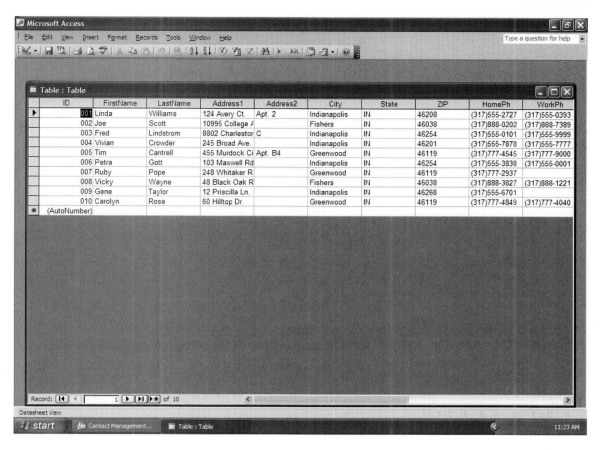

Figure 8.5. If you prefer, you can enter data in the table view.

When entering data, keep these pointers in mind:

- *Certain fields can contain only certain types of entries.* For instance, if the field type is set to numeric, you cannot enter text.

- *Data appearance may be set.* When creating a database, you can set up the format of a particular field. For instance, you might format a price field so that it displays as currency. You might use a specific format or template for entering phone numbers. If you are creating the database, take a look at some of the formatting options so that data entry is as clear as possible. If you are entering data in a database, keep in mind that you may not have to enter the formatting. For instance, if the format is set to currency you type 10.99, it will automatically appear as $10.99. Some fields require you to set the size of the field. You can count the characters in the longest entry and set the field size accordingly.

- *Data may have to meet certain requirements.* When setting up fields, you can set up rules, or parameters. For instance, an entry might have to appear within a certain range. Some fields require an entry; otherwise, you cannot add the record. If you are setting up the database, you can use these features to control data entry. If you are entering data, you might see an error message if you make an incorrect entry.

- *Select from lists.* To make it simple (and to limit entries), you can set up lists for fields. As an example, you might have a drop-down list from which to select the state. A teacher might select from a list of grades in a student database. Some fields may also have a default value. You can accept or edit the default entry in new records.

Updating Data

As mentioned, one of the benefits of using a database program is that you can easily update the information. You can change the address, add a new record, delete a record that isn't needed, and more. Here are just some of the common types of changes you can make to database records:

- *Change data.* You can edit any of the individual fields in a record. You might need to update a phone number, add an entry to an empty field, or make other changes.
- *Add records.* You can easily add new records to the database.
- *Delete records.* If a record is no longer valid, you can delete it. Doing so keeps the database free from unnecessary information.
- *Change the database structure.* You can delete fields that you don't use. Keep in mind that you delete not only the field, but all entries in this field in any records. You can add new fields if needed. Again, remember that this field will be blank in any existing records. To make changes to the structure, you usually change to a different program mode or view. For instance, in Access you change to Design view.

Viewing the Data

When you work with data, you may want to see different views of that data. As described, when entering data, you can select to view a single record or all the records in table view. (The name of this view may vary. For instance, in Access the view of the entire table is called Datasheet view.) Look for different view options in the View menu.

Also, you can scroll from record to record. Look for navigation features in the program window. In Access you can scroll using the scroll bar at the bottom (see Figure 8.6). You can also navigate from record to record using the Edit, Go To command. Most programs enable you to move from record to record as well as to the first and last records.

Figure 8.6. Use the Record scroll bar to move from record to record in Access.

 Keyboard shortcuts: You can also use keyboard shortcuts to scroll from record to record. Check the program's online help or manual to find out about keyboard shortcuts.

Most database programs enable you to sort the records as well as filter or display a subset of records. These features will be explained next.

SORTING DATA

One of the benefits of a database is its flexibility. You can sort the data using one or more of the fields. Sorting means to arrange the data in some type of order, alphabetical, ascending or descending within a field or fields. You could sort all the members of an organization first by the city they live in and then, within each city group, by the last name alphabetically. Being able to sort helps you show arrangements that best suit your purpose. Consider a database of videos. To see a complete list, you might sort in alphabetical order. If you wanted to see which movies were available in a certain category, you could sort by type. Then all of the movies would be grouped and displayed in this order (comedy, drama, action, and so on). If you were interested in recent movies, you might sort by release date.

The great thing about sorting is that you aren't stuck with that order. You can always select another sort order. You aren't changing the actual records, just the order in which they are listed.

Look for a Sort command. In Access you select Records, Sort. The exact command may be different in other programs. You also can choose a sort order: ascending (A to Z) or descending (Z to A).

 Return to original order: If you need to return to the original record order, consider using a counter field. You can then use this field to return to the original order in which the records were entered.

FILTERING A DATABASE

Another way to rearrange the records in a database is to filter the database. When you filter the database, you display a subset of records. Why do this? You might filter the list so that you can edit a group of records. Or perhaps you want to create a report from a subset of records.

For specific steps on filtering a database, check your program manual or online help. For instance, in ACT! you can use some predefined filters called lookups. You can look up a group of contacts by state, ZIP Code, sales stage, or other fields. In Access you can filter records or, as another method for grouping records, you can create a query (covered next).

Querying the Database

Querying refers to the idea of asking a question and getting a response. Basically, you query to see a set of records that match your request. Your results might be a set of records (all students signed up for Creative Writing) or a single record (the student named Michael in the Creative Writing class). Querying is the same as searching for a particular record or records.

To find a particular record, you can use the Find command. You can search on any field or set of fields in a database. Creating a query is a bit more complicated; however, most programs let you save the query. So once you've created the query, you can use it again when you want to work with the same set of records. Figure 8.7 shows the query design tools for Access. This query will look in the Contacts database table and find all records where the city is Indianapolis. These records will be sorted in ascending order.

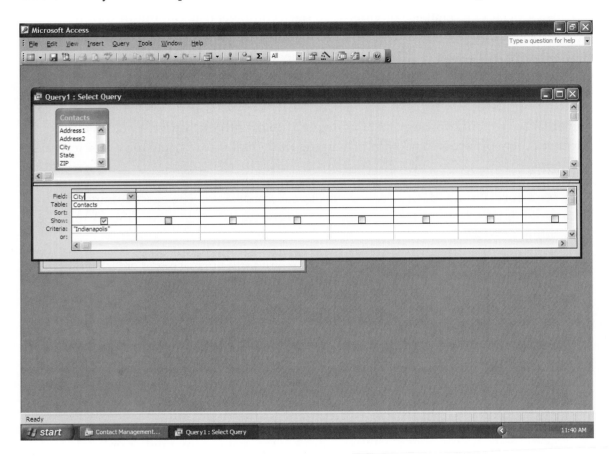

Figure 8.7. Build a query to pull specific data from the database.

You can create a query that is a statement of the criteria the record(s) must match. Most programs include templates or wizards to help you create the query. Most have a feature called query-by-example (QBE) that helps you build a query using a form. The program then takes your criteria and creates an SQL statement. SQL is a shortened form of SEQUEL (Structured English Query Language), a programming language. Database experts can use SQL to create sophisticated queries. Most end users don't need to learn SQL in order to query. Instead, they rely on the QBE features.

When you create a query, you can specify an exact match (all records where state=IN), or you can set up a condition or equation. For instance, you can find all records where the sales total is greater than (>) 5,000. To create this type of condition, you use Boolean operators. Common operators include the following:

=	Equal to
>	Greater than
<	Less than
>=	Greater than or equal to
<=	Less than or equal to
<>	Not equal to

Creating Reports

So far you've read about different ways to view and work with the data. You can view data in forms, useful especially for data entry. You can create queries when you want to see just a certain subset of records. When you want to present the information in some type of meaningful format, you can create another view—a report.

Most of the time the data in a database isn't useful in its straight record-by-record presentation. Imagine printing an entire list of all classes for all students, as presented and entered in a scheduling database. Not that useful. But if you can generate a report that lists each class, the time, the teacher, the location, and the students in the class, or perhaps just for the senior class, the information becomes much more useful.

As another example, consider a sales ordering database with tables for products, orders, and customers. All the information is important, but when you can create a report listing all back-ordered products, with customers who have ordered these products and their addresses, the information becomes invaluable.

Printing the report is easy: you simply select the Print command. Building the report is what takes some effort, but like other features, you will find tools to help you. Many programs include some predefined reports. You may also find features, such as wizards, which lead you through the process of creating reports. Figure 8.8 shows one of the steps in a report wizard for Access; here you select the fields you want to include in the report.

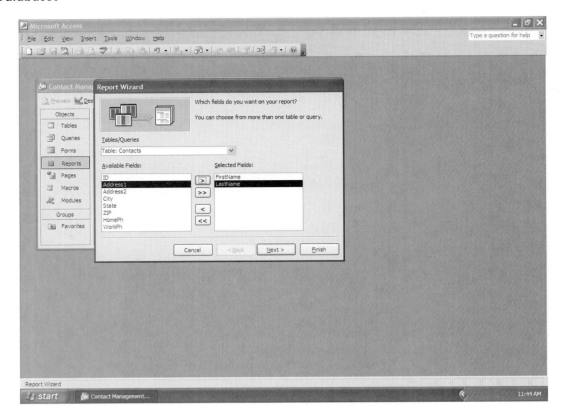

Figure 8.8. To help create reports, most programs include templates and wizards.

For high-end users, most programs offer sophisticated design tools for building reports. You can also do the following:

- In addition to including data, you can also create totals and subtotals.
- You can sort the data in an order appropriate for the report. You can also create a report from a query, that is, create a report that includes just a subset of data.
- You have a great deal of control over the look of the report, including formatting the headings, adding headers or footers, adding graphics, and more.
- Once you create a report, you can save it. Then when you want to create the same report again, you don't have to go through the steps to re-create it.

Programming Features

Forms, queries, and reports are types of common data presentations. In addition to these tools, most database programs include some programming elements. One example is the programming language and features for creating a query (covered earlier). In addition, you may be able to build macros that automate the update and maintenance of a database.

For more complex tasks, you can use the programming language of the database to build sophisticated subroutines (programs within the program). For instance, Access includes tools for building ActiveX controls and Visual Basic Applications (VBA). See Lesson 14 on programming for more information on these languages and topics.

Handling Database Files

A database file can be huge in size—and the contents are invaluable. You wouldn't want to reenter all the records in a database. For this reason, it's imperative that you take good care of your database. For business systems, companies usually have a database manager that takes care of the maintenance. If you are working with your own database, keep these tips in mind:

- You should periodically back up your database. Backup routines are essential to ensuring the integrity of your data. You may keep an extra copy of your database at another location; this safety practice is especially important for businesses.

- You may also need to perform other maintenance, such as purging the database (to gain space from deleted records) and reindexing (to update the index used to keep track of the records).

- Keep in mind that a database file may contain several components. For instance, in Access the database is the shell that houses all the other components. In addition to saving the database, you also save the database tables, queries, forms, and reports.

Summary

- Databases, although complex programs, are found in many types of businesses. Databases are used to keep track of information about a person, place, event, item, or transaction.

- You can create databases with programs such as Access or Approach. You can also hire a database programmer to create a customized database.

- A database consists of fields and records. Fields are the individual pieces of information—for example, the name in an address database. The records are one set of information—for example, all the address information for one person.

- Databases make it easy to keep data updated. They also enable you to quickly find information and to create subsets of the database (such as all clients in a particular state).

- You can sort a database on one or more of its fields.

- A query is a condition; the database program then pulls all database records that match the condition(s) in the query. Most programs enable you to create a query by example (QBE) rather than learn complex programming commands.

- You can create reports that summarize data.

LESSON 9: WORKING WITH IMAGES

Objectives

- ➤ **Create digital images**
- ➤ **Describe graphics programs**
- ➤ **Create drawings**
- ➤ **Work with photographs**
- ➤ **Use CAD programs**
- ➤ **Create animations**
- ➤ **Add graphics to Web pages**
- ➤ **Find sources of graphic images**

Getting Digital Images

If you work with images, you need a way to convert the image into a digital file (a file that you can open and edit on your computer). Before the arrival of digital cameras, the only way to convert a photograph into a digital file type was using a scanner. A scanner works like a copy machine, but instead of making a copy, the scanner converts the image into a digital file. You can use a scanner for photographs or any type of illustration.

More recently, digital cameras have become popular. This type of camera stores the image as a digital file. You can then copy or move the file from the camera's memory to the computer via a cable. Some cameras have a disk (or similar media like a card) as the storage device, and you can move pictures from your camera to other sources (the computer or printing kiosks, for instance).

Also, you can get traditional files developed as digital files on a photo CD (in addition to having the film developed as traditional pictures). Most film developers offer this option. You can then open these digital photo files and display and edit the photograph. Figure 9.1 shows a photograph from Kodak's PhotoCD (or PCD).

Figure 9.1. You can get versions of pictures on CDs and then display them on-screen.

USING A SCANNER

As mentioned, one way to get data into the computer is using a scanner. This type of input device is most commonly used to scan in pictures or illustrations. You can also use a scanner to scan text, but this requires special software. You can find special-purpose scanners, such as a bar code reader.

You can use a scanner to create an electronic file (and image) from a paper image. For instance, you can sell items at online auctions at eBay. To provide pictures of the items for sale, you can scan them. Scanners range in price from $100 on up. You can find two basic types of scanners: handheld scanners and flatbed scanners.

 WEB: Visit www.hp.com or www.epson.com. Use the links to navigate to the pages that cover the various scanners sold. What models are sold? How do they vary?

Handheld scanners are the least expensive. You create the image by taking the scanner and running it over the image or item.

Flatbed scanners work like copy machines. You place the image on the scanner and then scan or copy the image. Figure 9.2 shows a flatbed scanner.

Figure 9.2. You place the image on the scanner and then scan it,
much like making a copy on a copy machine.

Grayscale scanners can create images in black and white. Color scanners can process color images.

Once an image is scanned, you can include it in documents or on Web pages. You can print it using your printer. You can also use special software to edit or enhance the image.

You can also use a scanner to scan text. This task requires not only the scanner but also special software to translate the scanned characters into text that you can edit. This type of software is called optical character recognition (OCR) and can be quite expensive. The software allows you to edit the text as though it were word processing text. Without OCR software the text would scan as one whole picture. Usually you have to check the resulting text to be sure the results are accurate. As technology advances, you'll find OCR software that works better and is less expensive.

 TRY IT: When you shop at a store, the cashier may use a special bar code reader to scan the items you want to purchase. This type of scanner reads a special bar code (a pattern printed on products) and then enters the item and price. Bar code is also used with a remote-control wand to access tracks on a laser disc player.

DIGITAL CAMERAS

Another source of digital images is the digital camera. Rather than take a picture and then send the film out to be developed, you can use a digital camera. Then, with your computer and printer, you can print the resulting photographs. (Note that the quality depends on your printer.) You can also copy the digital photographs to your PC and insert them into documents or Web pages. With special editing software (covered later in this lesson), you can even edit the photographs.

 WEB: For information on digital cameras, visit www.kodak.com. Note the differences between cameras (as well as the prices). You can also visit other popular camera makers to find out about their digital model: Canon (www.canon.com), Nikon (www.nikon.com), Sony (www.sony.com), Olympus (www.olympus.com), and others.

Digital cameras cost from $150 to $7000 or more. Here are some pointers for working with this type of camera:

- The quality of the image is measured by its resolution (the number of pixels). The higher the resolution, the better the image quality. Cameras vary in the minimum and maximum resolutions they offer. High-end cameras offer resolution from 6-megapixel up to 11-megapixel. Lower-end cameras are usually in the 2 to 3.2 megapixel range.

- Digital cameras vary in the number of images they can store. You can expect to be able to store anywhere from 40 to hundreds of images.

- Images are stored in the camera's memory (a special card or disk). Most cameras have 16M to 64M of memory with additional memory media available up to 2G.

- You can take the images from a camera and have them printed at a traditional film developer. You can also print the images on your printer at home. Using special paper will help give you better quality. You can save money by selecting which images to develop or print. (You can delete any out-of-focus or otherwise "bad" pictures.) As another option, you can purchase special photo printers and print on traditional paper and size, with good results.

- To copy the images from the camera to the computer, you most often use a cable (connected via serial or USB port). The time it takes to copy the images (called the download time) varies. Some cameras include media cards, memory sticks, or disks that you can eject and then transfer to your computer or to printing kiosks.

- Digital cameras operate on batteries, and the cost and battery life vary from camera to camera.

- A good way to store pictures is to copy them to a CD. You can do this yourself. Or you can ask a local film developer to do this (copy your pictures from either actual photos or from digital images to a CD for safekeeping).

- Like traditional cameras, digital cameras vary in the features they offer such as focal range, controls for aperture, and so on. If you are a fairly advanced photographer, you may investigate these camera features.

 Photo printer: You can purchase special printers for printing photographs, including HP PhotoSmart, Kodak Personal Picture Maker, and Sony Digital Photo Printer. These range in cost from $90 to $700.

VIDEO CAMERAS

In addition to photographs, you can also create, edit, and play back videos using a video camera and video software. You can create your own home movies or include video clips on a Web site. (You learn more about video cameras in Lesson 11.) Some digital cameras enable you to shoot videos with audio. Keep in mind that the video features of a camera are basic; if you want to create home movies or other productions, you'll most likely want a video camera.

As another option, you might have a video camera on your PC. You can transmit live video images via the Internet. A common application of this type of input device is for videoconferencing.

 WEB: Go to www.logitech.com and see what cameras this company offers. Consider how you might use this type of computer component.

Graphics Programs

Now that you know some of the different types of equipment you might need to create digital images, let's take a look at the different programs you can use to work with this type of image as well as other graphic types.

Graphics software is a category that encompasses several programs, all dealing with images. You can use this type of program to create illustrations, edit images, and create special types of drawings, such as architectural drawings. This section explains the types of things you can do with these programs and also defines the various program types.

WAYS GRAPHICS PROGRAMS ARE USED

While word processing programs, spreadsheets, and databases may be used by a wide variety of people, you will find graphics programs are more specialized. That is, artists, photographers, illustrators, designers, architects, desktop publishers, and others use this type of program. This list gives you a general idea of the types of things you can create with graphics programs:

- *Artwork.* Artists use graphics programs to create artwork, logos, advertisements, and illustrations. For instance, a graphic artist created the line drawings in this book using computer programs (see Figure 9.3).

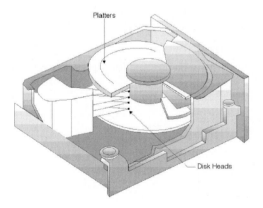

Figure 9.3. This illustration was created with Adobe Illustrator.

- *Photographs.* You can also display and manipulate photographs using graphics software. Photographers, designers, and artists use photo-manipulation software to take, store, and work with photos. For instance, the portrait in Figure 9.4 was created by a graphic artist (Kathy Hanley) from a photograph. You'll learn more about how you can display and work with photographs on the computer later in this lesson.

Figure 9.4. You can manipulate photographs.

- *Architectural drawings.* Architects, engineers, and designers use a special type of program called CAD (Computer-Aided Design) to create blueprints and other planning documents. For instance, clothing and package design can be done with this type of program.

- *Web graphics.* A Web page includes all kinds of graphics. In addition to photographs and illustrations, you may find buttons, logos, navigation tools, and animation on a Web page. These graphic parts of the page are created with graphics programs.

- *Animation.* Computers have made animation much easier than the original process of drawing each image. You'll find animation in films, cartoons, Web sites, games, and virtual tours.

TYPES OF PROGRAMS

As mentioned, the term "graphics programs" actually covers several types of programs, broken down into these main program types:

- *Paint and draw programs.* These programs are both used to create drawings, although they work in different ways. You can find high-end packages used by artists and illustrators. You can also find low-end packages, such as Paint, which you can use to create your own simple illustrations.

- *Photo manipulation software.* As mentioned, you can use scanners and digital cameras to create a digital file from a photograph. Then you can use this type of program to manipulate that photo. You may want to crop the image, sharpen the focus, change the lighting, or add a moustache to your Aunt Martha.

- *CAD programs.* This type of program is used to create technical drawings, the kind of drawing once created with a ruler and drafting table. Architects use these programs to create blueprints. Carpenters, electricians, and other construction workers use these documents to plan and create buildings. You'll also find other designers using these programs. For instance, engineers at a manufacturing plant can use this type of program to plan new products.

- *Animation programs*. If you need to create some type of animation, you can use this type of program to create, edit, display, and print your animations.

Paint Programs

Even if you are not an artist, you may still use paint programs to create illustrations. Paint programs include a palette of artist tools (paintbrush, pencil, eraser, for instance) that you can use to draw on the page. You select the tool you want and then draw on the canvas or page.

How do paint programs create the image? Think about a piece of graph paper. You can color in certain boxes or parts of boxes to create an image. That's how paint programs work. These programs "paint" individual tiny picture elements called pixels. The drawings are composed of little dots, giving you a great deal of flexibility in the shape and color of each individual drawing. But because the program thinks of each dot separately (not as one complete image), you cannot easily select, move, or edit the image. To make changes you have to work with the individual pixels. Although most programs enable you to add text, you cannot easily edit the text.

USING PAINT PROGRAMS

Popular paint programs include Paint Shop Pro (JASC Software), Adobe SuperPaint, and Paint (included with Microsoft Windows). To get an idea of the features of this program, take a look the Paint window shown in Figure 9.5. Other programs will vary, but they will contain similar tools and features. Notice these key areas and tools in Paint:

Toolbox

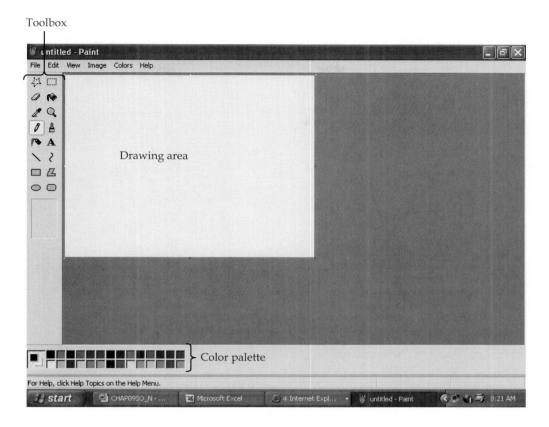

Figure 9.5. Paint, included with Windows, is a fun way
to experiment with your drawing skills.

- *Drawing area.* The main part of the program area is the drawing area. This area is your canvas on which you can draw using any of the tools in the toolbox.

- *Toolbox.* The toolbox is the rows of buttons along the left edge of the window. You can use these tools to draw in the drawing area. You can draw shapes using the Rectangle, Polygon, Ellipsis, and Rounded Rectangle tools. You can draw lines or curved lines using the Line and Curve tools. To draw freehand, use the Pencil or Brush. To add text, use the Text tool.

- *Color palette.* You can select a color for the object by clicking the color in the color palette. In Paint, click the left mouse button to select the color for the lines. Click the right mouse button to select a fill color for filled objects.

DRAWING AN OBJECT

To draw an object, you follow this basic process:

1 Click the tool you want to use.

2 Select any options for that tool. For instance, you can select the thickness of the line. For circles, rectangles, and polygons, you can select to draw a filled object or an empty object.

3 Click in the drawing area and drag to draw your object (see Figure 9.6).

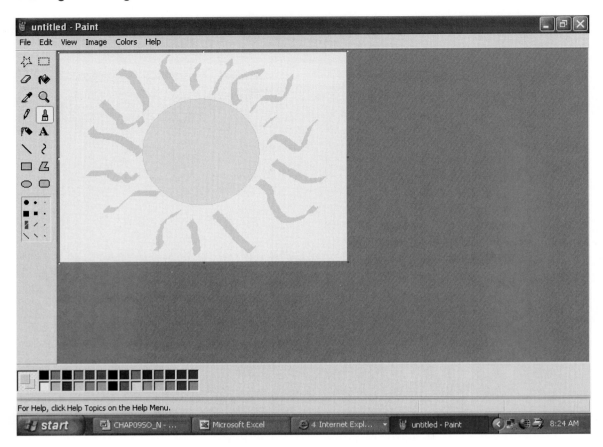

Figure 9.6. You can paint images using the tools in the toolbox.

 Draw circles, squares, straight lines: To draw a perfect square or rectangle or a straight line, hold down the Shift key as you drag to draw.

Most paint programs save the document as a bitmap (BMP) file. You may also hear this type of file referred to as a raster image. Many programs can open and display bitmap images. You can include them in other documents, such as word processing documents. You can also use them as Windows desktop wallpaper.

Drawing Programs

Drawing programs are used for the same purpose as paint programs, but they work in a different way. As mentioned, paint programs work by filling in dots to create the image. Drawing programs create images using mathematics. The programs use equations to define a line drawn from one point to another. The equation also determines the thickness and color. Each item is a discrete object, distinct from other objects. To understand the difference, take a look at a magnified view of a line in Figure 9.7. It is composed of dots. Now look at the line in Figure 9.8. It is defined as a line between two points and is not composed of a bunch of dots. It is a single element.

Figure 9.7. A paint program creates a bitmap image, consisting of dots.

Figure 9.8. A drawing program creates an image using mathematical equations.

Because the image is a discrete object, you can move, select, copy, and edit it. To make a change to the size or shape, you don't have to edit the individual pixels. Instead, you can click the item to select it and then drag the selection handles to change the size or shape. You can also select it and then make modifications—for instance, change the color.

Drawing programs are also better for handling text. In paint programs, text is not really letters, but dots put on the page to look like letters. You cannot go back and edit the text once you've added it. Drawing programs treat characters as objects so that you can edit the text if necessary. Another advantage is the file size; this type of image doesn't require as much storage space.

POPULAR DRAWING PROGRAMS

Popular drawing programs include Adobe Illustrator, CorelDraw, and Visio. You'll also find that other types of programs may include a drawing component you can use to add objects. For instance, in Word you can use the drawing toolbar to draw objects, such as lines or circles in a document. You can also do the same in Excel, PowerPoint, and Publisher.

 WEB: Visit Adobe's Web site at www.adobe.com. Notice the range of programs it includes for drawing and illustrating. Note the different features of programs, from the low-end for beginners or dabblers to the high-end for professional artists.

When discussing the technical aspects of a drawing program, you may hear this type of program referred to as an object-oriented program or vector-based program. This just describes how the program creates the image (with mathematics). These programs are also resolution-independent, which means that it doesn't matter what the resolution is; your image will look the same at different resolutions.

USING A DRAWING PROGRAM

To draw with a drawing program, you can use a mouse or a digitizer pad. You may also use special drawing devices, such as a light pen. (A light pen is shaped like a regular pen but uses photoelectric sensors. You use it to draw on a special drawing or digitizing tablet.) You can combine shapes to create a drawing. Most programs offer many predrawn objects, which you can insert into your drawing.

This program also includes features for adding special effects. For instance, you can flip, stretch, rotate, add shadow, and combine images. You can add layers and change the order of the layers. For instance, you can combine different shapes, layering each part of the drawing, to create an image.

Photo Programs

Illustrations aren't the only type of artwork you can create and work with on a computer. You can also tinker with photographs using photo-manipulation programs, such as Adobe Photoshop. Some programs, such as JASC Paint Shop Pro, let you work with illustrations and photographs . You can also find some programs which include tools for Web design.

 No more disorganized photos: Photo CDs enable you to easily store photos and to quickly review and select photos you want.

You can open up photos in your photo program and then make changes. You can edit each individual pixel (much like a paint program). Figure 9.9 shows a photograph opened in Paint Shop Pro.

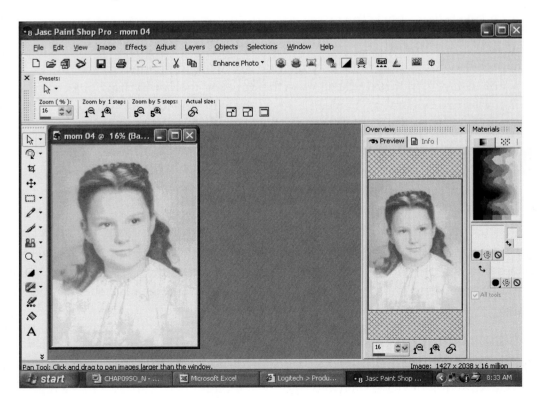

Figure 9.9. You can open and edit photographs using special graphics software.

Here are some of the common ways to edit a photograph:

- *Fix color problems*. Get rid of red-eye or smooth out problem areas, such as a face that is too dark or lighting that is too bright.

- *Crop the photograph*. You can crop the photograph to focus on a certain part of the image or to edit out part of the image.

- *Change the photograph*. You can combine images to create a special effect. You can take a photograph of yourself and put it next to one of the president. In fact, photographs can be changed so dramatically and realistically that most newspapers and magazines have guidelines over what types of changes can be made. Films often use this type of manipulation.

- *Print the photograph*. With a high-resolution printer, you can print images that are the same as those from a darkroom. If you do not have a high-resolution printer, you can send or take your images to a service bureau to be printed.

Design Programs

For technical drawings for blueprints or product design, you can use a special type of program called CAD. CAD can mean Computer-Aided Drawing, Computer-Aided Design, or Computer-Aided Drafting. These programs take the place of drafting tables, rulers, and mechanical pencils. Instead of drawing a blueprint, you can create one using a CAD program (see Figure 9.10).

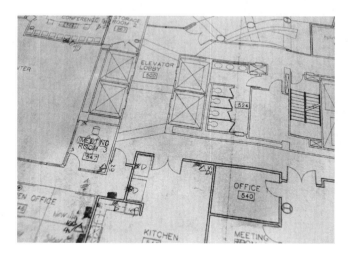

Figure 9.10. CAD programs can be used to create blueprints.

Unless you are in a specialized field, you may not have the occasion to use this type of program. If you pursue a career in construction, engineering, architecture, mechanical or other design fields, you may have access to a CAD program. It's not a program you can pick up cheaply or easily. You may require a special printer called a plotter to print CAD drawings.

For instance, the auto industry uses very high-tech, specialized computers to aid in the design, manufacture, and maintenance of automobiles. CAD programs are used to design new car models, down to the tiniest detail. These programs not only let the designer see how the car will look, but also enable the designer to make changes easily and to calculate the materials needed and the best way to manufacture the automobile.

Like drawing programs, CAD programs are vector-based. That is, they create the images using mathematical equations. With CAD programs, you get an incredible amount of accuracy. If you are in this field, you'll find this program offers many benefits, including the following:

- *Accurate scaled designs.* CAD programs are incredibly accurate. You can create a drawing that is accurate to the micrometer. You can also scale large objects and create full-scale designs.

- *Add layers.* You can add layers to a CAD drawing. For instance, a blueprint might include the physical or structural layout of the building, with added layers for wiring and plumbing. You can view the entire design or just the layer of interest.

- *Calculate size and materials.* Because the math requirements are so intensive, you can use a CAD program to quickly calculate room dimensions or volume. You can also create a list of materials, calculated to the requirements of the job.

- *3D design.* You can use CAD programs to create and display 3D designs. You can create wireframe models, showing the outside edges or solid models. You can render the image so that it looks "real" (adding shading and lighting).

 3D modeling: Most CAD programs include some 3D features, but you can also find and purchase 3D modeling software such as Discreet 3ds max, Ray Dream Studio, and LightWave 3D. You can use this type of program to create realistic 3D designs.

The most popular CAD program is AutoCAD from AutoDesk.

Animation Programs

Along with 3D design comes animation. In the past, animation was created by drawing an image frame by frame and then filming them one by one. Playing back the individual frames produced animation. This method was tedious and time-consuming.

Animation software changed all this. The same theory applies (frames filmed and then played back), but computer-generated imagery (CGI) provides tools to create animations quickly and realistically. Many popular movies use animation software for special effects.

WEB: Visit www.shockwave.com. Look at some of the examples and programs it includes for animations.

You'll find this type of software in film and television, as well as other fields. For instance, a realtor may provide a walk-through or virtual tour of a house using the same concept. Video games rely heavily on animation. Another type of animation is used in multimedia programs, such as HyperStudio, or presentation programs, such as PowerPoint.

Understanding Graphics Files

When you work with images, you have a great deal of flexibility in how you save the file, that is, the file type. You'll find graphic images in a variety of file formats, and some are more suited than others for special purposes. Let's take a quick look at the various types of graphics file types.

WEB GRAPHICS

You'll learn about creating Web sites in Lesson 10 on publishing, but keep in mind that graphics are an important part of a Web site. If you build a Web site, you should be familiar with the most common type of graphic images, as covered here.

To display an image, your browser must support that image type. To keep things simple, two file formats emerged as the most often used on the Web. These file formats are JPEG (or JPG) and GIF file formats.

JPEG stands for Joint Photographic Experts Group and is a bitmap file format. Photographs or complex images are usually in this file format because it works well for displaying colors and changes in colors. They are a popular file format because of the quality and file size.

GIF stands for Graphic Interchange Format and is used for simple images, especially those that need to be displayed often. For instance, a button on a Web page is most likely a GIF image.

A variation of this type of file is the animated GIF file. You see these in advertisements or logos that are displayed in a cycle (like a billboard that flips from one image to another every few minutes).

You'll also find other types of graphic content, including video clips, streaming video content (real-time video), and virtual reality modeling. For more information on Web publishing, see Lesson 10.

CLIP ART

If you are not an artist, don't despair. You can still add illustrations to your documents. To do so, you can use clip art. This type of artwork is created by professionals and then sold for your use. You can find a variety of clip art images in themes from cooking to business, sports to plants. You can purchase clip art libraries on CDs. You can also find clip art online. Also, many programs, such as Word for Windows and Microsoft Publisher, come with some clip art. Figure 9.11 shows the Clip Art task pane in Word for Windows. Here you can search for an insert clipart images stored on your computer as well as online (if you are connected to the Internet).

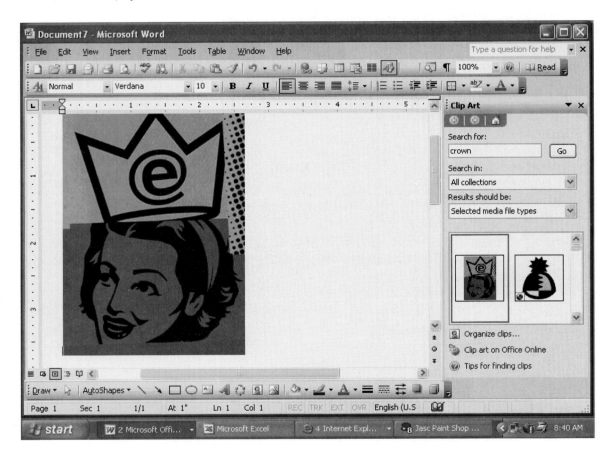

Figure 9.11. You can find precanned art called clip art and insert it into your document.

WEB: Visit www.clipart.com to view a subscription-based collection of clip art. Think about how you might use clipart in your work or home.

Most often clip art is licensed for your use. You can use it as often as you want. Other images are usually not provided free for your use. For instance, you cannot scan an image from a book and use it as your own without getting copyright permission. You also cannot copy a picture from a Web site that is copyrighted and use it without permission, even if you modify it.

Summary

- You can use a scanner to scan in a picture or photograph. You can purchase a grayscale or color scanner. Once the image is scanned, you can then edit it using a special graphics program.

- To scan text, you need a scanner and special optical character recognition software (OCR).

- Digital cameras enable you to take pictures with the camera, saving them in the camera's memory as a digital file. You can then download the images from the camera to your computer for manipulating or printing.

- Graphics programs encompass several types of programs. They all enable you to create, edit, and print some type of image.

- Paint and draw programs are used to create illustrations. Paint programs work by filling in pixels (picture elements) to create the image. Draw programs are mathematically based; an image is defined as a mathematical equation.

- Animation programs enable an illustrator to create animations. You'll find animations on Web pages, in film and TV, in games, and in presentations (such as a virtual tour of a home).

- To create technical drawings, such as blueprints for building, mechanical, or other designs, use a CAD program. The most popular CAD program is AutoCAD.

- The two most popular file formats for Web graphics are JPG and GIF. JPG is used for more complex images; GIF is used for simple illustrations and pictures that need to be displayed often (and therefore quickly).

- You can purchase illustrations created by professionals and distributed for your use. These types of images are called clip art, and you can find them on CD collections, at Web sites, and packaged with programs such as Word and Publisher.

LESSON 10: PRESENTATIONS AND PUBLISHING

Objectives

➢ **Create desktop publishing documents**

➢ **Create presentations**

➢ **Create Web documents**

Understanding Publishing

The computer has vastly changed the way information is published. The first revolution in publishing came with desktop publishing programs. These programs put the power of page layout in the hands of anyone with the right program and a decent printer.

Another change came in the area of presentations. While you can still use slides and a projector to give a presentation, you have a great many more options in not only the way the presentation is displayed, but in formatting and presenting it.

Finally, the Internet — in particular, the World Wide Web — has opened another avenue for publishing documents and manuscripts. With the appropriate software, you can create your own Web site.

This lesson covers the various types of publishing options, explaining where you are likely to encounter these publishing media and what benefits they offer.

Using Desktop Publishing Programs

Fewer than 10 years ago, a book like this one would have taken a major effort to get published and would have involved an entire team of production staff. Typesetters would format and print the text on special paper. Layout specialists would then cut the text and paste it onto pasteboards (hence the term paste-up). Figures and illustrations would also have to be inserted using a special screening technique. Color added another entire process. The final pasteboards were then sent to a service bureau and converted to film and then set to the printer to be printed. Not only was the entire process complicated and costly, but it did not enable you to easily make changes once the book was laid out.

Desktop publishing software changed all that. A much smaller production staff can accomplish the same process. Creating a book like this is quicker and cheaper. And this type of software is not just used for major publishing efforts like a book, but for any type of project. You can review this section to get an idea of what you can do.

TYPES OF DOCUMENTS

A book is just one example of a document that might be produced with desktop publishing software. You'll find a variety of documents suited for this type of program, including:

- *Newsletters.* You can create, print, and distribute newsletters. They might be a simple two-page document (printed on both sides) or several pages. You can include articles, pictures, illustrations, and other elements.

- *Advertisements.* You can create a wide variety of advertisements, including flyers, signs, banners, and print ads.

- *Brochures and booklets.* You can create brochures describing a product or service. You can make booklets on any topic imaginable.

- *Manuals.* Most how-to manuals are desktop published. The manual may include steps, technical information, tables, and other elements.

- *Business forms.* With a desktop publishing program, you can create professional business forms. For instance, you can make invoices or even your own business cards.

- *Personal stationery.* You can design your own stationery. Having a party? You can desktop publish an invitation. You can also create postcards and greeting cards.

Most programs, especially the low-end programs, were designed under the assumption that you may not be a layout expert. Therefore, they provide lots of templates for common publications. For example, Figure 10.1 shows just some of the templates and wizards you can use in Microsoft Publisher.

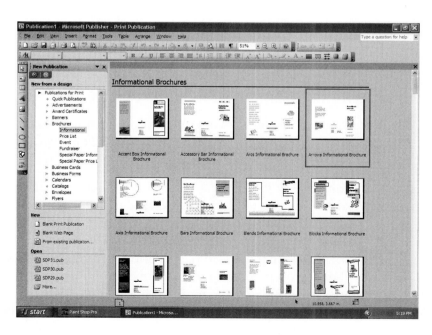

Figure 10.1. Desktop programs simplify creation by providing predesigned templates and wizards for a variety of publication formats.

TYPES OF PROGRAMS

As desktop publishing has become more popular, common applications, such as word processing and spreadsheets, have added desktop features to their programs. For simple documents, you may not even need a separate program. You may be able to use your word processing program. With a program such as Word, you can incorporate graphics, use columns, and add headers and footers. You can create a pretty sophisticated layout with the features of this program.

If the word processing program does not provide enough control or features to suit your publication, you can purchase a desktop publishing program. You can find programs ranging from the simple (Microsoft Publisher or PrintMaster) to the complex (Adobe PageMaker, QuarkXPress, Adobe FrameMaker).

WEB: To get an idea of the various programs, visit the Web sites for PageMaker (http://www.adobe.com/products/pagemaker/) and QuarkXpress (http://www.quark.com/products/xpress/). Compare the features and prices of these programs.

Visit the sites for the low-end programs (www.microsoft.com) for Microsoft Publisher and (www.broderbund.com) for PrintMaster.

Arts and Crafts: Broderbund also offers special-purpose printing programs for creating greeting cards, banners, scrapbook pages, and more.

PLACES YOU'LL FIND DESKTOP PUBLISHING

You'll find desktop publishing programs in small businesses that do their own publishing. For instance, a company may design its own forms, letterheads, and publications (internal newsletters, product catalogs, brochures, and so on). You'll also find this type of program used in publishing fields (publishers, editors, writers, advertising agencies, journalists and so on).

FEATURES AND BENEFITS OF DESKTOP PUBLISHING PROGRAMS

What does this type of program provide beyond a word processing program? It provides a great deal of control for handling text and graphics. Here are just a few of the features of this type of program:

- *Greater text control.* For simple one-column documents, your word processing program is great. You may also find features for adding columns and text boxes; but to place text anywhere on the page with utmost control, you need a desktop publishing program. As an example, think about a newsletter with stories that start on page 1 and then continue on another page. Think about two- or even three-column documents. Consider pull-quotes (quotations set off from the main body of text) or separate areas for a table of contents. While you can add these items using a word processing program, doing so would be cumbersome. Desktop publishing programs, on the other hand, are designed to work for just these types of layout features.

Still need a word processing program: Most desktop publishing programs concentrate on layout rather than text creation. Whereas you can type text, you will most likely create the text in your word processing program and then import it into the desktop publishing program. Why? Because your word processing program will provide much better features for editing and creating text.

- *More text formatting options.* Desktop publishing features offer more formatting options for text, including kerning (setting the spacing between characters) and hyphenation.

- *Better graphics placement.* While you won't use your program to create graphics, you will use a desktop publishing program to place a graphic in the publication. Not only can you place the graphic in the exact spot you want, but you can also control how text wraps around the graphic, add captions, use borders for the graphic, change the size, and so on.

- *Better output.* Desktop publishing programs offer the best output. You can print on your own printer, or you may prepare the publication and then send it to a service bureau or printing press. Desktop publishing programs offer great control for this type of printing. As an example, the program can prepare color separations for color documents.

- *Automatic references.* Because these programs are designed to handle long publications, you'll find features for automating the creation of indexes and table of contents. You can also generate lists of tables or figures.

- *Style consistency.* To ensure consistency with the formatting, you can create and assign styles. (Word processing programs offer the same style features.) Using styles also makes changing the design easier. You can update the style and all text formatted with that style will be updated.

 Learn the lingo: If you work with desktop publishing, you will need to learn the lingo for measurements. Publishers use points to measure type; there are 72 points to an inch. Twelve points make one pica, another measurement commonly used in desktop publishing.

UNDERSTANDING THE PROGRAM TOOLS

Although the looks of programs will vary, you can get an idea of how the program works by taking a look at one program and its features. Figure 10.2 shows the layout screen for Microsoft Publisher. Note these key features:

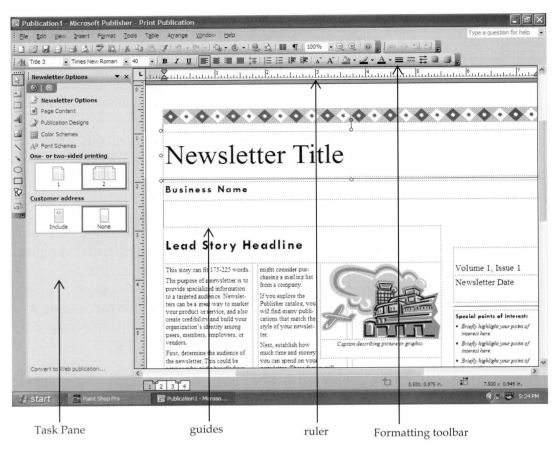

Task Pane   guides   ruler   Formatting toolbar

Figure 10.2. The tools for laying out a page are displayed in the program window.

- *Menu bar and formatting toolbar*. The menu bar and toolbars should look familiar; most programs include these elements. In a desktop publishing program, the toolbars include buttons for saving, printing, and viewing the publication. You'll also find typical buttons for formatting text and paragraphs.

- *Object toolbar*. In addition to the standard toolbars, you also see a toolbar with buttons for placing frames and other elements in the layout. In Publisher, the toolbar includes buttons for adding text frames, drawing tables, adding WordArt (special text), inserting pictures, adding clip art, and drawing common shapes (line, oval, rectangle, shapes).

- *Ruler*. The program window most likely includes a ruler. This element helps you align items in your layout. You can see the size and keep other elements on the page aligned using the ruler.

- *Guides*. Another helpful feature for placing items on the page is the page guides. Each element on the page is in its own "box" or frame. You can draw different frame types on the page: a frame for text, a frame for graphics, a frame for references. To see the placement of these frames, you can display guides.

- *Task pane*. You may find features to help you create the publication. For instance, in Publisher you can display the task pane, which guides you step by step through the process of creating a publication.

Hide on-screen elements: Just because a program displays tools doesn't mean you have to keep them displayed. Some features may be of help. Others may just be a distraction. For instance, you can hide the task pane in Publisher. To do so, click the Close (X) button in the title bar of the task pane. You can also turn on and off toolbars and status bar. Look for commands to make these changes in the View menu.

- *Status bar.* The status bar displays handy information, including the exact location (measurement-wise) of the insertion point. You can also display other pages in the publications using the page icons in the status bar.

 WEB: For more information, visit this site: www.microsoft.com and displaying the product information for Microsoft Publisher. You can find product information as well as design advice.

Using Presentation Programs

Desktop publishing centers mostly on printed media. If you are a speaker or need to make any kind of presentation, you'll find another category of software designed to meet this type of publishing.

Traditionally, a presentation is done with a slide show and screen. Presentation software has simplified the creation of slide shows and expanded the way presentations can be given. You can create presentations designed for the computer or the Web. This section covers the most important information about presentation programs.

PLACES YOU MIGHT FIND THIS PROGRAM

While you may think of teachers in a lecture hall when you think about presentations, especially slide presentations, this isn't the only place you'll find presentations. You might find them in other education areas; for instance, for job training. If the goal is education, presentation software comes in handy.

You'll also find them in companies, especially those involved in sales. A salesperson may make a pitch for a proposal or a new product in a presentation. A sales manager may review sales results and goals with a sales staff.

A company might also make presentations to its employees. For example, you might attend a presentation on new company benefits. At your annual company meeting you might have a presentation reviewing the organization, accomplishments, and goals of the company.

In addition to attending presentations, you may also be called on to give a presentation. If you are in school or have a child in school, you or they may have to make presentations as part of their class, for instance, report on a science project. You might have some fun and create a presentation of a vacation.

TYPES OF PRESENTATIONS

You know in what settings you might encounter a presentation. The types of presentations match up to these settings. For instance, you can find presentations for training, presenting a business plan, and selling a product. You can create presentations for an employee orientation, company meeting, financial overview, or project overview.

POPULAR PRESENTATION PROGRAMS

Popular presentation programs include Microsoft PowerPoint, Corel Presentations, and Lotus Freelance Graphics.

 WEB: Visit www.corel.com and display the product information for Corel Presentations. You can also get information about Lotus Freelance Graphics at www.lotus.com. For info on Microsoft PowerPoint, visit www.microsoft.com. At all of these sites, you'll have to navigate to the product page for that particular product. Also note that these programs are often included in program suites. For instance, Microsoft PowerPoint is included with all versions of Microsoft Office 2003.

FEATURES OF PRESENTATION PROGRAMS

Presentation programs naturally include features that help you in creating a presentation. But they go beyond that to add other elements:

- *Wizards.* Giving presentations is usually part of a job, not the entire job. Therefore, most people do not spend day in and day out creating presentations. Thus, the creators of this type of program provide wizards to help get you started. PowerPoint, for instance, includes wizards for popular presentation types (see Figure 10.3).

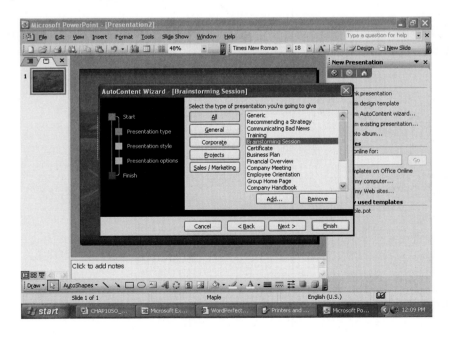

Figure 10.3. You can use the AutoContent wizard in Microsoft PowerPoint to create common presentation types.

- **Templates.** You can also select design themes to apply consistent formatting (background, headers and footers, logos, and so on) to your presentation. Figure 10.4 shows some of the design templates in Microsoft PowerPoint in the task pane.

Figure 10.4. A design template includes features, such as background, text formatting, and slide elements, such as titles and footers. *Consistent design.* In addition to templates, you can select from some predefined slide types.

- **Consistent design.** In addition to templates, you can select from some predefined slide types. For instance, you can select slides with placeholders for graphics, tables, bulleted lists, and so on.

- **Audience handouts.** Most programs enable you to create audience handouts, most often using the slides from the presentation. Your audience can use these handouts to follow along and to take notes.

- **Speaker notes.** To help the presenter, most programs enable you to create speaker notes. The note includes the slide as well as comments or points you may want to remember.

- **Special types of information.** In addition to text, you can create slides that contain graphics, animations, charts, tables, and organization charts. Figure 10.5 shows an organization chart from a PowerPoint presentation.

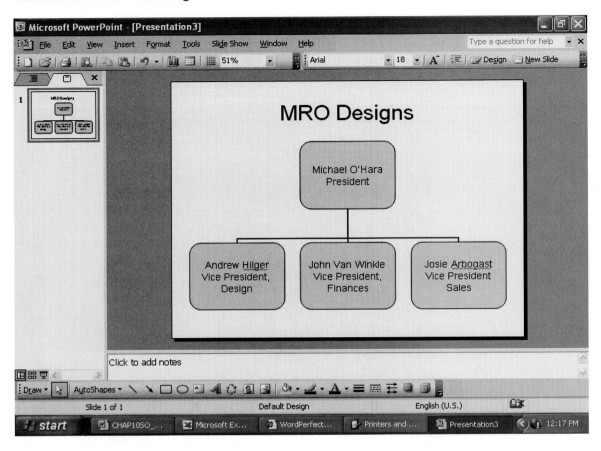

Figure 10.5. You can add special elements like an organization chart, shown here.

- *Special effects.* You can add special effects, such as transitions or animations. Transitions add special effects when moving from slide to slide.

UNDERSTANDING THE PROGRAM TOOLS

Again, various programs have different interfaces. You can get an idea of what to expect with this type of program by taking a look at PowerPoint and its program window. Figure 10.6 shows a title slide in PowerPoint. Note these key features:

 Create presentations from an outline: Some presenters prefer to work from an outline. You can create a presentation from a word processing outline. You may also be able to create a presentation in different views. For instance, in PowerPoint you can create a presentation in Outline view.

Outline   Menu bar   Toolbar

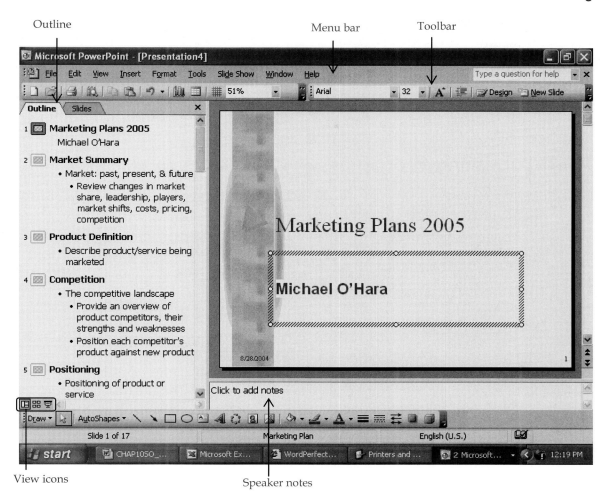

View icons   Speaker notes

Figure 10.6. Presentation programs include tools for adding and viewing the slides in a presentation.

- *Menu bar and toolbars.* Like other programs you've come across, the menu bar contains the names of the menus, and the toolbars provide quick access to frequently used commands. Note that a lot of the buttons in a toolbar are the same from program to program (for instance, the buttons for copying, cutting, and pasting text). The buttons that are different are those that are pertinent to that particular program. For instance, in PowerPoint you see a button for Common Tasks. Using this button you can add slides, change the layout of the slide, or apply a new design.

- *Outline.* To keep track of the organization of the presentation, you may be able to display an outline. PowerPoint, for instance, displays an outline listing the titles and bullets for all the slides in the presentation.

- *View icons.* While working on a presentation, you want to see the slide and perhaps the outline. To check the flow and special effects, you will want to view the slide show. If you are changing the order of the slides, you may want to see a thumbnail view. To make formatting changes to all slides, such as inserting page numbers, use the Master Slide view. You can change to various views using the view icons (or look for commands in the View menu).

- *Notes area*. As mentioned, you can add speaker notes to a slide. These will not be displayed as part of the presentation, but can be used by the presenter for notes, comments, points, and other hints for discussing any particular slide.

Web Publishing Programs

The popularity of the World Wide Web has opened another avenue for publishing: the Web. You don't have to be a business to have a Web site. You can create your own personal Web site, listing your favorite things or displaying your resume, for example. You can find programs to help you create and manage your Web site. You can also find services to publish your Web site (place it on the Web so that others can visit the site). This section explains this new type of publishing.

WHY CREATE A WEB SITE?

Lesson 12 covers browsing the Internet and gives you a good idea of the types of sites you can visit. You'll find sites for reading current news, selling items (cars, houses, shoes, books, you name it), offering services (job hunting, loans, online trading, travel planning), providing reference information, expressing opinions (book reviews, movie reviews, political essays), and just plain having fun (see Figure 10.7). Sites are created to inform, educate, entertain, sell, and prompt to action.

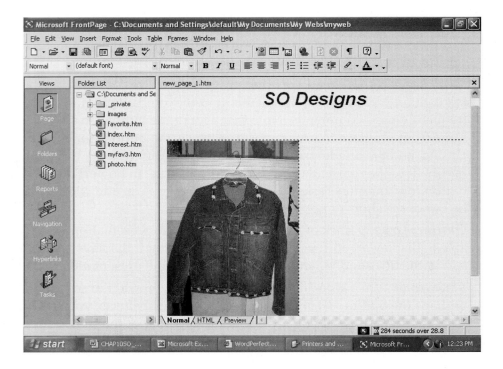

Figure 10.7. Anyone can create a Web site and include any type of content.

In addition to browsing other Web sites, you may want to create your own Web site. You might be involved in a project for setting up a Web site for someone. Perhaps your school has a Web site (or is thinking of creating one). Maybe you just want a forum to express your thoughts. Perhaps you have some business or service you want to advertise. Whatever the reason, you can create a Web site.

WHAT YOU NEED TO PUBLISH A WEB SITE

To publish a Web site, you need the following: a program for creating Web pages and a host or provider that will publish your Web site. You may also need programs for creating other special multimedia Web page elements, such as animations, videos, or graphics.

Web pages are most often a special type of document called HTML. This stands for HyperText Markup Language, the special formatting language used to define the look and contents of a Web page. Don't panic and think you have to learn programming. You can find programs that simplify the creation of HTML documents.

For simple pages, you may be able to use your word processing programs. As Web publishing has become more popular, more programs are incorporating features to aid in designing and publishing Web pages. For instance, Word includes a Web Page template and a Web Tools toolbar. You can also create and save any document as an HTML file.

If your needs go beyond the capabilities of a word processing program, you can purchase Web publishing programs such as Microsoft FrontPage .

You can also find Web sites that provide templates and allow you to customize your own Web page, for instance Yahoo!'s GeoCities and Homestead. You can also place your page on site for little or no charge.

 WEB: Visit the sites for publishing simple Web sites include Yahoo!'s GeoCities (http://geocities.yahoo.com/) and Homestead (www.homestead.com).

In addition to the program, you need a way to take the documents you create and make them accessible from the Web. To do so, you need an Internet or online provider. If you have Internet access, you already have an account with an Internet provider. Most provide some type of Web hosting or publishing service. For instance, America Online (AOL) offers this service, as does EarthLink. Some offer free hosting services. For others, you may pay a fee. Also, the free sites may be limited to a certain size. If you go beyond this size, you may have to pay. For business sites, you may also be able to hire designers or programmers to help create and maintain the site.

Web sites are more than simply text. Most contain graphics and links to other sites. (A link is an image or text that, when clicked, takes you to another Web page or Web site.) These features are easy to add. You can include a variety of graphics. The most popular format for graphic images are JPEG and GIF. (See Lesson 11 for more information on graphic programs.) You may also add animations or video clips. To develop these features, you might want to get a multimedia authoring program.

Two of the most popular programs are Macromedia Flash (for Web designing and Web graphics) and Macromedia Studio MX 2004 (a comprehensive suite for Web development, which includes Dreamweaver and Flash).

 WEB: For more information on Web publishing programs, visit www.macromedia.com. Review the product information for both Flash and Studio MX 2004.

FEATURES OF WEB PUBLISHING PROGRAMS

What can you do with a Web publishing program? Why do you need this type of program? The following list gives you an idea of some of the key features:

- *Wizards and templates.* Like other publishing programs, most users need some help in creating a publication, especially if it's not something they do full-time. To aid in creating sites, most programs provide wizards and templates. For instance, FrontPage includes a wizard for creating a personal Web site. You make selections for the content, and it creates a layout with pertinent sections. You then edit these sections to include your own information.

- *Links.* Your Web site should contain links to other sites. You can find features for inserting, formatting, and managing the links (also called hyperlinks) in your program.

- *Graphics and other media.* To create an inviting Web site, you want to include more than just text. Your program should simplify adding graphics, banners, forms, pictures, animations, and other multimedia elements.

- *Preview and publish.* The program should include commands that enable you to preview the page, to see it as it will appear in a Web browser. You should also find commands for publishing the site on your Web server. You may have to request the specifications from your Internet Service Provider (ISP).

- *File management.* A Web site may consist of several pages and several types of documents, including text, graphics, photographs, tables, charts, animations, sounds, and other elements. Most programs offer features to help you keep track of these elements.

- *Navigation.* If your Web site contains several pages, you want an easy way for your visitors to navigate from page to page. You can find tools for adding navigation panes. You can also view a roadmap of the site so that you see how pages are interconnected. You can make changes to the organization or flow of the pages.

- *Reports.* To keep track of all the page elements, you can use the reporting feature. In FrontPage, the site summary report includes the number of pictures, linked files, unlinked files, older files, recently added files, hyperlinks, broken links, errors, and tasks. You can use this feature to troubleshoot problems with the site.

Summary

- Desktop publishing revolutionized the print industry, making it less expensive and easier to create professional-quality publications from a computer.

- Popular desktop publishing programs include Adobe PageMaker, QuarkXPress, and Microsoft Publisher.

- Desktop publishing programs provide more control over text and graphic placement. You can also use more advanced formatting features, such as text kerning.

- Presentation programs simplify the creation of a presentation. Most programs provide some templates and wizards to help you get started.

- Popular presentation programs include Microsoft PowerPoint, Lotus Freelance Graphics, and Corel Presentations. These programs are included within program suites from each company.

- Another popular form of publishing is Web publishing. To do this, you need software to create the Web documents and also a server on which to publish the content.

- Some Internet providers include free Web site hosting. If yours doesn't (or if you have needs beyond the free services), you can sign up for more complete Web hosting services.

LESSON 11: ENTERTAINMENT

Objectives

> ➤ **See how entertainment (music, TV, games) has evolved**
> ➤ **Learn how to play, download, and copy music**
> ➤ **Learn how to play and create videos**
> ➤ **Play games**

How Entertainment Has Changed

Technology has also changed how we get our entertainment. Back in the 1970s, we didn't have VCRs or cable TV or Gameboys. We had three channels: ABC, NBC, and CBS. Occasionally, we could get a local channel (in Indiana WTTV-4), but the reception was horrible. We had antennas on our TV and broadcasts were not 24 hours a day. In the middle of the night, if you turned on the TV, all you saw was static.

We listened to records (LPs and 45s). The 8-track tape was popular in the 1970s but quickly became obsolete. Cassette tapes were something new.

You can see how quickly technology has changed how we spend our leisure time by looking at some of the key events highlighted in this section.

MUSIC

How do you listen to music? How did your parents? Technology has also changed (and will continue to change) how music is distributed. Note these key developments over the years:

- In 1948, the LP was introduced. The next year, 45 RPM records debuted. These records were called vinyl and remained popular until the introduction of the CD.
- In 1954, transistor radios hit the market. (They had been developed and patented earlier, but they became a popular home item in the 1950s.)
- Audio cassettes became a viable way to distribute music in the 1960s. They are still used today. Although they were new, they did not make the LP obsolete.
- Portable music became possible in 1980, with the introduction of the Sony Walkman tape player.
- Next came the compact disc players and music on compact discs (mid-1980s). These are still popular today.
- In the late 1990s a new music medium, the MP3 format, was developed and used for distributing music over the Internet. You can download music to

your computer or to a portable MP3 player. (This topic is covered later in this chapter.)

RADIO AND TV

Depending on your age, you might remember black-and-white TV and if you are a Senior Citizen, you may even remember radio shows and when TV was first introduced. Now you have 24-hour TV, hundreds of channels, cable or satellite service, pay-for-view, and even Web access on your TV. Want to see how quickly things have changed? Review the following TV timeline:

1901	First radio message sent across Atlantic
1927	TV is demonstrated at Bell Labs
1948	"Ed Sullivan" show debuts
1948	Earliest cable systems are started in remote areas of Pennsylvania and Oregon (CATV or community antenna television)
1951	"I Love Lucy" debuts
1953	Color broadcasting begins
1954	"The Tonight Show" with Steve Allen debuts
1964	1 million homes wired for cable
1969	Neil Armstrong walks on moon, shown on TV
1971	"All in the Family" debuts
1972	Pay TV launched with HBO
1976	Betamax (Sony) format introduced
1977	VHS (JVC) format introduced; becomes industry standard
1979	ESPN debuts
1980	CNN and MTV launched
1982	Home Shopping Network
1987	Debut of the FOX network
1997	DVD players enter market

Newer innovations include HDTV (high definition TV) and digital cable. With digital cable, you can get thousands of channels as well as On Demand movies. You can also view on-screen program listings. With TiVo systems (a special box and service), you can find and digitally record up to 140 hours of the programming you want. You can also pause, rewind and play back live TV in slow motion.

VIDEO GAMES

Video games, another form of entertainment, have seen the ups and downs of several companies. What's interesting about this market is that the companies still have proprietary formats. That means you can't play a Sony PlayStation game on a Nintendo system. These companies have effectively kept the market segmented. Here's a brief history of video games:

1962	First video game written
1972	First home video games; Atari releases Pong
1980	Pac Man
1985	Nintendo
1988	Gameboy
1989	Sega Genesis
1991	Super Nintendo
1995	Sony PlayStation
1996	Nintendo 64
2000	Sega Dreamcast, Sony PlayStation 2
2001	Microsoft X-Box

Let's take a look at how entertainment components have merged and combined with computers to provide even more usability and flexibility.

Playing Sounds and Music

In the not so distant future, sound on a computer was a new feature; now sound cards and speakers are standard equipment. You can use these hardware components to not only play computer sounds (like the sound you might hear when you receive an email), but also to sample tracks on a CD or to even play an audio CD. In addition to listening to music, you can visit online music sites and purchase music, downloading it to your computer. From your computer, you can then transfer the music to a portable device such as an iPod, or you can burn your own CDs (from music you've purchased online as well as "regular" music CDs you already own). This section describes all the sound and music options you'll find on a typical computer.

SOUND CARDS AND SPEAKERS

You need a sound card and speakers to play sounds, and most computers come with these components. The quality of the playback is determined by the speakers. Most speakers are fine for playing voices, but if you want to play CD-quality music, you may need to upgrade to a better set of speakers.

PLAYING SOUNDS

Sounds are stored like other data on a computer, in a file. For instance, WAV files are a popular sound file format. You can play back WAV files using the Sound Recorder included with Windows. To start the program, click Start, All Programs, Accessories, Entertainment, and then Sound Recorder. You can then use the File, Open command to open the sound file you want to play. Note the Sound Recorder window, shown in Figure 11.1, has buttons similar to a tape player. You can play, rewind, and stop the playback, for instance.

Figure 11.1. To play simple sound files, you can use Sound Recorder, included with Microsoft Windows.

 Record sounds: With a microphone, you can record sounds and save them as audio files. You might record a message and attach it to an e-mail message.

Windows (and other programs) play sounds for certain events (such as when an alert message is displayed). As another sound feature, you can select the events for which sounds are played as well as select the particular sound. You can select a set of sounds, called a sound scheme. You might make this change to customize the sounds to something unique. Open the Sounds and Audio Devices Properties (click Start, select Control Panel, click Sounds, Speech, and Audio Devices, and then click Sounds and Audio Devices). You can then click the Sounds tab and select a sound scheme to use (see Figure 11.2).

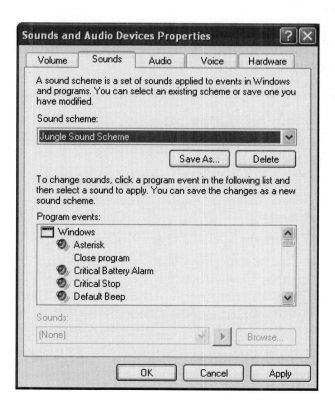

Figure 11.2. You can customize the sounds that Windows plays for key system events.

PLAYING MUSIC

With the Media Player included with Windows, you can also play audio CDs on your computer (see Figure 11.3). You can use the Media Player to do any of the following:

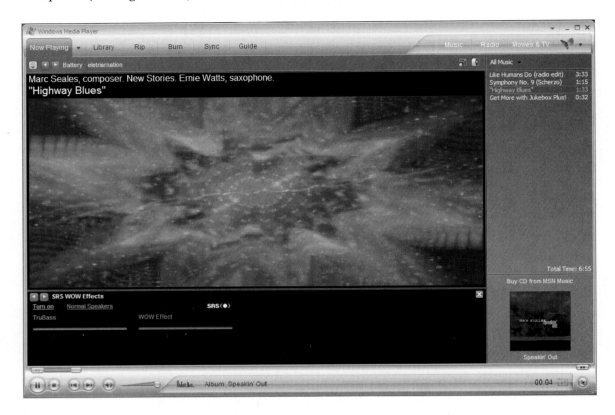

Figure 11.3. You can use Windows Media Player to play music.

- To see what's currently playing, click the Now Playing button. You can also choose to display different visualizations (moving graphic images) in the Now Playing window. To do so, use the buttons directly beneath the Now Playing button.

- You can play the next or previous track, stop or pause the playback, and adjust the volume using the controls along the bottom of the Windows Media Player window.

- To play a different track, click the track name in the list on the right.

- You can copy music from the CD and store it in your Music Library. You can then create custom CDs with music from a variety of sources. To copy music from the CD to your computer, use the RIP button. To view the music you have on your computer, click the Library button.

- You can create your own playlists of favorite songs. You create playlists from the Library.

- You can create your own music CDs by "burning" them to an audio CD or by transferring them to a portable music device such as an Apple iPod. Use the Burn and Sync buttons to access these features.

- Tune into favorite radio broadcasts using the Radio button. Watch the latest news, sports, and entertainment by clicking the Movies & TV button.

- Visit Windows Media site by clicking the Guide button. (You must be connected to the Internet.) In addition to browsing or searching for music, you can also view video clips and other media files (for instance, a trailer for an upcoming movie). Figure 11.4 shows WindowsMedia.com.

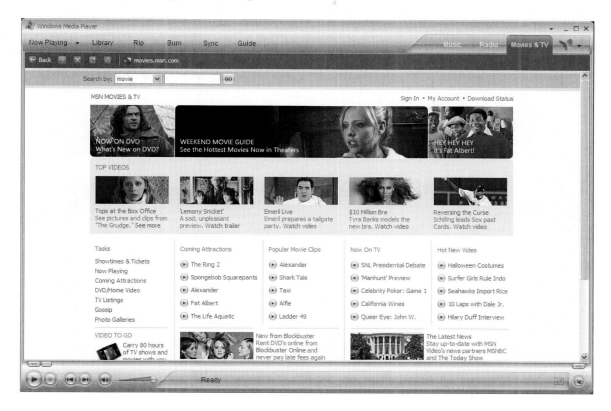

Figure 11.4. To find music or videos for playback with Windows Media Player, visit the WindowsMedia site.

FINDING MUSIC ONLINE

In addition to WindowsMedia.com, you can find music at a variety of other online sources. For instance, if you want to purchase a CD, you can visit a CD online store and usually sample the songs to see if you like them. Initially when music hit the Internet, you could find and download songs free via services such as Napster. Music producers and artists, though, put an end to free music access. Now you must purchase the music (although most sites offer a free weekly song). You can purchase an individual song or a complete album and download the music from that site to your computer. In Windows Media Player, you can access popular online stores by clicking the online stores button, located to the right of the Movies & TV button.

One thing that can be confusing about online music is the different formats and players. One popular format, MP3, became popular in the late 1990s. MP3 was developed by the

Moving Pictures Expert group and is a format for audio compression without sacrificing quality. Compression is necessary because audio and video files tend to take up a lot of disk space.

In addition to Windows Media Player (included as part of Windows), you can also use other media players including Apple's iTunes, MusicMatch Jukebox (www.musicmatch.com), shown in Figure 11.5, and RealPlayer (www.realone.com). Most often you can download the player for free (or purchase an enhanced version of the player). You can also access and download songs. The problem is that some players won't let you play music from another site or source. Each player wants to be your "default" music player. For instance, you can't play iTunes on MusicMatch's Jukebox. This should change, though, as pressure from consumers demand compatibility.

 Copyrighted music: Keep in mind that the music is copyrighted and may be limited in how you can use it. Check the particular music site for information about use of the downloaded music.

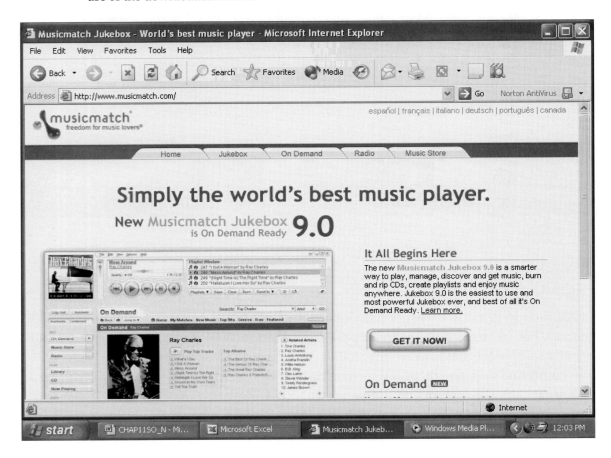

Figure 11.5. You can download the music player and music from Musicmatch's site.

CREATING MUSIC CDS AND USING PORTABLE PLAYERS

If your CD drive can record, you can copy songs from your computer to an audio CD (often called "burning a CD"). You can mix and match music from your own CD collection to songs purchased online to create your own music compilations.

Another popular add-on is a portable music player. You can download all or part of your music collection to a digital audio player. Much like computer media players, you can create playlists, adding or deleting songs. These cost from $200 on up and vary depending on the amount of music you can store and the features. One of the most popular players is Apple's iPod which you can use on both PC and Macintosh computers. You can also find other portable devices from Sony, Rio, and other electronic companies.

Movies & TV

The line between entertainment and computers is getting even blurrier, and it's not uncommon to find information about entertainment components such as HDTV or a home theater system in computer magazines.

In addition, you may also want to explore the possibilities of digital film recording, using a digital video camera and software. This section discusses these two entertainment avenues.

WATCHING TV & HOME THEATERS

If you enjoy watching TV, you may consider purchasing or adding to your computer the capability to receive and display TV channels. Many new monitors (and its companion piece, the adapter) include this added feature. You can then hook up your TV service and view TV from your computer.

In addition, you may find that your cable company provides more than just your TV options, but also perhaps your Internet connection (see Lesson 12 for more information on the Internet). You'll find a variety of television options including HDTV and TiVo (covered earlier in this lesson). Like buying a computer, purchasing this type of system may require a little homework so that you can distinguish among the different TVs and services offered. You can often find this information in computer magazines. For instance, PC World included in its May 2004 issue an article called "HDTV Answer Guide," providing a review of the differences and a list of frequently asked questions. You'll also find reviews of home theater systems. The latest trend is to sell the equipment as a package so that you are assured of compatibility. Most home theater systems include speakers, a DVD player, and a receiver. The receiver is the hub that unites several essential components and decodes the various formats. Often, the DVD player functions as both a player and receiver.

PLAYING MOVIES

In addition to playing music, you can also playback videos using your computer. For instance, you can use Windows MediaPlayer to view media clips including trailers for upcoming movies, interviews, and more. If your computer has a DVD drive and DVD player, you can also use your computer to view DVD movies. This is especially handy for portable computers and long airline flights! Most computers come with the equipment you need to take advantage of these media types.

MAKING MOVIES

In addition, you'll find that video capturing and editing features are also incorporated into new computers. With a digital camcorder and video editing software, you can create your own movie. You can then distribute the movie on your own Web site, at an independent site, or at studio sites.

And you no longer have to have expensive equipment to make your own movies, and these movies no longer have to be amateur presentations. With the right equipment and software, you can edit and create professional movies right from your computer.

What do you need? Here's a checklist of equipment:

- *Digital Camcorder*. To capture your film, you need a digital camcorder. You can copy the digital film to the PC, edit it, and then copy it back to the digital videotape (DV) without any loss of quality. As digital camcorders become more popular, prices become more affordable. And as with other electronic components, the more features and higher the output quality, the more expensive the camcorder.

- *Computer*. Because video editing is such a demanding task for a computer, you need a pretty fast PC and a lot of memory. If you are using your computer specifically for movie making, you may want to investigate in some upgrades to a traditional computer setup. For instance, you may want a bigger and better monitor and a higher-end processor.

- *Editing software*. You can purchase the editing software separately or purchase an integrated package of digital capture card and editing software. Popular editing programs include VideoStudio, Adobe Premiere, Studio DV, InterVideo WinDVD Creator, and MGI Software's VideoWave. You can also use the movie program included with Windows, Movie Maker (see Figure 11.6).

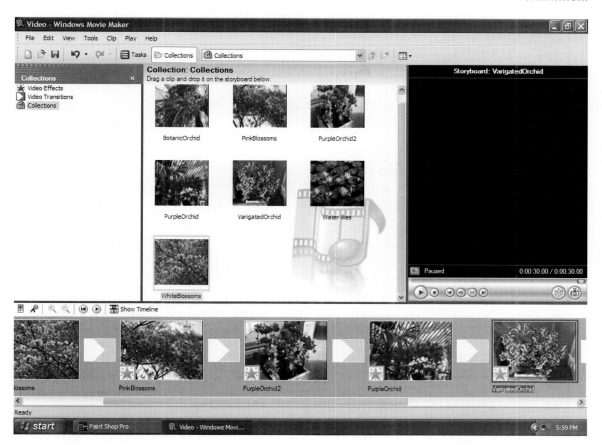

Figure 11.6. You can create your own movies using Windows Movie Maker.

Games & Hobbies & More

Beyond the traditional productivity software lies an endless world of other possibilities for games, hobbies, home, and more. To start, you may use your computers to play games. For instance, Windows includes some familiar card games such as Hearts and Solitaire (see Figure 11.7). You can find games that let you build cities, fight crime, ride skateboards, play basketball, and more. If there's a popular program for a gaming system you are interested in, there's probably a computer version of that or a similar program.

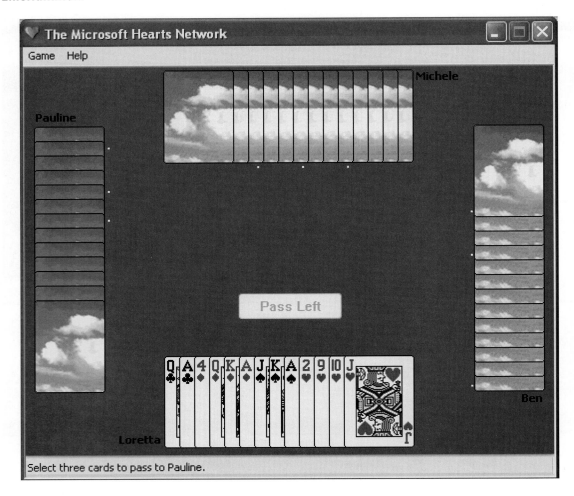

Figure 11.7. Try some of the games included with Windows, including Hearts.

In addition to playing games alone, you can join others in online games, which opens up many avenues of exploration including role playing ongoing games, fantasy football leagues, and more.

If you have some hobby, there's probably a software program for you. You can find software for creating quilts, creating scrapbook pages, going deer hunting, and so on. You can find programs for designing a deck to planning a garden. You'll also find a wide range of educational software that can teach you to type, for instance, or speak Spanish. Check out the programs advertised in magazines or your local Sunday paper. Visit an electronics or computer store and browse the program aisle. You'll also find that popular stores like Target, Wal-Mart, and K-Mart sell software (and other supplies).

When buying any new software (especially games), be sure to check the system requirements. Do you have the equipment you need to run the program on your computer? Is the program compatible with your version of Windows? The system requirements are listed on the software package.

Summary

- Technology also greatly impacted entertainment. You can play audio CDs on your computer, copy music from your CDs to your computer, download music, and create your own audio CDs.

- If you are a home movie fan, you'll be delighted with the newest equipment for making movies using your computer and a digital video recorder.

- Video games have evolved immensely, starting with a simple game of ping-pong (Pong) to sophisticated games with 3D graphics and virtual reality.

LESSON 12: THE INTERNET & EMAIL

Objectives

- ➤ **Define the Internet**
- ➤ **Get connected**
- ➤ **Browse Web pages**
- ➤ **Search the Internet**
- ➤ **Send e-mail and instant messages**

What is the Internet?

The Internet is a network of networks, literally thousands and thousands of networks connected to thousands and thousands of computers. By accessing one network on the Internet, you gain access to all of the other networks and all of the information and services provided on that network. The Internet has revolutionized the way we get and provide information. The Internet can provide a wide source of information, all from the convenience of your home. For instance, suppose that you were interested in Leonardo da Vinci. You could go to the library to look for books or articles on him. Or you can go online and take a look at some of da Vinci's most famous artwork, find books relating to your topic, get biographical information, research related topics, such as the Renaissance period, find articles about current showings or studies of da Vinci's work, and more.

As another example, maybe you are thinking of purchasing a car. Before the Internet, you had limited access to information about cars, mostly provided in publications like *Consumer Reports* and by the dealer or salesperson. Now you can look up a blue book value for a car, get information about different loan rates, check the safety rating for a vehicle, research the list and invoice prices, review a list of options for particular car models, and perhaps even find a car online.

The Internet is a grand resource that is exploding. More and more people are getting connected each day. With the Internet, you literally have the world at your fingertips.

HISTORY OF THE INTERNET

Here's a brief history of the Internet:

1968	Defense Department contracts with a computer design company to build ARPAnet, a network to link research computers
1985(86)	National Science foundation formed the NSFNET, linking five supercomputer centers
1985	America Online founded

1989(90)	Tim Berners-Lee, a researcher at CERN, developed HyperText Markup Language (HTML), the language used to create the World Wide Web
1990	The World is the first commercial provider of Internet dial-up access
1991	Gopher (menu-driven search tool for Internet) developed
1993	First Web browser (Mosaic) developed
1993	50 World Wide Web servers
1993	White House has a Web page and e-mail address
1994	Netscape launched
1994	Yahoo! was launched as an Internet directory
1995	AT&T introduces WorldNet, providing Internet access to its AT&T customers
1998	30 million households purchase goods over the Internet
2000	150 million to 200 million people worldwide use the Internet
2001	A survey estimated the size of the Internet at 2.5 billion documents and growing by a rate of 7.5 million documents per day
2004	Estimates put the number of people connected to the Internet (and this is just a guess) at 605+ million people

 Check latest statistics: For the latest information about the Internet's demographics, visit Nua Internet Surveys (www.nua.ie/surveys/).

WHAT YOU CAN DO ON THE INTERNET

The reason the Internet is so popular is that you can do so much, including sending electronic messages (called *email*), browsing for content, and connecting with other users either live (via a chat) or by posting messages on an electronic message board (called newsgroups).

Email is the most common activity on the Internet. You can send a message to anyone else with an e-mail address. E-mail has several benefits. First, it's quick. Once you send the message, it is available to the recipient pretty much instantaneously. Second, it's inexpensive. You do not have to pay for your e-mail messages. Third, it's convenient. You can send messages at any time. Fourth, it's versatile. You can include more than just messages. You can attach documents, photos, or send Web pages with your message. You can read more about e-mail later in this lesson.

In addition to e-mail, the Internet is a rich resource for all kinds of information. You can read the latest news, listen to new CDs, or purchase anything from an autographed football from Brett Favre to textbooks. You can research papers, search for a job, get advice for computer problems, find apartments for rent, look up current stock quotes, or listen to a live radio broadcast. The possibilities are endless. You'll read more about some of the things you can do on the Internet later in this lesson.

The Internet is an optimum tool for research. Not only can you find information on almost any topic, written by authorities from all over the world, but the information is updated and you can find the most current data that is available.

 Check your source: A word to the wise: it is important to check your sources. Not everything you read on the Internet is correct or accurate.

The Internet is an excellent publishing tool. You have the ability to share your ideas, work, and opinions with the world.

Last but not least, the Internet is a means for connecting to other users. In addition to e-mail, you can send and receive instant messages. You can also send instant messages (covered in more detail later in this lesson). You can also participate in chats (online discussion groups). Chats are like a party or meeting, only you aren't physically present. Instead, you type your comments. You can connect with people across the world.

As another example, you can participate in newsgroup discussions. A newsgroup is a message board. You post comments, and others respond, creating a conversation through these messages. Newsgroups are different than chats; chats are "live," or real-time, communication, newsgroups are not. You can find everything from groups about biochemical engineering to Elvis sightings. Both chats and newsgroups enable you to find other Internet users with your same interests.

Internet phones are also becoming popular. In the past, the sound quality was not good, but it has improved, and you can find telephones and programs that let you use the Internet to make long distance calls.

WHAT IS THE WORLD WIDE WEB

When you hear the Internet discussed, you may also hear the term "World Wide Web." The Internet encompasses all the various types of information and activities you can do. The World Wide Web isn't a physical part of the Internet, but more the way the information is presented. On the Web, information is presented in a graphical hypermedia format. What's that mean? It means a Web site will contain text, pictures, video clips, sounds, animation, and other multimedia elements.

A Web site also includes links (also called hyperlinks). These links are connections to other sites, to other pages at the current site, or to other places in the current document. With links you can explore related information by simply clicking the link. Figure 12.1 shows MSN's home page. You can click any of the links in the left column to view that information. For instance, Travel to view travel articles as well as links to other travel-related information.

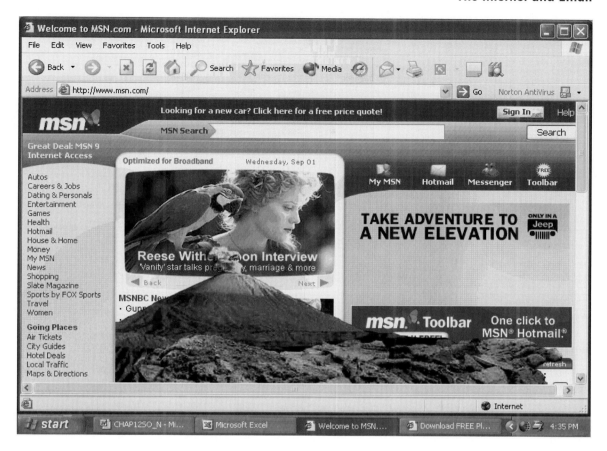

Figure 12.1. A Web page presents information in a graphical format and includes links to other sites.

Getting Connected

To do any of the activities (send mail, browse the Web), you need to get connected. Getting connected requires these things:

- A modem or network connection
- An Internet provider
- Programs for reading mail and browsing the Web

MODEMS: CONNECTING TO THE INTERNET

Many users connect to the Internet with a special hardware device called a modem. Modem stands for MOdulator-DEModulator and is a device used for connecting to other computers via the phone lines (see Figure 12.2). Phone lines transmit data using an analog signal; computers transmit and store digital data. Therefore, to use the phone lines to transmit data, you need a device to translate the digital data (from the PC) to an analog format (which the phone lines can handle and transmit) and then back to digital format (on the receiving PC). This device is the modem.

Figure 12.2. You can use a modem to connect to the Internet.

Today most computers come with a modem. Also, you may have a modem that can also function as a fax machine. Connected to the phone line, you can fax documents from your computer.

Modems differ basically in speed, and the speed is measured in how much data is transmitted per second (bits per second, or bps). This measurement is often confused with baud, but baud rate is not really the correct terminology.

Early modems could transmit data at around 300 bps. As modems became more popular, speed increased to 1200, 2400, 9600, 14,400 (sometimes called 14.4K), 28,800 (or 28.8K), and 33,600 (33.6K). The newest modems can transmit 56,000 bps or 56K, which is effectively as fast as this technology will get with existing phone technology.

Speed is limited: You can only go as fast as the device to which you are connecting, and the speed is limited because of phone technology.

To get around the phone-line bottleneck, new modem types have been developed. You can access the Internet via your cable company. To do so, you can use a cable modem. You may also be able to get connected via a special type of phone line called a DSL line. Originally these services were not available everywhere and were pricey. Now this type of access (often called broadband access) is common. You can check your local cable or phone company to see what type of Internet service they provide, as well as the cost.

The need for speed: You want the fastest Internet connection so that you can display pages and move from link to link without a lot of waiting. Speed is measured in kilobytes per second (KBps) and megabytes per second (MBps). The amount of data that can be transmitted is often referred to as bandwidth. Faster connections are referred to as broad bandwidth or high bandwidth.

WEB: To see what DSL services are available, visit the site www.dsl.com.

PICKING A PROVIDER

In addition to a connection, you need a company that provides access to the Internet. This company is called the Internet Service Provider, or ISP . Internet providers are your on-ramp to the Internet; they provide the link to the various networks of the Internet.

Your ISP also handles your mail and provides a list of newsgroups which you may want to join. For these services, you pay a subscription fee.

Many consumers get access to the Internet through an online provider, such as America Online. In addition to providing a link to the Internet, America Online (AOL) offers its own content and features. With America Online, you can get instant messages, participate in chats, and review content, all within the America Online community. Microsoft Network (MSN) is similar to AOL; you've probably seen TV advertisements about this online service.

While America Online does provide Internet access, it is not a dedicated Internet provider. You can find companies that are just that: Internet providers. You can find national providers, such as EarthLink. You can also find local providers in your area. Also, as mentioned, your cable and phone company probably now offers Internet service. You have lots of options, so be sure to shop around if you are signing up for a new service.

When choosing an Internet Service Provider, it's important to check out these factors:

- What are the fees? Is it a flat fee? Is there a startup fee? Do you have a free trial period? Any extra charges?
- What types of connections do they support? If you have a special connection (say a DSL), your provider must support that connection.
- Is the connection call local? You want a local or toll-free call. If the call isn't local, check out any fees for the actual phone call.
- What support is provided? Does the provider have phone support? Online support? Does the provider charge for support?
- What other services are provided? Some provide Web hosting services so that you can publish your Web pages through the provider. Some even give you free publishing for a page within a certain size (not physical size, but size of the files).

CHOOSING A BROWSER

In addition to the connection and the provider, you need the software to access and display Web pages. The software for displaying Web pages is called a browser, and the most popular browser is now Internet Explorer, which is included as part of Windows.

 Originally Netscape had the biggest share of the Internet market. Enter Microsoft, which by including Internet Explorer as part of Windows, stole most of the market. That was part of the reason for all the Justice investigation into Microsoft in 2000.

Figure 12.3 shows the Internet Explorer program.

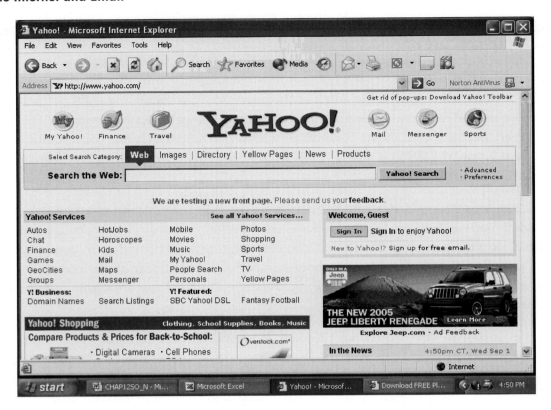

Figure 12.3. Internet Explorer is a popular Web browser.

In addition to a browser, you need a program for reading mail, and if you participate in newsgroups, you need a newsreader. Most browsers now include all of these components in one package. Windows users can send and receive email and participate in newsgroups using Outlook Express (another program included with Windows). You can also find and use other email programs. For instance, a more full-featured version of Outlook Express (called Outlook) is included with Microsoft Office. You can also find other popular mail programs, including Eudora.

SETTING UP YOUR COMPUTER

Once you have all the things you need to get connected, you are ready to set up your computer. This involves installing any software that is needed and setting up dial-up access to the Internet. You need only do the setup once. Setup does involve entering technical information, such as your username, password, mail protocol, phone number to dial, and other information. Your Internet provider should supply this information to you. You can also use Windows' Internet Connection Wizard to get connected; this wizard leads you step-by-step through the process.

Once everything is set up, you log on. The procedure for logging on will vary depending on your setup, but it usually involves double-clicking the connection icon and entering your username and password. For 24/7 connections (for instance, cable modems), you are always connected and don't need to log on. Once connected, you see your browser and your home page (the first page that is displayed each time you log on).

 Change your home page: Most browsers enable you to select the home page you want to use. In Internet Explorer, for instance, you can select your home page by selecting Tools, Internet Options. On the General tab of the Internet Options dialog box, type the address of the home page you want to use. Then click OK.

Your home page is your starting point, and most home pages include lots of helpful links. You may even be able to customize the home page. For instance, if you use Yahoo! for your home page, you can set it up to display weather in your area, stock quotes, your horoscope, news stories of interest to you, and so on.

If you have a cable connection, you are always online and don't need to log on and off. Because of this 24/7 connection, you do need to take some security precautions to prevent others from accessing your computer. Lesson 13 covers this topic as well as other security and privacy issues relating to the Internet, email, and computers.

Browsing Web Pages

There's no way you can summarize all the information you can find on the Internet. There are huge telephone-like books that list sites and books that cover specific features, such as finding a job or trading stock online. If there's something you are looking for, you can most likely find it. All you need is a few basic skills for navigating, and this section introduces those skills.

UNDERSTANDING A WEB PAGE

A Web page consists of text, graphics, links, and other multimedia elements. What you see when you visit a particular site varies from site to site. Some may include video clips or sounds. You may find animations. Some may include cool graphics; others may be mostly text. Many sites include advertisements. Almost all sites include links to other sites. These links usually appear in a different color and are underlined. You can use these links to navigate from site to site, as covered in the next section.

A Web site is a collection of pages, and each Web site has a unique address called a URL, or uniform resource locator. Here's the address, for instance, of the White House:

www.whitehouse.gov

Most addresses follow this format. They start with www, which is an indication that the page is a Web page (as opposed to other site types). You might see http:// before the www, but this part of the address is usually assumed. HTTP stands for HyperText Transfer Protocol and is the language, or protocol, used for displaying Web pages.

FTP sites: Another common site you may find are ftp sites. FTP stands for file transfer protocol; these sites are used to download information. They usually follow a hierarchical structure, much like documents stored in folders on your hard drive.

The next part of the address is the name of the site. Usually this accurately reflects the content. What's the page for the NBA? www.nba.com. What's the site for the NFL? www.nfl.com. Even if you don't know a page name, you can usually take a guess.

The final part of the address indicates the type of network. Here's a quick list of the most common extensions and their meaning:

- com   Commercial
- edu   Education
- gov   Government
- mil   Military
- net   Networking (like your service provider)
- org   Private (usually not-for-profit organizations)

Foreign sites also often include a country code as part of the address. Here's a list of common country codes:

- us   United States
- uk   United Kingdom
- fr   France
- au   Australia
- ca   Canada
- ie   Ireland

Each site has a unique name as does each page. Sometimes an address includes the address name and a page name, as in this example:

www.pearsoneducation.com/us-school/index.htm

This address is similar to a path to a particular document. Notice that the backslash is used to separate the site name from the path name. Also, the page (document) name may include an extension. HTM (or HTML) is the most common format for Web pages.

 Create your own Web page: You can get information about Web publishing in Lesson 10 of this book.

BROWSING USING LINKS

As mentioned, most Web pages include links or hyperlinks, and these links often appear in a different color or are underlined. Sometimes a graphic is also a link. A collection of links, each assigned to particular part of a picture, is called an image map.

 Check pointer: You can tell when you are pointing to a link because the pointer should change shape (most often to a hand). Also, the status bar may display the address of that link.

To use a link, you click it. When you click a link, you may be taken to another part of the current Web page, to another page at that site, or to another site entirely. You can click any of the links on this page to go to another site or page. Going from page to page using links is called navigating or browsing or surfing the Web (or Net).

USING TOOLBAR BUTTONS

When you are browsing using links, you aren't really sure what you'll see when you click the link. You'll see a page, but whether that page is what you are looking for or contains information you seek is hard to tell until you actually see the page.

To help you navigate, most browsers include toolbar buttons to help you move among the pages and sites you have visited. For instance, Internet Explorer includes these toolbar buttons for navigating:

Button	Name	Description
Back ▼	Back	Click this button to go back to the last page viewed. You can click this button more than once to go back several pages.
⊙	Forward	If you've gone back, you can then go forward by clicking this button. If the button is grayed out, you have not gone back, so you can't go forward.
✕	Stop	If a page is taking too long to display, click this button to stop the display.
↻	Refresh	To update the information on the page, click this button. Some sites continually update the information. As an example, if you are looking at stock quotes, the prices will continually be updated. You can refresh the page to get the most recent information.
⌂	Home	To return to your home page, click this button.

GOING TO AN ADDRESS

In addition to browsing, you can go directly to a site. This is the fastest method to go to a site of interest, but you must know the site name. You can find addresses advertised in print and TV ads. You'll also find sites in books, such as this one. To go to a particular site, click in the Address bar, type the address, and press Enter.

 Guess: If you aren't sure what the address is, guess. Most sites try to stick to an easily recognizable name. For instance, the address for MTV is www.mtv.com. If you guess wrong, nothing bad will happen. You may get an error message or you may see a page you didn't intend.

Searching the Internet

If you know a site name, you can go to that site. You may also find sites of interest as you browse, but if you are looking for a particular site or if you want to see what sites are available for a certain topic, you can search.

To search the Internet, you use a search tool. These tools vary in how they search; you can use search engines, which are large databases, or search indexes. That distinction isn't really that important, and the distinction is somewhat blurred. Just be aware that you may hear or read these terms.

BASICS OF SEARCHING

The basic steps to search include the following:

1   Go to the search page. Some start pages include a search feature. Or you can go to any of the popular search sites covered later in this section.

2   Type the word or phrase you want to find.

3   Click the search button. The name of this button will vary.

4   View the results. The results will be a list of links to sites that match your entry. You can click any of these links to go to that site. Some search tools display information to help you decide which link is the closest match. They may have some percentage indicator. You may also see a short description. Some search tools provide reviews of sites. Figure 12.4 shows the results of searching for "U.S. Tennis Open" using the most popular search tool, Google.

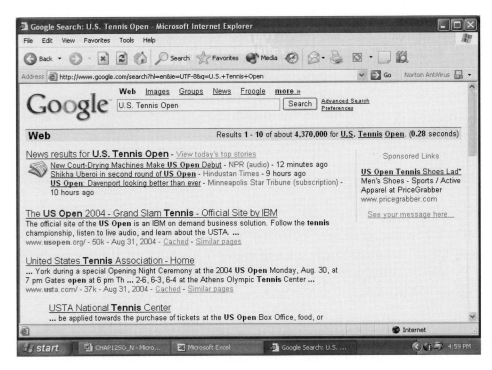

Figure 12.4. You can search for topics using any of the Internet's search tools.

POPULAR SEARCH TOOLS

The Internet is full of search tools, and new ones are offered all the time. Here's a list of some of the most popular sites and their addresses:

- Google   www.google.com
- Yahoo!   www.yahoo.com
- AltaVista   www.altavista.com
- Teoma   www.teoma.com
- AlltheWeb   www.alltheweb.com
- HotBot   www.hotbot.com

SEARCH TIPS

Finding what you want can be like finding the proverbial needle in the haystack. For most effective searching, consider these tips:

- If you get too many matches, try narrowing the search by using different words. Also, be sure to pick a unique word or phrase. If you search for too broad of a topic, you'll have too many matches to wade through. For instance, if you search for music, you'll never find what you are looking for. If you search for Celtic music, though, your odds of locating what you desire are increased.

- Try search options. Most tools provide options for refining the search. You may be able to select what parts of the Internet are searched. You can limit searches to match all words entered. Look for a link for search options or something similarly named.

- Use Boolean operators. You can create searches using Boolean operators, such as AND and NOT. As an example, if you search for "Latin" AND "Music" the search will find sites that include both Latin and music (not one or the other). You can find more information about search options by clicking the advanced search link for that particular search tool.

- Use search channels. Some search sites include channels or categories, which you can browse. Looking for travel information? Visit the travel channel.

- Try other search tools. If you don't find what you like with one tool, try another one. The results will vary. You'll also find that you will prefer one site to another.

- Look for people and places. Most tools also include features for finding physical addresses and e-mail addresses. You can also get directions and maps using the search tools and look up businesses in Yellow Page-like resources.

Sending and Receiving Email

E-mail is by far the most popular activity on the Internet. You can send messages to anyone with an e-mail address, including people that use the same service (like other AOL members), people that use different services, people in your city, and people across the world. It's fast, convenient, and free.

YOUR EMAIL ADDRESS

When you sign up for Internet access, you receive an e-mail account and an e-mail address. This address is in the following format:

sohara@aol.com

The first part of the address is the username. You can usually select your e-mail username (unless it's taken by someone else). The two parts of the address are separated by an at sign (@). The second part of the address is the domain name, usually the name of your Internet provider. In this example, aol.com is the ISP, or Internet network.

READING AND RESPONDING TO EMAIL

When someone addresses a message to you, basically, the message is sent to your Internet provider's network. When you check your mail, the message is then copied from that system to your system. To read mail, you need a mail program (see Figure 12.5). Windows, for instance, includes Outlook Express, a program for sending and receiving email. You can also find and use other mail programs. Most mail programs include similar features.

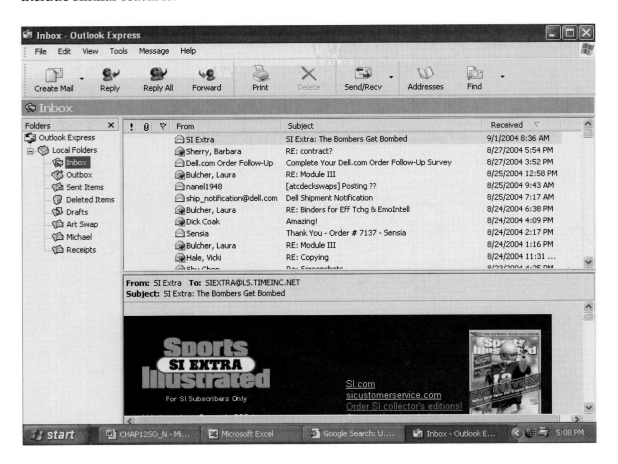

Figure 12.5. You can check and read your mail using your mail program.

You can check your mail and download messages from your mail server to your system. Messages are displayed in your Inbox, marked in bold. The number of new messages may also appear.

From the list of messages, you can click the message you want. In Outlook Express, you can view part of the message in the preview pane (the lower half of the window). To open a message in its own window, double-click the message (see Figure 12.6). You can review the message and then decide how to handle it.

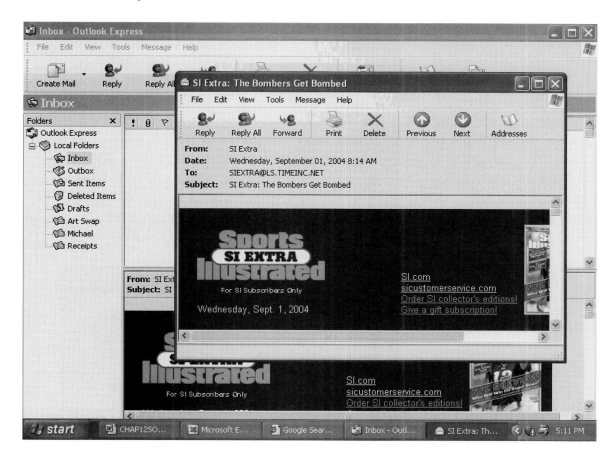

Figure 12.6. You can open and read the messages you receive.

When you receive a message, you can choose to do the following:

- To reply to the sender, click the Reply button. Doing so creates a new mail message with the address and subject line complete. Depending on your mail settings and program, the new message may contain the text of the original message. You can type your reply and then send the message.

- If the message was sent to several people and you want to reply to all recipients, click the Reply All button. Type your response and then send the message.

- If you want to forward the message (jokes and inspirational stories are the most commonly forwarded items), click the Forward button. You can then type the address of the person(s) to whom you want to forward the message. Or you can select the recipients from your address book. See the next section on creating and sending messages.

- To delete the message, click the Delete button. You can also select messages from the Inbox and click Delete to delete them. Note that, in Outlook Express, deleted messages are moved from your Inbox to the Deleted Items folder (unless you have made a change to the default settings). You can click the Deleted Items folder to recover any messages you have deleted by mistake.

- To view other messages in your Inbox, click the Next or Previous buttons. To close the message window and return to the mail program, click the Close button in the message window.

CREATING AND SENDING EMAIL

In addition to receiving and responding to email messages, you can create new messages and send them. When you create a new message, you need to type the address, subject, and content. Because it's easy to make a mistake when typing an email address, you can set up an address book. You can then select names from this list when you create a new message. When the message is complete, you can then click the Send button to send the message (see Figure 12.7). Depending on your setup, the message is either sent immediately or placed in your Outbox and sent when you click the button for sending and receiving messages.

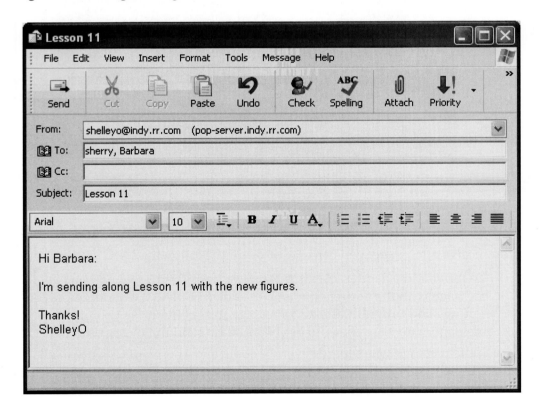

Figure 12.7. You can create and send new messages.

When you create messages, you also can do the following:

- *Attach files.* Most programs enable you to attach files and photos to a message. For example, when authors submit chapters of a book to the editor, some send a message and attach the document file. To attach a file in Outlook Express, click the Attach button and then select the file to attach (see Figure 12.8). Note the recipient needs the appropriate software to open the attachment. For instance, if you send a Word document, the recipient needs either Word or another word processing program that can open Word documents.

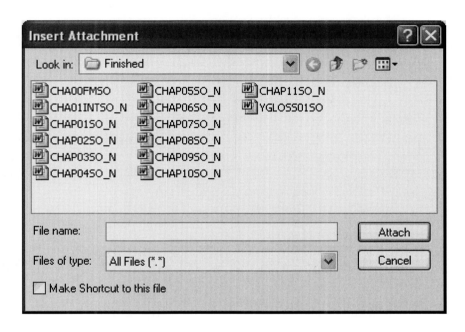

Figure 12.8. You can attach files to an email message.

- *Change the appearance.* Depending on the message type, you may be able to make changes to the appearance. For instance, you can make text bold, indent text, change the color, and make other changes in Outlook Express for Rich Text (HTML) messages. Keep in mind that your recipient's mail program may not be able to display (or display properly) your formatting changes. Also, formatting makes the message larger (and therefore it takes more time to send/receive). Keep your formatting to a minimum.

- *Check your spelling.* Even though email is an informal communication, it's still a good idea to check your spelling and grammar. You'll find in very informal communications people often use abbreviations such as LOL (laughing out loud) and BTW (by the way). That's fine for communications with friends, but probably not a good idea for business communications.

 Junk mail: Junk mail is called Spam. Some mail programs help you filter out this type of message. Lesson 13 covers more about handling junk mail and dealing with privacy issues.

EXPRESSING EMOTIONS IN E-MAIL

Because an e-mail message can't convey your tone of voice or facial expressions, someone came up with a way to show emotion using "emoticons," or smiley faces. The basic smiley face is:

:)

(Turn the page sideways to see the face.) You'll find an entire gallery of faces you can use in your message. This article highlights some popular, some weird, and some creative emoticons for your e-mail messages.

Symbol	Meaning
: (	Sad
;)	Winking
B -)	Person wearing glasses
8 -)	Excited (bug-eyed)
: - D	Laughing
: - O	Oh No!
: - P	Sticking tongue out
: - J	Tongue in cheek
: - #	Censored
: - &	Tongue-tied
: - *	Kiss
: - x	My lips are sealed
<:-)	Dunce
| - (	Late night
: ^)	Big nose
: - (=)	Big teeth
: - {#}	Braces
O : -)	Angel
C=:-)	Chef
= | :-)=	Uncle Sam
[:-)	Wearing a Walkman (or Frankenstein)
%-^	Picasso
***** :-)	Marge Simpson

Other Communications

In addition to email, you'll find several other types of popular ways to communicate including instant messages, chats, and newsgroups. These topics are covered briefly in this section.

INSTANT MESSAGES

With instant messaging, you set up a list of your friends and family and when someone from your list is online at the same time you are, you are notified. You can then type and send messages instantly using instant messaging programs. Instant messaging is like a phone conversation, only you type your comments.

One popular instant messaging program is AOL's Instant Messenger (AIM). Windows also includes Windows Messenger. Note that these two are not compatible; you cannot send messages to AOL members via Windows Messenger unless the recipients also have signed up with Windows Messenger. Expect this to change as new instant messaging programs let you instant message anyone, regardless of the program they use.

CHATS

Like Instant Messages, chats are a form of live conversations, and to participate, you type comments. You can visit general chat rooms or chat rooms devoted for special topics. You can also participate in private chats in private chat rooms.

 Be safe: You should never give out personal information in a message or chat. Don't tell your real name, address, or other personal information.

Moderated chats have a person that monitors and feeds questions, usually to a guest speaker. For instance, you can find celebrity chats where you can submit questions to the celebrity and if your question is chosen by the modurator, the celebrity will respond.

NEWSGROUPS

Still another form of communication is newsgroups. These are not live, but they are online discussion groups. Anyone can post a message to a particular newsgroup, and anyone that reviews that message can respond. You can reply to existing messages or start your own "conversation" with a new message.

The collection of newsgroups is called USENET, and you can find literally thousands of newsgroups devoted to a range of topics. Each newsgroup has a unique name, and you can get a pretty good idea of the content of the newsgroup by its name. The first part of the name is the domain name, and each domain is divided into subcategories. For instance, here's one newsgroup devoted to tennis:

    Rec.sports.tennis

Netiquette: When you communicate online, you are expected to follow certain etiquette rules. For instance, it's rude to type in all capital letters because that is similar to screaming. In newsgroups, look for a FAQ (frequently asked question) list to get an idea of any conventions.

Here is a list of common domain names:

- Rec   Recreation
- Sci   Science
- Alt   Alternative
- News   Relating to newsgroups (not news)
- Soc   Social and society
- Misc   Miscellaneous

To participate in newsgroups, you need a newsreader. Most mail programs also serve as a newsreader. You also need to set up your news server; you get access to a particular set of newsgroups from your Internet provider. To participate, you subscribe to the newsgroups of interest (you don't have to pay a fee). Then you post messages, much like creating and sending e-mail.

Summary

- The Internet is a network of networks providing information, entertainment, news, education, and many other types of resources.

- You use the Internet to send e-mail messages, browse the Web, do research, publish information and creative works, and communicate with other users in chats or newsgroups.

- To get connected to the Internet, you need a connection, an Internet provider, and the software for browsing and handling mail and other communications (newsgroups, for instance).

- The most common way to get connected is using a modem. You can then connect via a regular phone line, a special line (such as a DSL line), or a cable connection.

- The World Wide Web is a means for distributing information on the Internet. World Wide Web pages contain text and graphics and may also include animations, video, and sound. Web pages also include links (or hyperlinks) to other pages at that site, to other parts of that page, or to other sites entirely.

- Each Web site has a unique address called a URL (uniform resource locator). This address usually starts with www and includes the site name and type of site. For instance, the address to Amazon.com (a popular online bookstore) is www.amazon.com.

- To go to a site you can type the address of the site in the Address bar. You can use the toolbar buttons in the browser program window to go back among pages you have viewed.

- To find a particular site or to find sites that relate to a certain topic, you can search the Internet. To do so, you use a search tool, and the basic process is to go to the search page, type what you want to find, and click the search button. The search tool then displays a list of matching sites. You can click any of the results to go to that site.

- Your e-mail address consists of your username, an at sign (@), and the name of your network or Internet provider (for example, ladygodiva@msn.com).

- To send and receive mail, you use a mail program. Some mail programs, such as Outlook Express (included with Windows), also work as a newsreader, for joining in newsgroup discussions.

LESSON 13: SECURITY AND PRIVACY

Objectives

> **Learn about computer crime**
>
> **Keep safe from computer viruses**
>
> **Learn how to browse the Internet safely**
>
> **Learn environmental-friendly computing**

Computer Crime

Statistics on computer crime are hard to come by. First, it's a fairly new avenue for crime. Second, many defrauded companies don't want you to know that they were compromised. A news story in March 2000 revealed that some 485,000 credit card numbers were stolen from an e-commerce site and then stored on a U.S. government agency database. The banks didn't notify the customers of the threat because the cards were not used to commit fraud. E-commerce sites want you to feel secure in purchasing goods online, so they don't want to publicize breaches in security to cause a panic. (More on these safety issues later.)

Most crimes targeted on the general public are harmless (annoying, maybe, but not destructive). Hackers most often commit these crimes.

HACKERS, CRACKERS, AND PHREAKERS

A hacker is a person that uses his or her extensive computer knowledge to illegally access private computer systems and databases. The hacker wants access for a number of reasons: to show off his or her skills, to play a practical joke, or to simply make a statement. Sometimes the purpose is destructive, but usually a hacker does not gain financially from the attack.

Criminal hackers, often called crackers, do seek to profit from their hacking. They might break into a system to steal credit card numbers or other sensitive data. This type of hacker seeks to defraud a company or industry. For instance, one of the most hunted hackers was Kevin Mitnick, who served 4 ½ years in prison after pleading guilty to computer fraud.

Yet another distinction is phreakers. These hackers specifically target national telephone systems to reroute lines, steal telephone services, elude police, sell wiretaps, and perform other illegal activities. A phreaker, for instance, may bill long-distance calls to another number or sell calling card numbers to others to use fraudulently.

Originally all hackers were phreakers: Initially, communication services were expensive and limited, making them the first target for hackers. The hackers wanted access to this new computer communication line, so they hacked in and stole the services.

SECURITY AGAINST HACKING

To prevent any type of access (criminal or otherwise), companies take many security measures. These range from simple to complex security systems. Here are a few of the security measures used:

- *Passwords*. A basic form of protection is the use of passwords. Passwords help ensure that only legitimate users have access to information and programs.

- *Data encryption*. To ensure that data cannot be obtained, many computer systems encrypt data. Basically, the data is scrambled so that even if the data was accessed, it wouldn't make sense. To understand the data, it has to be decrypted. Most shopping sites use data encryption for credit card information.

- *Firewalls*. A firewall is a system of software and hardware that protects a company's network from outside networks (including the Internet).

Firewall: If you have a 24/7 connection, for instance, through a cable modem, you need to install and use a firewall. Windows XP includes firewall protection, as covered later in this lesson.

SOFTWARE PIRACY

Another computer crime that a common person must safeguard against is software piracy. This is the illegal copying or use of software. For instance, suppose that you purchase a word processing program. You have the right to use this program on one computer and make one backup copy. That doesn't give you the right to copy the disks and give them to coworkers, friends, relatives, or even to use it on another computer at home. Doing so is illegal. Companies license software for a certain number of users; this agreement is called a site license. If users install or allow access to more than the licensed amount, they are committing a crime.

Licensing agreement: When you purchase software, you aren't buying the software but the license to use this software. Most programs have a detailed licensing agreement that you agree to when you install the software (called EULAs for end user licence agreements). If you are unsure of when/how you can use the software, review this agreement.

Commercial software is copyrighted and protected by the Software Piracy and Counterfeiting Amendment to the Copyright Act and the Software Act of 1980. Some countries are notorious for not enforcing the copyright act. Purchasing software from such a source is also illegal. Software piracy is a felony offense. It also is responsible for rising costs for end users.

Computer Viruses

A computer virus, like a biological virus, spreads from computer to computer, infecting the computers it comes in contact with. Sometimes the virus is harmless; it might display a message on-screen. Other times, the virus can be destructive (deleting all the files on your hard drive, for instance). A virus works by attaching itself to a "legitimate" file. Once you run this file, the virus is activated and duplicated.

The main concepts about viruses are that:

- Viruses are programs, and you must run the program to be infected. That means you won't get a virus from reading an e-mail message. You may get a virus if that message contains a program attachment and you open that attachment.
- Some viruses are harmless, but others may be destructive.
- When you get infected, you need a program called a vaccine to clean up your system. Deleting the suspect file is not enough because this program has attached itself and made changes to other files that "appear" normal.
- You can take precautions to safeguard your computer from viruses, as covered in the next section.

 Like viruses: You can find other types of programs that are like viruses. For instance, a worm is a program that enters usually through a network and then replicates itself. A Trojan Horse looks like a helpful program but instead is destructive. A timebomb stays on the system until a specific date or event; then the timebomb program is executed.

USING VIRUS PROTECTION PROGRAMS

One of the best ways to protect your system from viruses is to use virus protection software, such as Norton AntiVirus (see Figure 13.1). This program scans your system for known viruses, including new programs or e-mail attachments. If a virus is found, the antivirus cleans up the infected system with a vaccine program for that particular virus. You can get updates to protect against new viruses that pop up.

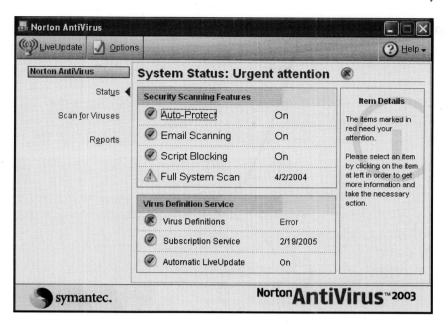

Figure 13.1. You can scan your hard drive for viruses.

Another popular program is McAfee's VirusScan. This program also scans for viruses and then displays any suspected files. If a virus is found, you can use VirusScan to remove and clean up any infected files.

 WEB: Visit www.symantec.com to see the various virus and other security software offered by Symantec.

PROTECTING YOUR SYSTEM FROM VIRUSES

In addition to using software, you can follow these tips to protect your system:

- Don't run program attachments unless you check them.
- Don't open attachments from someone you don't know.
- If you use an antivirus program, check for periodic updates on viruses. Usually you subscribe to a service, and then the program periodically checks for new updates via your online connection. You can then keep your virus protection software up-to-date.
- If you do get infected, seek a cure quickly. You can use the Internet to search for information about a particular virus and even get vaccines at nominal costs.
- If you get a floppy disk from someone else, scan it for viruses before you open any files or run any programs on the disk.

USING WINDOWS SECURITY CENTER

To emphasize the importance of security, the newest service release (2) of Windows XP includes the Security Center. You can use this feature to check the status of your computer's virus protection as well as Internet security (covered next). To display the

Security Center, click Start, All Programs, Accessories, System Tools, and then Security Center. You can then view the status of the key security elements on your computer (see Figure 13.2).

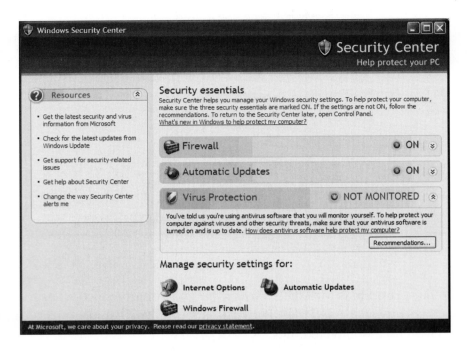

Figure 13.2. If you have the latest release of Windows, you can use the Windows Security Center to review and change security settings.

Getting Security Center: If you don't have the Security Center, you may want to upgrade to the newest release of Windows. As mentioned in Lesson 5, Microsoft periodically releases updates to Windows. If there have been a lot of updates, Microsoft combines them into a Service Pack. At the time this book was written, Service Pack 2 had just become available. You can check out updates to Windows by visiting windowsupdate.microsoft.com.

Safe Internet Browsing

In addition to protecting against viruses, you also need to take some precautions when using the Internet. If you have a 24/7 connection, you need to set up a firewall. You may also want to use security programs to block unwanted email (called spam) and unwanted programs (called spyware). Also, if you purchase items online, you want to ensure you are shopping at a secure site.

USING A FIREWALL

One of the conveniences of a cable modem is that you are hooked up to the Internet 24/7; you don't have to log on. On the downside is that your computer may be vulnerable to outside attacks. To prevent someone from accessing your computer, you can use a firewall.

Windows XP includes a firewall and it's simple to turn on this feature. The easiest way to do so is using the Windows Security Center (refer to Figure 13.2). Follow these steps:

1   Click Start, All Programs, Accessories, System Tools, and then Security Center.

2   If you don't see ON next to the Firewall option (or you want information about how this feature works), click the Windows Firewall link at the bottom part of the window.

3   Make any changes in the dialog box (see Figure 13.3). For instance, if this feature is not on, select On (recommended).

4   Click OK.

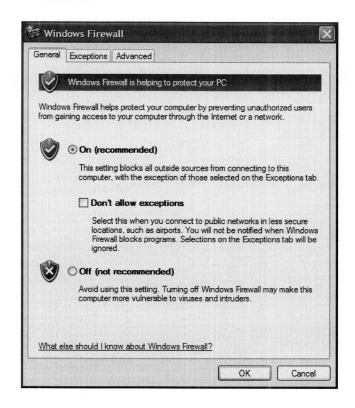

Figure 13.3. Use a firewall to prevent unauthorized access to your computer.

CHECKING FOR SPYWARE AND BLOCKING ADS

Other nuisances of Internet browsing are spyware programs and pop-up advertisements, and often these are related. Spyware programs are installed without your knowledge or consent and track where you go on the Internet. This information is then relayed to other companies. The spyware program is installed automatically when you visit a site. For instance, you may visit a golf site and unwittingly pick up a spyware program. That program may then track what sites you visit and display pop-up ads based on your browsing preferences. The marketing and advertisers argue that this type of program helps them customize ads to suit your interests. But most users don't agree.

In fact, you may be bombarded with pop-up advertisements. These may appear as system messages, or they may appear when you visit a particular Web site. You can easily close the ad windows, but it's annoying.

Windows includes some features to prevent spyware and to block ads. You can also purchase spyware programs (Spy Sweeper or STOPzilla) or suites of security programs such as Norton Internet Security that bundles several features (virus protection, ad blocking, spamware, and so on). As another alternative, you can find some free or shareware versions of programs designed to check for and delete any found spyware programs. One popular program is Spybot's Search and Destroy (see Figure 13.4). You can download a version of this program from http://safer-networking.org/en/index.html.

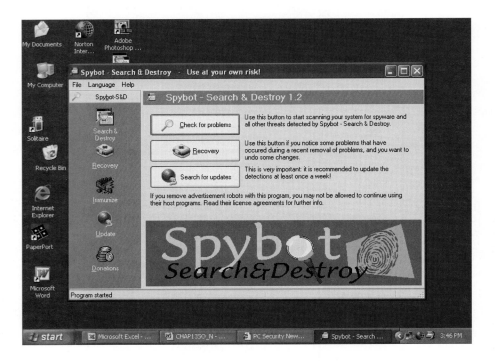

Figure 13.4. You can check for spyware programs and then remove them using anti-spyware programs such as Spybot's Search and Destroy.

AVOIDING SPAM

Once you start visiting sites (and especially shopping online or signing up for contests or polls), your name gets added to the marketing list, and you will see messages in your Inbox for deals, special offers, and so on. This type of e-mail junk mail is called spam.

How do you avoid spam? Some e-mail programs include spam filters where you can automatically place unsolicited mail in a special Junk Mail folder. You can also find spam blocking features in security suites such as Norton's Internet Security. Or, you can purchase or download software designed specifically for dealing with spam, such as Spam Inspector and Spam Catcher.

You can cut down on spam by keeping your online information to a minimum. That is, don't give out your personal information at sites. Don't fill in survey forms or participate in contests. And if you order something online, be sure to turn off the automatic e-mail solicitations.

If you receive spam, you can delete the messages. You should also look for a way to get off the mailing list. Usually you respond to a certain e-mail address and unsubscribe.

SECURE SHOPPING

Is Internet shopping safe? For the most part, yes. At least as safe as giving your credit card number and information over the telephone. Most sites use a secure server software (SSL) for transmitting sensitive information such as credit card numbers. The data is encrypted so that even if the data were intercepted, it would not be of any use. The secure site then decrypts the data.

 Check the icon: Most browsers use a special icon to indicate a secure site. For instance, in Internet Explorer you see a closed padlock when the site is secure.

If you are not sure about a site, check out its policies. Figure 13.5 shows the security information for Amazon.com. You can also consult reviews of the site. For instance, one popular reviewer is BizRate (www.bizrate.com). This company reviews customer service and other features of an online merchant and ranks them accordingly.

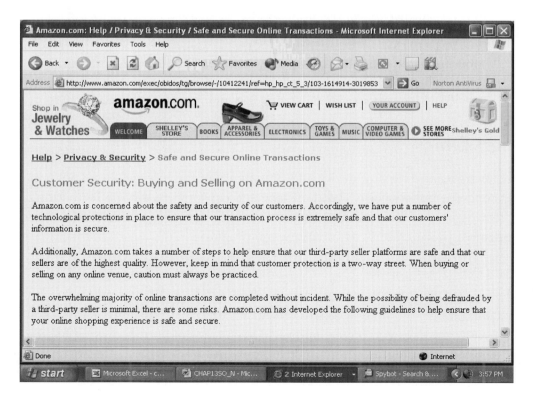

Figure 13.5. Shopping online? Review the store's security procedures.

Still worried: If you are still worried about ordering online, most sites provide access to a toll-free number, a fax order line, or other methods for placing an order.

SAFE BROWSING FOR KIDS

Younger children and even teens may require some set guidelines for Internet access. Some parents may want to purchase and use some type of Internet security software, such as NetNanny (www.netnanny.com) and Cyber Patrol (www.cyberpatrol.com). These programs monitor and may even block access to certain sites. In addition to software, it's a good idea for parents to establish some guidelines for computer use:

- *Don't give out personal information,* including your phone number, address, or school. You should also not give out information about your daily schedule, names of friends or teachers, sports teams, or photos of yourself.

- *Don't ever agree to meet anyone.* Chats and instant messaging are online activities that kids love, but be sure not to give out personal information or to agree to meet anyone, no matter what that person promises. You should also inform a parent or teacher of any offensive activity.

- *Adhere to limits.* It's a good idea to set time limits for online time, especially online chats. If you are the parent, be sure to discuss what things your child can and cannot do, including handling e-mail messages, visiting Web sites, and participating in chats. If you are the child, be sure you know what your restrictions are and stick to them.

WEB: As another option, visit the Center for Missing and Exploited Children at www.missingkids.com and review its suggestions for online safety.

More options: If you want even more tracking power, you can buy programs for homes and small businesses that will record email, instant messages, Internet activity, and so on. One such program is Spector Pro (www.spectorsoft.com).

Internet Ethics

With the ever-expanding popularity and prevalence of the Internet come not only security concerns but concerns about privacy and censorship. What information about you is floating around the Internet? How do you both provide free speech but also protect against pornography, defamation, and plagiarism?

PRIVACY, PLEASE

The Internet enables you to get information, shop, send e-mail, and more. But what are the associated risks? Who has access to this information? For instance, should someone be able to view the sites you have visited and keep track of your browsing habits? Several companies (using programs such as spyware) track where Internet users go and then build a database of consumer information. These companies then sell this information to marketers.

More privacy acts: In addition to online privacy, you can also find policies and regulations as they relate to computer data. For instance, the Freedom of Information Act gives you the right to request data files that the federal government has on you. The Right to Financial Privacy Act determines what rules federal agencies must follow when they review bank records.

Expect forums, discussions, and possibly some regulation of privacy policies in the future. As of now, you are personally responsible for ensuring your own privacy. To do so, consider these pointers:

- *Don't give out personal information.* You'll come across sweepstake entries, surveys, polls, and other forms that request information. If you submit the information, make sure you know how it will be used.

- *Check for e-mail solicitations.* If you purchase products online or complete surveys, you usually see a checkbox on the form that allows you to accept or decline e-mail solicitations. If you leave the option on, you agree to accept offers for deals, new products, newsletters, or whatever marketing material that site wants to send. If you turn off the option, that company should honor your request to stay off the mailing list.

- *Read privacy policies.* Many sites include a specific privacy policy that explains how they use data they obtain. Check out this policy. Look for a link called Privacy Policy or something similar.

Many sites follow set guidelines for privacy, and the most common are the guidelines established by TRUSTe. In the site's own words, "TRUSTe® is an independent, nonprofit organization dedicated to enabling individuals and organizations to establish trusting relationships based on respect for personal identity and information in the evolving networked world." It licenses a special seal or logos to Web sites that follow its set privacy principles. This seal marks companies that adhere to TRUSTe's strict privacy principles, and comply with the TRUSTe Watchdog dispute resolution process. Principles include:

- Creating a **privacy policy** to be reviewed by TRUSTe
- Posting **notice and disclosure** of collection and use practices of personally identifiable information
- Giving users **choice and consent** over how their information is used and shared

 WEB: Visit the Web site for TRUSTe at www.truste.com to view the current status of computer and privacy issues.

CENSORSHIP

Another issue relating to Web content is censorship. Like privacy, there are no hard and fast rules that apply to Web censorship, but you can find lots of discussion on the topic. Should Web content be monitored? Rated? If so, who should do the rating? What about sites that distribute pornography? What about sites that promote violence?

Again, until specific guidelines are in place, you are responsible for protecting your own interests. Most networks, especially ones at work or at school, will have policies regarding censorship. Do not make the mistake of thinking that anything you send over the Internet is private.

PLAGIARISM

The Internet provides a wealth of content, but just because that information is online doesn't mean it is free for your use. The rules of plagiarism still apply: you cannot use ideas and words as your own if they are not your own.

Likewise, some images are copyrighted. You cannot use them without permission from the artist or publisher. Or you may be able to use them only in a restricted sense. For instance, the Fair Use Policy for Education and Non-Profit organizations allows use as a long as the use of that work does not interfere with the rights of the author. If you have any doubts, check with the artist for permission.

 Netiquette: The Internet is a community, and while there is no moderator or censor, it does make sense to follow some Internet etiquette (called netiquette).

WORK ETHICS

In addition to ethic standards for personal use, you should also keep in mind that if you use a computer at work, you have certain responsibilities (legally and ethically). Your e-mail is not private, at least according to court decisions. Your employer has legal access to your e-mail and can review it. Also, protect your company's confidentiality. Be sure you do not give out any confidential information about your company either advertently or inadvertently. Even if you delete your e-mail, there is a chance that it may have been saved inadvertently, which could cause some embarrassing situations.

COMPUTERS AND THE ENVIRONMENT

Finally, computers affect the environment, and the main issues are energy consumption and disposing of computer parts (especially monitors). Computers are the fastest growing load on electrical power, and most computers are left on most of the time. Newer computers take advantage of energy-saving features, such as putting the computer and monitor on standby if it is not used for a set period of time. Most companies belong to the Energy Star program, sponsored by the EPA. This program sets the maximum energy consumption for a computer in an idle state. PCs that comply are sometimes called Green PCs.

Another issue is recycling. Recycling supplies relates not to just paper and disks, but also to other computer products, such as toner cartridges and old hardware. Check out the local resources in your area for recycling for more information.

Summary

- Computer crime involves illegal access of services, systems, databases, or other computer components. These crimes may be committed for fun or for profit.

- Users that access a computer illegally are called hackers. If the intent is criminal, these users are often called crackers.

- Companies and organizations employ security systems to protect the integrity of the system. These usually involve passwords, data encryption, and firewalls.

- It is illegal to copy software and give or sell that copy. Doing so is software piracy. It is also illegal to purchase pirated software.

- A computer virus is a program or file that infects a system. The purpose may be a prank or some destructive action (such as formatting your hard drive). To protect against viruses, use a virus checker program, such as Symantec's Norton AntiVirus or McAfee's VirusScan.

- The Internet has opened several areas of debate. Two of the biggest concerns relate to privacy and censorship.

- You can shop confidently on the Internet as long as you stick to secure shopping sites; these use secure server software (SSL) to encrypt data. If you are not sure about the safety of a site, check out its security policies.

- E-mail is not private. If you send e-mail from work, that e-mail can legally be reviewed by your employer.

- Most people leave the computer running, which wastes power, one of the environmental issues relating to the use of computers. To deal with this problem, computer manufacturers have started to build in energy-saving features. These computers are Energy Star-compliant. (Energy Star is a program developed by the EPA.)

LESSON 14: PROGRAMMING

 ➤ **Define the purpose or programming**

 ➤ **Examine the development of the first computer languages**

 ➤ **Discuss the basics of programming**

 ➤ **Review common programming languages**

The Definition of Programming

Most dictionaries define the term "program" or "programming" as follows:

> A set of coded instructions for insertion into a machine, in accordance with which the machine performs a desired sequence of operations

While this definition is accurate, let's explore the concept of "programming." Take, for example, using a microwave oven to pop popcorn. After placing the popcorn bag in the oven, you select the temperature (perhaps) and the cooking time from the control panel on the microwave. Basically, you have just programmed the microwave to perform a task.

Although it is a simple example, it does demonstrate the programmer's purpose. Simply stated, "programming" is the process of giving instructions to a device that will then perform the programmed task. The device could be anything from a computer to an automated shoemaker. The important part is "how" the device is going to be programmed.

For the most part, programmers use a "language" to program a device. Language is the list of instructions that the programmer creates. The programmer enters this list into the device to complete a set of operations. Languages are usually designed to make life easier for the programmer.

To get a better feel of what a language is, let's develop our own using an automated shoemaker. This is the information you will work with:

- The automated shoemaker operates by moving levers up and down in a certain order to produce shoes of a specific color.
- For each color of shoe, different levers are pulled in different orders.
- As the programmer, your job is to create a list of instructions that describes which levers are to be pulled to create a certain shoe color.
- New employees using the automated shoemaker will use this list to create the shoes.
- The shoemaker has four levers, numbered 1 through 4, that can be set either up or down.

Your list might look similar to the following:

For Red Shoes

1.   Move lever 1 down.

2.   Move lever 2 down.

3.   Move lever 3 up.

4.   Move lever 4 down.

For Blue Shoes

1.   Move lever 1 up.

2.   Move lever 2 down.

3.   Move lever 3 down.

4.   Move lever 4 up.

For White Shoes

1.   Move lever 1 down.

2.   Move lever 2 down.

3.   Move lever 3 down.

4.   Move lever 4 down.

For Black Shoes

1.   Move lever 1 up.

2.   Move lever 2 up.

3.   Move lever 3 up.

4.   Move lever 4 up.

In this list, each color of shoe requires four instructions. Using this list, anyone could create the shoe of his or her color choice. Let's say that the automated shoemaker can make 200 differently colored shoes. The previous list would grow to several pages in length. Employees using the list would be forced to wade through all those pages searching for the correct combination.

To improve this list, you must improve the programming language. Knowing that each lever is labeled, from left to right, with a number from one to four, you can consolidate your instructions into something like this:

1=up, 0=down

Red – 0010

Blue – 1001

White – 0000

Black – 1111

By creating this "code," you have simplified the process of finding the correct combination for the desired shoe color. Your new set of instructions has increased the performance of the employees making the shoes.

You can even add another layer to this example. Imagine building a mechanical device that can read the "code" from your instruction sheet instead of having the employees pull the levers. The programmer could feed the "code" to the machine and it would automatically move the levers to the correct position.

The preceding example describes the "essence" of programming. One person develops a device to accomplish a task, and then someone else develops a method of programming that device. Over time, the language is improved by other programmers to add features and improve its performance.

An example of this is the PC. The PC would be the device and the list of instructions is the operating system. Computer operating systems have evolved radically since the first, basic systems.

While some programmers spend their time developing languages, most programmers spend their time using a language that has been previously developed to solve problems and perform tasks.

History of Programming

Here's a quick overview of key dates in the history of programming:

1833	Charles Babbage created what was considered the first "computer," an invention he called the Analytical Machine. This was programmed by feeding special cards that had instructions punched into them.
1930s	The first digital computer was designed. It still required manual programming and led to the development of the first programming language.

1940s	Bell Telephone Laboratories designed its first digital computer. This system used binary coding. (Binary numbers are numbers with a base of 2 and are written using 1's and 0's.) During the 1940s computers and programming quickly evolved.
WWII	Many notable computers were developed during this time. Alan Turing's Colossus computer was designed to crack German coding. The Mark I was designed to calculate artillery trajectories. The Mark I computer, like many computers over the next few years, was a huge device filled with vacuum tubes and mechanical relays. Grace Hopper, considered one of the first modern-era programmers, became famous for her work in the computer field. She programmed the first Mark I.
1950s	As computers became more advanced, better methods of programming were needed. The first symbolic languages were introduced: Symbolic assembly language (Assembler) and Intermediate Programming Language (PL).
1950s on	After the introduction of the first languages, a flood of new languages emerged, mostly designed for special purposes. For instance, COBOL (Common Business Oriented Language) was designed for data processing programs, and FORTRAN was designed for engineers and scientists.

Thousands of languages have been developed, including C, Basic, Java; these are only a sample of the languages available to the programmer. When programming projects are considered, the language plays an important role in the outcome of the project. The Internet has also had a profound effect on programming and programming languages.

Programming Basics

Programming is a skill that's highly in demand and offers many different avenues for careers. The Internet has played a big role in the increasing demand, as well as changing the face of programming as a whole. This section looks at the skills a programmer needs and the steps a typical programmer follows to create a program.

SKILLS NEEDED

Programmers require the following skills:

- Organizational skills. That means keeping good notes, keeping and updating program flowcharts, and maintaining good communication with other members of a programming team.

- Project management skills. Every programmer needs to be able to manage the project, or portion of the project, to which he or she is assigned. Programming means meeting deadlines and resolving problems as they arise. Project management means not only working with team members, but also with customers.

- Documentation skills. Many programmers add comments to their code to help the debugging process. The comments explain what function the particular line of code is performing. It's easy to forget what you were thinking when you wrote a line of code after writing thousands of lines. Therefore, documenting your code is incredibly helpful.

- Programming language skills. Language skills involve knowing the commands, functions, and syntax (proper format) for a language. As mentioned, most languages are designed for a specific purpose and have a specific programming structure, which varies from language to language. It's important to know which language is suited for a particular program project as well as how the languages relate.

- Logic skills. Computers do exactly what you tell them, in the order you tell them. Logic skills tie closely in with language skills and are arguably the most important skill. You may know all the commands and functions of a language, but without being able to formulate the logic, the language is useless.

THE PROCESS OF PROGRAMMING

There is a logical procession of steps in writing a program, starting with the program design and ending with distributing the program. Here's a quick look at how the process works:

1   Design Program Logic. The programmer designs the logic of the program. Most programmers create very detailed flowcharts that contain data structures, user interface requirements, and complete program logic. While flowcharts aren't mandatory, documentation or design notes are critical to help the programmer remember key items.

2   Write Code. After the program is designed, the programmer then uses an editor to write the code, using the language of choice. An editor can be a simple "text" editor or a program designed specifically for programming (called a Development Environment or Software Development Kit).

3   Translate Program. Computers operate using binary or translated machine code. So once a programmer writes a program, it must be translated so that the computer can execute it. This can be done by using a compiler or a translator.

4   Test and Debug. After the program has been coded, the next phase is testing and debugging. Testing the program involves running the program through its paces over and over again. When

a problem is discovered, the programmer then debugs and recompiles the program to start testing again. This testing phase is often broken down into categories known as "alpha" testing and "beta" testing. Even with extensive testing and debugging, most software still includes bugs. Most companies release patches or updates to fix these problems that pop up after the program has been released.

5   Distribute the program. When the program passes its final testing phase, it can be distributed. Most programmers include a help file or manual to assist in installing and using the program.

Programming Languages

As mentioned, you can find a variety of programming languages, and most are designed for a specific task or setting. Choosing the right language is part of the process of creating an effective program. Many times the type of project dictates the language(s) used. As an example, consider designing a Web page. In doing so, a programmer may use several languages including:

- HTML. HyperText Markup Language, used on the Internet, lets the programmer create the basic Web page. The language is limited, so only basic design and graphics are created using HTML.

- Jscript and VBScript. To add enhancements, additional scripting may be required. Two languages used to make Web pages more user-friendly include Jscript and VBScript.

- Java. To create a Web-based application for the customer, the programmer may use Java. Java is a popular programming language for creating application front-ends for the Internet. This application talks to the database that contains all of the customer's products, for instance, and then displays them for the end user.

- SQL. SQL is a standard database engine that can store and manage large amounts of data. The programmer ties the Web site and Java programs together with the database.

As you can see, programmers may use a variety of languages to create a program. For some projects, though, a single language will suffice. The "right" language is the one that best suits the purpose of the programmer. The following table summarizes the popular programs of the last several years.

Level of Language	Description	Examples
Low-level	• Most difficult to learn • Most flexible and powerful • Offers complete control of computer and operations • Offers best performance results	Machine code, Assembler

	• Requires many lines of code to complete a single task • Generally used for operating systems, scientists, and engineers	
Mid-level	• Generally not for beginners • Easier to learn than low-level languages • Offers flexibility and performance • Does not require as much logic • Has been used for operating systems for Unix, Windows, and the Macintosh OS • Flexible enough for general application programming	C, C++ (one of the most widely-used languages of all)
High-level	• Excellent language for beginners • Designed as a training language, simple and easy to learn • Has become more powerful	Visual Basic
Web programming	• Designed for Web applications and design • Used to embed software resources inside web pages • Some programs able to create 3D elements	Java, JavaScript, Virtual Reality Modeling Language (VRML)

Summary

- The professional programmer needs a variety of skills including organization, project management, documentation, programming language, and logic skills.

- The basic process for creating a program includes these steps: design the logic of the program, write the code, translate the program using a compiler or translator, test and debug the program, and distribute the program.

- You can find a variety of computer programming languages, most designed for a specific purpose or environment. Part of designing a program is picking the "best" language in which to write the program.

LESSON 15: NETWORKING

Objectives

➤ **Learn about networking**

➤ **Get familiar with types of networks**

➤ **Learn about network devices**

What Is a Network?

The primary method of networking PCs in the early 1980s was "sneaker net." Sneaker net was the process of copying files from computer to computer using a floppy disk and then carrying the disk from computer to computer. This, of course, wasn't very efficient, and the results of the needs of sharing data and resources created networked computers. Although the idea of networking seems simple, it can be fairly complex. Until recently, networking required a complex technological architecture, but with the popularity of home networking growing, some types of networking have become simpler.

A network is the connecting together of computers to share resources and information. That information can come in a variety of forms including worksheets, documents, email, graphics files, sounds, movies, presentations, Web pages, help files, books, and more. A computer can store just about any kind of information, and a network can share that information with those connected. Sharing information is a critical component of networking.

In addition to information, networks also enable those connected to share resources, which can mean both software and hardware. For instance, you can install a computer program on a network so that those connected can use that program. (Note that to run programs on a network, you need licenses for all those that will use the program. You cannot legally just purchase one copy and share it on a network.)

Hardware resources are also easily shared on a network and include printers, scanners, storage devices, communication devices, fax machines, plotters, backup drives, Internet connection, video equipment, and other components. If it can be plugged into the computer or network, it probably can be shared.

Sharing saves not only money, but also helps in productivity. Instead of having an inexpensive printer on every desk, a business can have a shared high-quality printer (perhaps with a few local printers scattered throughout the office also). Users can print to a high quality printer, and the company needs to purchase and maintain this one printer. (Note that you aren't limited to one printer. You can actually hook up several printers to a network. This is just a simple example.)

Networks also centralize services and can provide the following:

- Email
- Printing
- File management, including backing up data

Types of Networks

Networks are often described by how they are connected and/or what area they cover. You'll also hear them distinguished by what function each computer plays and what protocol the network uses. This section looks at the various terms and features that distinguish different types of networks.

LANS VS. WANS

You may hear the terms LANs and WANs used to describe a type of network. LAN stands for local area network and is usually small in size. A LAN may incorporate an office, a floor of a building, or a small building. LANs are usually hard-wired—that is, connected by cables.

WAN stands for wide area network and often covers a large geographic area from a portion of a city to a global network. WANs are often connected via phone lines, modems, or satellites. The Internet, for instance, is an example of a WAN.

CLIENT/SERVER NETWORKS

A network can include anywhere from one other computer to several hundred. In a network, different computers serve different purposes. In one setup (server/client), the main computer(s) is called the server. Computers hooked up to the server are called clients or workstations. Let's take a look first at the role the network server plays in this type of setup.

A server contains the network operating system and all the shared applications and files. Shared components such as an Internet connection or printer are connected to the server. The server not only provides access to the applications and files, but also to these resources. For instance, if you are connected to the server, you can run any programs on the server, open any shared files on that computer, and use any of the hardware connected to it (like a printer) as if the server were part of your computer. You can save files, for instance, to the server. Your files can also be made available to others connected to the network. So if you and a co-worker are teaming up on a project, you can keep and access one set of files via a network rather than try to coordinate different versions of the same file.

The server manages the activity of the network, keeping track of who's connected, what data is being accessed (and can be accessed), and what tasks need to be performed. The server manages, for instance, any print jobs sent to the printer, keeping them in a queue and sending them in turn to the printer.

Computers connected to the server are often referred to as clients or workstations. When a network has a separate server and clients, it's referred to as a client/server network.

Client/server networks are typically larger networks that require more performance and security. This performance and security comes from each computer's having a specialized function rather than trying to do everything.

PEER-TO-PEER NETWORKS

When a computer functions both as a server and a client, it's referred to as a peer network. Peer networks tend to be small and each computer can access the hard disks of each of the other computers. This type of network is often used when the network includes only a small number of users. Also, this network is cheaper and easier to install and maintain. Peer networks have some drawbacks: they use more resources (such as memory) and security can be an issue.

NETWORK PROTOCOL

Protocols are the rules and standards used in network communications. The most well-known network communication protocol is called TCP/IP (Transmission Control Protocol/Internet Protocol). IP defines the addressing of the network. This is a fundamental and important part of how a network gets information to the intended recipient.

The IP address of a computer gives the computer a unique identifier on the network (like a Social Security Number identifies a person). The IP address has two parts: the network address and the host address. These consist of a series of numbers such as 123.23.44.15. Memorizing all the numbers for all the computers is difficult; it's much easier to remember their names. TCP/IP uses the Domain Name Service (DNS) to convert the domain name to the IP address of the computer and also converts the addresses to names. When you use the Internet, this type of conversion goes on all the time. While the IP address for a site may be 165.193.130.107, DNS converts this name to www.pearsoneducation.com (for instance). And if you type www.pearsoneducation.com, DNS converts this back to the number.

NETWORK TOPOLOGY

A network's topology is a description of how the network is laid out and physically connected and how data travels on the network. The following lists common network topologies:

- **Bus or daisy chain**. In this type of topology, all devices on the network connect to a single cable. This single cable is the conduit through which all data travels. Each computer (also called a node) has a transceiver that can send messages in either direction.
- **Ring or Token Ring**. This topology is similar to a bus except that the wire is a continuous loop on a circular path. The ring network uses a token, which circulates around the ring until a node sends a message.

- **Star**. This type of topology is the most common type used in networks. In a star, all devices connect to a central point.
- **Hybrid**. In this type, two or more of the topologies are combined into a single network.

NETWORK ADMINISTRATOR

Maintaining a network involves many different types of tasks. Most often, one person is the network administrator. This person sets up and sustains the network. The network administrator also sets up network accounts for each computer connected; the administrator also controls the level of access to the network. For instance, some users may only be allowed to view, but not change certain data. (You wouldn't, for instance, want a data entry person who is entering in orders to be able to modify the price or inventory in a product database.)

The administrator also takes care of installing and maintaining the software, setting up shared services such as email or the Internet, and performing maintenance tasks (such as backing up files).

Network Hardware and Operating System

A network requires special hardware that not only connects the computers on the network, but also enables them to communicate. Typically, a network includes these hardware components:

- Network interface cards (NIC). This is an electronic card that is inserted into an expansion slot inside your system unit. All of the computers require a network interface card; also, these cards must be compatible with each other and with the network operating system used. When information is requested or sent over the network, this card receives the information, determines whether this computer made the request, and either passes it along to the processor or ignores it.
- Hub. The hub is the central device in the network, and each computer connects to the hub.
- Connection. The networked computers need some way to communicate to the hub (and to other computers). This can be through a physical connection such as a phone line. Newer technology uses a wireless connection. The computers may communicate via laser, infrared, satellite, or radio frequency.

In addition to the hardware, a network is managed by a network operating system (NOS). This operating system is just like Windows (in fact, it may *be* Windows), but the operating system also provides and manages the services on the network.

 Home network: Home networks have become more popular and Windows XP includes a Network Setup Wizard that guides you through the process of setting up a network. Because most networks differ (different number of users, hardware, setup, and so on), you'll need to follow the specific directions for your situation to set up your network.

Summary

- A network allows users to share both computer resources as well as hardware. You can, for instance, share printers, Internet connections, data files, software programs, and so on.

- LAN stands for local area network; this type of network has computers that are close together (such as on the same floor or in the same house). WAN stands for wide area network; the Internet is an example of a WAN because the networked computers are widely dispersed (across the world!)

- Client/server networks use a dedicated server as the central computer. Clients or work stations are connected to this server.

- In a peer-to-peer network, there isn't a dedicated server. The networked computers access all of the other computers.

- For a network, you need a network interface card (NIC), a hub, and some type of connection. Wireless connections have become more popular and common place. In this type of network, computers are not physically connected with cabling but instead communicate through wireless transmissions (and a hub).

- To manage the services of the network, you use a special network operating system (NOS). Windows, for instance, has network versions of its operating system.

Introduction

This glossary covers hundreds of the most important computer terms you need to understand and use, including terms about the Internet and World Wide Web. Like other dictionaries, this one presents terms in A to Z order. Along the way, you'll find special elements that highlight key information:

 This icon appears beside the name of any term that deals with communications, including networking, connecting computers via a modem, or connecting to the Internet.

 Tip boxes like these highlight extra tidbits of information, or ideas and steps to save you time.

This glossary presents command choices by giving the menu name, followed by subsequent command names, all of them separated using the | (pipe) character. So, Insert | Picture | Clip Art means to click the Insert menu, click the Picture command, and then click the Clip Art command in the submenu that appears.

Characters

3.5" disk A floppy disk that has its magnetic storage media encased within a 3 ½" square rigid plastic case (see Figure 0.1). You can copy your computer files onto a floppy disk to create a spare copy of the files or to move files from one computer to another.

Figure 0.1. 3 ½" floppy disks

A

Abort To stop a program or command before it finishes, often by pressing Esc, Ctrl+C, or the Break key on the keyboard. Sometimes, when an operation "hangs," or stalls your computer, it presents a dialog box offering a button you can click to abort the operation. In Windows you can stop a program by clicking End Task in the Task Manager.

About dialog box A dialog box you can display to find out what version of a program you're using and to view the registered serial number for your copy of the program. You typically display the About dialog box by choosing the About (*program name*) command from the Help menu in the program.

absolute reference In a spreadsheet program, an absolute reference in a formula always refers to the same cell, even if you copy the formula to another location.

Access (Microsoft Access) This database program, published by Microsoft, enables you to store lists of information, such as a list of customer names and addresses or a list of all the audio CDs you've bought. Database programs are covered in Lesson 10.

accounting software Software you use to perform accounting functions. Business accounting software like Peachtree or QuickBooks typically enables you to track assets, expenses, inventory, and payroll, as well as providing invoicing and reporting features. You can use personal accounting software such as Quicken or Microsoft Money to record transactions for your bank accounts, print checks, monitor credit card balances and investment returns, and review reports such as net worth reports.

active Active indicates that a program window, file window, dialog box, or area within a program holds the insertion point.

Add or Remove Programs A feature in Windows that enables you to install and remove programs more easily. When you use this feature, Windows deletes all the program files and cleans the vast majority of references to the program from Windows system files.

 To display the Add or Remove Programs dialog box, choose Start| |Control Panel, and then click the Add or Remove Programs link (Category view) or double-click the Add or Remove Programs icon (Classic View).

address An address, depending on the context, can mean different things. In a spreadsheet program, the address is the location of the cell and is comprised of the cell's column and row. For the Internet, you type an address to go to a particular Web site. This type of address is also known as a URL. For email, you type the recipient's email address in this format (personname@domainname.ext).

Address Book Most e-mail programs, whether used for an internal network or for Internet communication, offer an Address Book into which you can enter the name and e-mail address for each person with whom you correspond.

alignment Refers to how information lines up relative to the document margins or the boundaries of a cell or text box in a document. Figure A.1 illustrates various alignments.

Left-Aligned Text
CENTERED TEXT
Right-Aligned Text
JUSTIFIED TEXT STRETCHES TO FILL THE AREA BETWEEN MARGINS

Figure A.1 Most applications enable you to align text in various ways.

alphanumeric characters Labels, words, or phrases that include both letters and numbers, as in *A139X*.

alphanumeric sort A sorting method that considers both letters and numbers in a label, word, or phrase. For example, an alphanumeric sort might sort items beginning with punctuation marks or symbols first (!,$, %, or &, for example), then items beginning with numbers. Items beginning with letters are sorted last.

Alt key A key you press in conjunction with another keyboard key to select a command or run a macro. For example, in most applications you can press [Alt]+[F] to open the File menu. You can also press [Alt] in conjunction with one of the Function keys at the top of the keyboard to perform a command or action.

America Online (AOL) One of the world's leading online services. Users can log on to share information and e-mail, or connect with the Internet.

animation A moving computer image that combines multiple objects that change in position. You may have seen animated banners and graphics on Web pages, or you may have seen special animated mouse pointers in programs. Numerous programs enable you to create various types of animations and animated objects.

> Animated graphics consume considerable system and video RAM. If your system bombs out when you try to run an animation or if the animation runs in a jerky fashion, you may need to upgrade your system's RAM or video RAM.

antivirus This term applies to any software or software feature that scans your system and files for viruses. Most antivirus programs can also clean or remove the virus from the affected system areas or files. Typically, you can choose to scan for viruses either automatically or manually.

append To add information to the end of an existing file or database table.

Apple Computer, Inc. The company that manufactures Macintosh desktop PCs and PowerBook notebook PCs. Apple also makes a popular digital music player called the iPod.

application window The window that opens on the Windows desktop when you start an application. The application window holds a separate window for each file you open and create in the application.

archive Traditionally, this term refers to a specialized backup file created by a backup program. More commonly, however, the term also refers to a special type of file that holds multiple compressed files.

argument A value or text string you include in a programming statement or in a command within a program; the statement or command uses the argument information when it runs. You also use arguments in spreadsheet formulas that include functions. For example, the argument(s) you specify for the SUM function tells the spreadsheet program what values to add or which cells hold those values.

arrow key Literally, the keyboard keys that have arrows on them. Most keyboards offer up, down, left, and right arrow keys, but some also include diagonal arrow keys.

ascending order Ascending order refers to text information alphabetized in A to Z order or numbers ordered from the smallest value to the largest.

ASCII (pronounced as-key) ASCII stands for American Standard Code for Information Interchange. It refers to a standard set of characters that virtually all programs understand. The ASCII character set consists of mostly letters and numbers, but also includes a few symbols and codes for controlling the computer. Many applications enable you to save your files in ASCII or plain text format, which exclude special formatting and characters, but make the files easier for other programs to open.

attribute Windows records key attributes about any file you save, such as its name, how large the file is, the date you created it, whether you've set the file to be read-only (so others can't change it, etc.). Within an application, the term attribute describes formatting you apply to text or some other object. For example, you can apply the bold attribute to selected text.

audio Sound produced by your computer or another device.

audio CD An audio CD holds audio data in a format developed for playback via a boom box or your home stereo. Computers also can play audio CDs using audio or CD player software.

autosave The autosave feature on an application will save all open files at a specified regular interval. Then, even if your computer loses power or has a problem, you'll lose only a few minutes' worth of work, rather than a few hours' worth.

B

background The background is what appears on your desktop in Windows. You can change the image or colors used to display the desktop. This term also refers to how tasks are handled. Most computers today can handle multiple tasks simultaneously (multitask). In such a case, the task or application you're currently using occupies the foreground, and the task or application carrying out prior instructions continues operating in the background. Finally, the term background also applies to documents or graphics. You can apply a background color or pattern to many types of files.

Backspace key A keyboard key that deletes the character to the left of the insertion point in a document, spreadsheet cell, or text box in a dialog box.

backup A special type of file that serves as a spare copy for one or more other files. You should backup your work often. You can manually copy your documents, or you can use special backup programs and media to speed the backup process.

bad sector On a hard or floppy disk, a damaged area that can no longer accept data. Normally, your system marks bad sectors so that it doesn't try to write data to them. However, a sector can go bad after the system has stored information in it. In such a case, you can use a utility to try to get the data from the bad sector. These utilities move the data from the bad sector to another location on the disk.

 The primary culprits that cause floppy disk damage include metals, magnets, and dust that can damage the magnetized material on the disk media. Even though a floppy's media is encased in harder plastic, damaging materials can make their way in through the sliding metal cover over the opening on one side of the disk. So, keep your computer area clean, and keep metallic objects like paper clips and magnetized objects away from your floppy and other removable disks.

beta software Preliminary or test versions of a software program, distributed by the software publisher for testing. With the great interest in computers today, eager users seek out many beta software versions. Be careful with betas, though.

Installing a beta can prevent other software on your system from working, so you should always back up your system before installing a beta. Many betas expire after a certain number of uses or after a certain time period.

bitmap A method of displaying information on the screen dot-by-dot. Each on-screen dot (pixel) displays a particular color, based on the setting for one or more corresponding bits of information.

bitmap font A font drawn using a pattern of dots, so that the font isn't scalable. If you try to double the size of text formatted with a bitmap font, the computer in essence increases the size of each dot so that you see unattractive jaggies or a stairstep appearance.

bitmap graphic Bitmap graphics, like bitmap fonts, consist of a pattern of colored dots. The file name extensions .BMP, .TIF, and .PCX often identify bitmap graphic files.

bold A formatting attribute applied to characters in an application. Making a selection bold (or applying boldface) turns the characters thicker and darker. Bold formatting can be applied to headings and titles in a document to make them stand out from the rest of the text.

bookmark In a word processor document, you can mark an area in the document by creating an electronic bookmark. Later, you can select the bookmark to jump to that area in the document. In Netscape's Navigator Web browser, you can create a bookmark to note the address for a favorite Web page. You can then select the bookmark rather than typing the full Web address when you want to display that Web page.

boot To start or power up your computer. When you boot the computer, it performs a number of actions to test the system, such as the POST (Power-On Self Test), and loads the operating system so the computer will be ready to accept your commands. A special read-only memory (ROM) chip on the motherboard typically stores the computer's boot instructions.

browser software Software that enables you to view graphical Web pages stored on Web sites on the Internet. The browser loads each Web page, complete with graphics and text formatting. You can click linked text, buttons, or graphics to jump to other pages. Or, you can enter a Web page address to go to that page. Microsoft Internet Explorer is the most widely-used browser.

BTW An abbreviation you can type instead of "by the way" in an e-mail message. For example, you might type, "BTW, I received your fax yesterday." You also might see and use other abbreviations like CU (see you) and B4 (before).

bug An error in a program or macro that causes it to stop working, display an error message, return an inaccurate result, or shows some other operating problem.

bullet A dot, box, check mark, or other small graphic used to set off each item in a list, as in:
- Apples
- Pears
- Bananas

button An on-screen shape you click to execute an action in a program. Buttons may be as simple as a rectangle or oval with text in it, or as fancy as a colored image. You often find buttons in dialog boxes or on a special toolbar near the top of the application window.

byte A group of eight bits of information. Because each bit only represents either a 1 (on) or a 0 (off), computers need a combination of bits to define more complex information. Each byte represents a particular character. A *kilobyte* equals 1,024 bytes, a *megabyte* equals 1,048,576 bytes, and a *gigabyte* equals 1,073,741,824 bytes.

> The base-2 math used for bits and bytes results in the actual number of bytes in a kilobyte and megabyte being more than an even thousand (a value identified by the kilo prefix in decimal or base-10 math), million (the mega prefix), or billion (the giga prefix).

C

cable An external connecting wire that carries data between your computer and another device, such as a printer, monitor, network hub, or phone jack. Each cable plugs into a port on the computer. The type of connecting device and the available ports on the computer determine the type of cable needed to make the connection.

calculate To perform a mathematical operation. In most spreadsheet programs, you can manually recalculate the open file so that its formulas reflect results based on the most recent values you've entered.

Caps Lock key Press the Caps Lock key on the keyboard to begin typing in ALL CAPITAL letters. Press the Caps Lock key again to return to typing in upper- and lowercase letters.

 Most keyboards include an indicator light to tell you when Caps Lock is on. Also note that with Caps Lock on, you still need to press the Shift key to produce certain characters, like !, @, and all other "shifted" characters on the number keys along the top row of the keyboard.

cancel To stop or abort an operation in progress. Often, you can press [Esc] to cancel the command or process. For example, in most Windows applications you can press [Esc] twice to close a menu you've opened (and deselect the menu name) if you no longer want to choose a command from it.

Cancel button A dialog box button you click to close the dialog box without applying your choices in the dialog box.

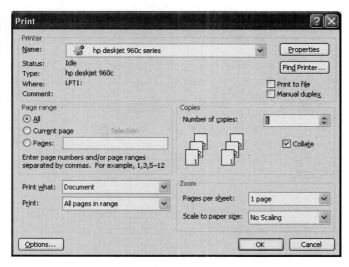

Figure C.1. Click the Cancel button in a dialog box to close the dialog box without applying the choices you made in it.

cascade To arrange open windows on the screen so that they overlap like a fanned stack of cards, with the title bar for each window visible. You can then click the title bar for any window to select that window. To cascade, right-click the Windows taskbar and then click Cascade Windows.

case-sensitive In some computer environments or online environments, you must enter commands or addresses using exact punctuation. Often, passwords and user logon names are case-sensitive, too. In such an instance, if you assign a password like *TodaY* to a file, you must enter *TodaY* to open the file, not *TODAY* or *today*.

CD-R A type of compact that you can record information to. You can, for instance, create a music CD by copying (or burning) songs from your computer to a CD-R disk (in a CD-R drive). The R indicates that you can only record once; you cannot rerecord information (see CD-RW).

CD-ROM Compact Disc Read-Only Memory disc. CD-ROM discs are about 4.75 inches in diameter and have a polycarbonate wafer coated with a metallic film that holds the data; the wafer and metallic coating together are coated with polycarbonate. One side of the CD-ROM holds printed label information. The metallic coating remains visible through the other side. Each CD-ROM disc holds about 650M of data.

CD-ROM drive A drive that reads—but cannot write to—CD-ROM discs. The CD-ROM drive uses a laser to read the shiny side of the CD-ROM. The laser bounces off *pits* and *lands* in the metallic coating visible on that side of the disc, and the drive reads the reflected light. The reflected light varies in intensity depending on whether it came from a pit or land, and the drive translates each reflection into a data bit that the computer can understand.

CD-RW A type of compact disk and drive that enables you to record and rewrite information to a disk. You can erase a disk and record over the current information. Contrast this type of drive/disk to CD-R which can only be recorded once.

cell The intersection of a column and row in a spreadsheet (worksheet). You can enter text, values, dates, and formulas into each cell.

Spreadsheet programs identify each column with a column letter and each row with a row number.

cell address The cell address identifies the specific location of a cell in a spreadsheet (worksheet) using the cell's column letter and row number. For example, the address G15 identifies the cell in column G, row 15.

center To position selected information so its center point is equidistant from the left and right margins of a document or the left and right boundaries of a cell or other text box.

central processing unit (CPU) The microprocessor chip that executes commands and controls the data that moves through the computer. The CPU's power defines the capabilities of the PC as a whole. The most popular type of CPU is Intel's Pentium 4 processor.

character When you press a keyboard key (or Shift plus another key), the specified character appears on the screen. Characters include letters, numbers, punctuation marks, and other symbols.

chart (also called graph) Representing groups or series of data in a graphical form to clarify how values compare or what trends may have developed over time. Most spreadsheet programs and presentation graphics programs offer charting capabilities. You also can insert a chart or graph into a word processor document by copying it from a spreadsheet program into the document. Common chart types include a bar or column chart, line chart, or pie chart (Figure C.2).

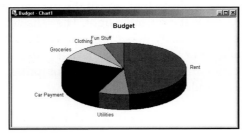

Figure C.2. A pie chart shows you how individual values in a group compare with the total for the group.

clear To remove the selected text or object from a file, usually by pressing Delete or choosing Edit | Clear in a program. Note that clearing information does not place it on the Clipboard.

click To move the mouse pointer over an on-screen item and then press down and release the left mouse button once.

clip art Predrawn artwork that you can insert into your files. Most major word processors include clip art. You also can buy clip art collections from other resources or download clip art from the Internet.

Clipboard In Windows, a holding area in memory that stores information you cut or copy from a file using the Edit | Cut or Edit | Copy command. You can then paste the information from the Clipboard into another location in the same file or into another file altogether using the Edit | Paste command.

clock An internal clock circuit that generates regular pulses spaced at small intervals. Each pulse represents a single cycle in the system. The computer uses the pulses to synchronize the CPU's activities and information flow in the computer.

close To use a command to remove a file or program from the computer's screen and thus from the working memory (RAM) for the system. Closing a file or application frees up RAM so the computer can use it for other purposes. To close a file in an application, choose the File | Close command. To close an application, choose File | Exit.

Close (X) button In Windows, one of three buttons at the right end of the title bar for a file window or application window. The Close button has an X on it. You can click the Close button to close the file or application window.

column In a table in a word processor or Web document, a column is a vertical block of cells spanning the whole table height. In a spreadsheet program, a column represents each vertical group of cells. As shown in Figure C.3, spreadsheet programs identify columns using column letters.

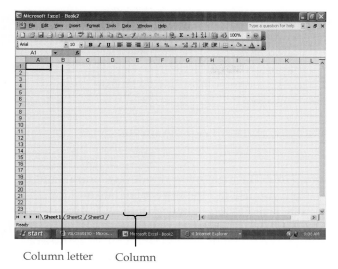

Column letter   Column

Figure C.3. Spreadsheets organize information in columns and rows of cells.

column border A decorative boundary applied around a column in a word processor table, Web page table, or in a spreadsheet program. In a spreadsheet program, the column border also means the dividing line between column letters at the top of the spreadsheet. You can usually drag the right column border for a column in a spreadsheet to resize the column.

command button In a dialog box, a button you click to carry out an action. If the command button name includes an ellipsis (...), the command button displays another dialog box. Most dialog boxes include an OK button, which you click to close the dialog box and apply your choices from the dialog box. The Cancel button in a dialog box closes the dialog box without applying your choices.

Command Prompt A Windows accessory that lets you access a DOS-type window and type commands. Click Start | All Programs | Accessories | Command Prompt to display this window.

compress To use a special utility program to reduce the amount of space a file occupies. Compressed files take up less space and transfer more quickly over the Internet or a network. Typically, you compress multiple files into a single compressed file. For example, you can compress 10, 100K files (1M of data) into a single file that might only take up only 300K.

 You can use Windows Send To | Compressed Folder command to compress the selected files into a folder.

compressed folder This is a "container" folder that typically holds the contents of several files. You extract the original files from the compressed file (decompress the file). In Windows, you can double-click a compressed folder icon and then select and copy the files to another drive or folder to decompress them. Some compressed files are self-extracting and have an .EXE extension.

configure To change settings for a piece of hardware or software so that it works correctly when you first install it, or so that it works as you prefer at a later time. For example, after adding more RAM to your system, you need to reconfigure a setting for the system to ensure that it can find all of the new RAM.

Control (Ctrl) key A key you press in combination with other keys to perform a command or make a selection in an application. For example, in recent versions of Microsoft Word, you can press and hold the Ctrl key and click a sentence to select the whole sentence.

Control menu The menu that opens if you click the small icon to the left of the application name or file name in a window title bar. The Control menu contains commands for working with the window. For example, if you click the Close command on the Control menu, Windows closes the window.

Control Panel An area in Windows that you can use to change Windows settings and hardware settings. For example, you can use the Control Panel to access the Mouse Properties to change your mouse settings. To open the Control Panel, choose Start | Control Panel in Windows. You can display the features in Classic view (as icons) or in Category view (as links and listed by task).

copy To duplicate selected text, selected cells, or a selected object, typically using the Edit | Copy command or Copy button.

crash When a computer or program stops working or "locks up." You can try to exit the program that is causing problems from the Task Manager (press Ctrl+Alt+Delete). You can also try to restart by clicking Start and then Turn Off Computer. Click

Restart. If the keyboard and mouse have stopped responding, however, you must reset the computer by turning it off and then back on. Do this only as a last resort.

cross-hair pointer A mouse pointer that appears after you select a command or button for inserting an object (like a chart) or drawing a shape in an application (Figure C.4). Drag the cross-hair pointer to define the approximate size, shape, and position for the object.

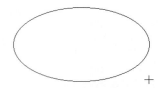

Figure C.4. Use the cross-hair pointer (the small plus) to draw or define a boundary for an object.

current cell or selection In a spreadsheet program, you click a cell to make it the active cell. If you drag to select a group (range) of cells in a spreadsheet or database table, text in a word processor, or an object in any kind of application, the selection becomes the current selection. Any command or formatting you specify next applies to the current selection.

current file The active file that's ready to accept the next information you type or command you give. The current file holds the insertion point or current selection.

cut To remove a selection from a file and place it on the Clipboard using the Edit | Cut command or Cut button. You can then paste the cut selection to another location using the Edit | Paste command or the Paste button.

Cyberspace The vast online world where users interact and exchange information without physically meeting.

D

data Information you enter into a computer. You can then use the computer to store or manipulate the information.

database A file that holds an organized list of information. For example, a database might list all your audio CDs. The database file divides the list into records and fields. The user could sort the list to find a particular record (CD) listed in the database.

database program A program you can use to compile and manipulate databases (database files).

Date/Time The icon in the Windows Control Panel that you use to reset the actual date and time displayed at the right end of the Windows taskbar.

default The initial or normal setting for a feature or object. For example, most software prints one copy of a file unless you change the default and specify that it should print more than one copy.

defragment When you save a file to disk, the disk drive attempts to write all the information in the file to contiguous clusters on the disk. Over time, as you delete and add files on the disk, the groups of contiguous clusters become smaller, and sometimes the drive has to store different parts of a file in non-contiguous clusters, which fragments the file. The more fragmented files a disk holds, the slower the disk runs. You can run a defragmenter, a utility that reorganizes the information on a disk until every file spans contiguous clusters, enabling the drive to retrieve files more efficiently.

delete To remove selected information from a file, usually by pressing the [Del] key or choosing Edit | Clear. Deleting information does not place it on the Clipboard.

descending order Text information alphabetized in Z to A order or numbers ordered from the largest value to the smallest.

deselect To remove the check beside a dialog box check box. Or, to click outside selected text, cells, or an object in a document to remove selection highlighting or sizing handles.

Desktop In Windows, the working area or screen background that holds the taskbar, icons, and program windows.

desktop publishing (DTP) Creating publications that integrate text and graphics—typically brochures, newsletters, annual reports, and sales flyers—on a computer. While most word processors offer at least limited DTP features, such as the ability to insert graphics, rules, and other design elements in a document, precise work calls for a separate desktop publishing application such as Microsoft Publisher, QuarkXPress, or Adobe PageMaker.

dialog box If you choose a command with an ellipsis (...) after its name, the command displays a dialog box. The dialog box presents options or choices that you make to control what the command does. Figure D.1 shows an example.

Figure D.1. A dialog box gives you choices for completing a command, in this case changing the font of text in a Word document.

digital camera A camera that saves a still image directly to digital format. You can transfer the images from the digital camera to a PC. Then, as with any other graphic file, you can insert the picture file in a document, print it with a color printer, or include it on a Web page.

disk One of many types of rewriteable magnetic media that holds files created by computer applications.

A disk drive reads information from and writes information to the disk.

document A file created in a word processing program. Web pages also may be called documents.

documentation The instruction books and any online how-to demonstrations that help you use a new PC or program.

domain name The alphanumeric, friendly name for a Web site or other Internet site. For example, home.microsoft.com, www.house.gov, www.writer.org, and www.butler.edu are all domain names for Web sites.

> The suffix for a Web sites gives you a clue about what type of organization operates the site. The .com suffix typically represents a for-profit company, while .org usually identifies the site for a non-profit organization, gov stands for a government body's site, and .edu stands for an educational entity's site.

double-click To move the mouse pointer over an item on-screen and press the left mouse button twice, quickly.

download To transfer a file from another computer to your computer, usually from an online service or the Internet.

> If you're downloading a file from an unfamiliar online source, it may have a computer virus. You should use virus checking software to scan downloaded files for viruses and remove those viruses.

drag and drop A technique where you drag something to perform a command or action in a program. For example, you can drag a file icon from one folder and drop it onto the icon for another folder to moves the file from its original folder to the folder on which you dropped it. In a word processor or spreadsheet, you can drag a selection from one location and drop it into another location to move the selection.

drop-down list A text box in a dialog box or on a toolbar that includes a drop-down list arrow at the right side. When you click the drop-down list arrow, a list of choices opens. You can then click the choice you want in the list.

DVD (digital versatile disc). A type of drive often included on computers or the disc used in that type of drive. DVD drives use a different technique for storing data on the disc and can store a lot more data than CDs. Like CD drives, though, you can find DVD drives that can just read discs (for instance, play a movie). Or you can find drives that can record data once (DVD-R) or drives that can record, rewrite, and erase data on the disc (DVD-RW). The speed for rewriting data is slower than reading or recording.

E

e-mail A message that you send via a network, online service, or the Internet using special e-mail software like Outlook Express. You also can attach a file such as a spreadsheet or graphic to the e-mail message.

e-mail address A unique address used to send and route messages to a particular recipient. Most email addresses follow this format: a unique user name, followed by the @ symbol and the domain for the ISP or company on which the user has his or her e-mail account: *username@isp.net*.

edit To make a change to information in a file. Many programs offer editing commands on an Edit menu.

embed In OLE, embedding means inserting an object in one application that you created in another application. For example, you can insert a chart created from Microsoft Excel into a Microsoft Word document.

End key Use the End key to navigate in programs. For example, pressing $\boxed{\text{End}}$ in a word processor moves the insertion point to the end of a line. You often can press $\boxed{\text{Ctrl}}$+$\boxed{\text{End}}$ to move to the end of a word processor document or to the last cell that holds text in a spreadsheet.

enhanced keyboard Enhanced keyboards include a keypad to the right of the main group of keyboard keys. Computer users that type a lot of numbers, such as financial professionals and bookkeepers, can use the 10-key keypad to enter numeric information more quickly. While desktop systems usually come with an enhanced keyboard, most notebook system keyboards typically lack the separate numeric keypad.

Enter key Press $\boxed{\text{Enter}}$ to start a new paragraph in a word processor or finish an entry in a spreadsheet or database table cell. You also can press $\boxed{\text{Enter}}$ in most dialog boxes to close the dialog box and apply your dialog box selections.

error messages An operating system or application displays an error message (Figure E.1) when a problem occurs or when you request an action that can't be completed. For example, you might see an error message if you enter a spreadsheet formula incorrectly. Usually, the error message includes a description of the problem and gives you options for proceeding.

Figure E.1. Error messages alert you when there's a problem and give you options for how to proceed.

Esc key You press $\boxed{\text{Esc}}$ to cancel actions, in most cases. For example, if you open a menu in an application, you can press $\boxed{\text{Esc}}$ twice to close the menu and deselect the menu name. You also can press $\boxed{\text{Esc}}$ to close an open dialog box without applying your choices in the dialog box.

Excel The Microsoft Excel spreadsheet program, also part of the Microsoft Office suite, leads the spreadsheet market. Like other spreadsheet programs, Excel provides many functions that you can use to perform complex calculations.

Exit The command typically found on the File menu that you use to close a program. The term exit refers to shutting or closing down any application.

expand When you're working with the folder tree in a file window, expanding means redisplaying all the folders and files that have been hidden or collapsed within a particular folder. When you're working with the outlining feature in an application, expanding means redisplaying all the subheadings and body text hidden or collapsed under a particular heading.

extension The extension appears as a suffix on the file name and consists of a dot (.) followed by three characters, as in .EXE or .DOC. The file name extension enables Windows and Windows applications to identify the file type.

external drive Unlike an internal drive installed within the case of your PC, an external drive has its own case and connects to the PC via a cable. Some external drives connect to the parallel port. Others may require that you install a special card to make the connection.

F

FAQ This acronym for "Frequently Asked Questions" refers to a list of questions and answers about a topic provided on a Web site, newsgroup, or as a file that comes with software. Experienced Internet newsgroup participants first compiled FAQs as a reference for new users to prevent the same questions from appearing repeatedly on the newsgroup.

fax software Fax software enables a fax/modem to send and receive faxes. Create a coversheet in the fax software and then attach the file to send. When you send the fax, the fax software tells the fax/modem to dial the fax number specified, send the cover sheet, and send the attached file, page by page. Similarly, faxing software tells the fax/modem to respond to incoming fax calls and store fax pages electronically so you can later view or print them.

field In a database, a field represents a piece of information common to all the entries. For example, if you create a database to list all your audio CDs, the fields might be *Title*, *Artist*, *Genre*, and *Price*.

file A named unit of information stored on a disk. Each application creates a specific type of file. The Word word processor creates document files, each of which has the .DOC extension. The Excel spreadsheet program creates workbook files, each of which has the .XLS extension.

file attachment When you send an e-mail message or newsgroup message, you can send a particular file with the message (Figure F.1). This is called *attaching* the file or adding a *file attachment*. You can attach document files, spreadsheets, graphics, or any other type of file.

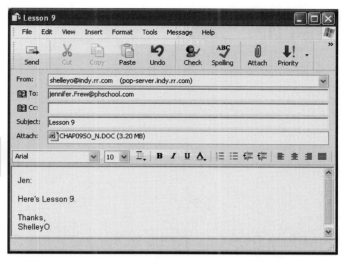

Figure F.1. You can attach files to an email message.

file size The number of kilobytes or megabytes of information in a file. You may need to know the file size to know if a file will fit on a floppy disk. You also must consider the file size for any file attachment you send via e-mail. Many ISPs will not send a message with very large file attachments.

file window When you open a file in an application, it opens in its own window, called a file window. Each file you open appears in its own window and becomes the current file.

> To switch to another open file (and its file window), open the Window menu in the application with which you're working and click the name of the file you want to use.

fill Many spreadsheet programs offer a fill feature, which lets you copy an entry from one cell across the row or down the column. Also, in many programs, you can apply a fill, or background, to an object you draw, a selected range, or a selected paragraph.

find A find operation selects each matching instance of a word or phrase you specify. After the program finds the first matching instance, click a Find Next button or choose a Find Next command to select the next match. Most applications provide some type of find or search capability.

 To start a find, look for the Edit | Find, Edit | Search, or Tools | Find command in your application.

firewall A system of software and hardware that protects a company's network from outside networks (including the Internet). If you have a 24/7 (cable) connection, you should use a firewall to prevent unauthorized access to your computer.

flowchart This type of chart, often used in programming, illustrates how a process works using different box styles and connecting lines. Flow charts show how a process branches or proceeds in different directions based on whether the answer to a particular question is yes or no.

folder You can divide the space on any disk into named file storage areas called folders. The folders help organize the information on the disk, because you can save files covering the same topic in a single folder.

Folders list In file and folder windows, you can display a hierarchical list of the drives and folders on your computer. To do so, click the Folders button. Figure F.2 shows the Folders list displayed. Click the plus sign beside a disk or folder to view the folder's contents. Click a minus sign beside a disk or folder to hide the folder's contents.

Figure F.2. You can display a Folders list in a file or folder window.

font Traditionally, a font refers to a particular set of characters in a particular size and style, such as the bold Times New Roman characters in the 12-point size. In most applications today, however, the font choice refers more generally to the typeface, such as Times New Roman. After you choose a font from the Font list, you can choose the size and styling separately.

footer You can create a footer to appear at the bottom of each printed page from a word processor document, spreadsheet file, graphics presentation, or database form or report. The footer might include such information as the file name, date, and page number. Footers and headers help the reader pick up key information about the document from any page.

format When you format selected text or a selected object, you change settings that control the text or object's appearance. For example, you can change the font, size, or color of text. Or, you can apply a colored border around an object and a fill within it.

formula In a spreadsheet cell, you enter a formula to perform a calculation on the values held in other cells. Formulas resemble mathematical equations. You enter an equals sign (=) to start each formula, then use numbers, cell addresses, mathematical operators, and functions to complete the formula. For example, the formula =(C1*5)+C2 multiplies the value held in cell C1 by 5, then adds the value held in cell C2.

FrontPage Use the Microsoft FrontPage software to design your own Web pages.

FTP FTP stands for File Transfer Protocol, a method of transferring files over the Internet.

function In a spreadsheet program, a function serves as shorthand for a more complicated calculation. For example, you can use the AVERAGE function in Excel to average a list of numbers, rather than building a formula to perform the calculation. In programming language, a function typically returns a value on which the program you're creating can then act.

Function keys Sometimes called F-keys, these keys appear in a row above the numbers at the top of the keyboard. Software publishers use the function keys as shortcut keys for accessing program features.

G

G (gigabyte) A gigabyte equals roughly 1,000M of information.

grammar checker Top word processing programs can check the grammar used in a document in addition to checking the document's spelling. The grammar checker compares each sentence to a set of grammar rules and highlights any sentence that may violate a rule. You can then decide whether or not to change the sentence.

graphics Electronic still images that you can create and display using a PC are graphics, also called graphics files. "Graphics" also refers to a PC's capabilities for displaying graphical images and data.

grayscale An image using shades of gray in addition to pure black and white to represent shapes and shadows more realistically than a pure black and white image.

gridlines Gridlines separate cells in a spreadsheet, database table, or a table in a word processor document.

H

halftone A halftone image is a black and white photo prepared for printing. A scanner can create a digital halftone. The scanner and its software convert the continuous shades in the photo to dots of varying sizes. Larger, more dense dots create the darker areas of the image, while smaller, more sparse dots represent the lighter areas.

hard disk The series of magnetic storage platters within a hard disk drive. The hard disk holds the files for the computer's operating system, program files, and files you create with programs.

hard disk drive The hard disk drive holds the hard disk platters. Its read/write head reads the information from and writes the information to the

sectors on the hard disk. A hard drive holds the disk platters in an airtight case, making the hard disk data less prone to damage than a floppy disk.

 Remember, you can't save a file to a "drive," the mechanical device that reads and writes disks. You save a file to a "disk," the magnetic media that holds your data.

hard page break A page break that you insert manually in a chosen location in a document, usually by pressing [Ctrl]+[Enter]. For example, you could insert a hard page break to create a title page in a document, shifting the body information to the top of the next page.

hardware The circuitry and other physical components that make up a PC's system unit and the devices connected to the system, like the printer, monitor, and keyboard.

header You can create a header to appear at the top of each printed page from a word processor document, spreadsheet file, graphics presentation, or database form or report. The header might include such information as the file name, date, and page number. Like footers, headers give key information about the document on every page.

Help The Help feature in a program explains how to use a feature, provides background information, or supplies definitions. Figure H.1 shows the Help window for Windows XP. You can display help by choosing Start | Help and Support. In most programs you can find a term by topic, by using an index, or by searching for a keyword.

Figure H.1. You can use Windows online help feature to get information.

History list By default, your Web browser keeps a list of Web sites you have visited during recent browsing sessions. To return to a site, you can select the site name from the History list.

Home key Use [Home] to navigate in programs. You usually can press [Home] in a word processor to move the insertion point to the beginning of a line. You also can press [Ctrl]+[Home] to move to the beginning of a word processor document or to the first cell in a spreadsheet.

home page Sometimes, home page refers to the first page your Web browser loads when it connects to the Internet. More often, it means the main page for a Web site, from which you can connect to other pages the site offers.

HTML The acronym for Hypertext Markup Language, the coding scheme for creating Web pages. Web browser software can read the HTML coding, convert the codes, and display attractively formatted Web pages. While Web page authors used to have to code Web pages manually, more friendly programs like FrontPage enable users to create Web pages using a method similar to creating a Word processor document, where you enter text, apply formatting, and insert graphics.

http:// and https:// These are content identifiers appearing at the beginning of an Internet address, or URL. A content identifier tells you to what type of site the Internet address leads. The http:// content identifier stands for Hypertext Transfer Protocol, meaning any site with an address beginning with http:// holds HTML information, or Web pages. The https:// content identifier leads off the address for a secure Web site.

hyperlink A link you click to display another Web page or document. Most often, hyperlinks appear in Web pages and can consist of specially formatted text, buttons, and hot spots on graphics. You can also insert hyperlinks within the files you create or even within e-mail messages. For example, you can insert a link to a Web page in a Word document or even a link to another file on your hard disk; clicking the link displays the linked Web page or file.

I

icon These small pictures represent files, folders, programs, and features in Windows and Windows applications. Figure I.1 shows icons on the Windows desktop. Double-click an icon to open the file or run the program.

Figure I.1. Icons appear on your desktop.

import To use information from one program in another, completely different program. For example, you might import financial data from Access into Excel.

inbox The folder in your e-mail program that displays newly received e-mail messages.

indent To set one or more lines of a paragraph in from the left or right margin in a word processor document. If you indent the paragraph's first line from the left margin, you create a first-line indent. If you indent the paragraph from the left margin, except the first line, you create a hanging indent. You can also indent the entire paragraph from either or both sides.

insert To add or move text into existing text, or to add a graphic or other object into a document.

insert mode In a word processing program, you use insert mode to insert new text within existing text at the insertion point. Text to the right of the insertion point moves further right to make room for the inserted text.

insertion point The blinking vertical line that appears in a document, spreadsheet cell, database field, or text box to indicate where the next text you type will appear.

install To copy program files from the program disks to your computer's hard disk. Most programs include an installation or setup program that handles the copy process, as well as making certain changes that enable Windows to find and operate the newly installed program properly.

Intel The company that designs and manufactures the most widely used central processing unit (CPU) chips and motherboard chipsets, enabling personal computers to process program instructions.

interface The commands, buttons, graphics, and other program features on your computer monitor that you use to navigate in a program. The interface also provides feedback, such as the page you're currently working with in your document.

Internet  The worldwide network of computer networks to which an individual PC can connect for communication and information exchange. Users connect to the Internet to send and receive files and private e-mail, find information from online resources, participate in public message and chat areas, and even shop and transact other business, such as stock market transactions.

Internet Explorer  The Web browser software published by Microsoft and distributed with Windows and other Microsoft program bundles. Figure I.2 shows Internet Explorer.

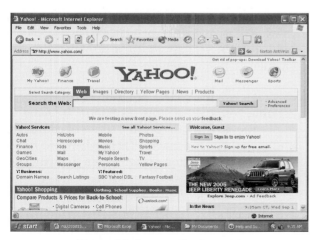

Figure I.2. Internet Explorer 6.0

intranet  An intranet is an "Internet within a company," although it may not be connected to the Internet. Intranets are ideal for communicating information to employees, such as new product and inventory information.

italic An attribute or style you apply to text to make it look *slanted*, or *italicized*. In many applications, you can press Ctrl+I to apply italics to selected text.

J

.JPG (JPEG)  .JPG (Windows) or .JPEG (Mac) files are types of graphic files typically found on Web pages.

justify A type of alignment that inserts spacing between words and letters to expand each line of text to span between document margins or the sides of a cell (see J.1).

> This text in this paragraph is **justified**. Justified text means that the text in both the left and right margins will line up evenly. The last line in a justified paragraph may not go all the way to the right margin.¶

Figure J.1. This is an example of justified text.

K

KB This abbreviation, like K, designates a measurement presented in kilobytes.

Kbps  *Kbps* stands for *kilobits per second*, or 1,000 bits per second. A 56K modem generally can transfer about 56,000 bps, but some are capable of transferring data at 57,600 bps (with the extra transmission speed provided via data compression and other features).

 The FCC limits data transmission speeds over phone lines. Although some modems can work at 56K, the FCC limits data receiving speeds to 53K, so your modem generally won't connect at a speed greater than 53K on a regular phone line.

keyboard The keyboard is made up of all the letter, number, and character keys that you use to enter information into the computer, as well as special keys that you can use to select commands.

 You can buy split keyboards that help you hold your arms at more comfortable angles. There are also keyboards with built-in wrist rests to reduce the repetitive-motion injury called carpal-tunnel syndrome.

L

label Text that you enter in a spreadsheet cell to identify data below or beside it.

LAN (local area network) A Local Area Network connects a number of computers so that they share resources on a dedicated file server. A single LAN can serve a few computers or hundreds, but usually the LAN serves only one location or company.

landscape orientation A wide page format that turns the page so that the longer side runs along the top edge. Landscape orientation fits more information on each line or row of the document.

laser pointer A pen-sized device that emits a beam of red light, which you can use to point to information on a projection screen or other large board during a presentation.

laser printer Laser printers print high-quality hard copies. Laser printers achieve high-print resolutions by using electrostatic reproduction. A fine laser charges areas on a photostatic drum or belt. As the drum or belt rotates, it applies the toner that was attracted to the charged areas to the page. A laser printer offers better print quality than an inkjet printer and also prints faster.

launch Another word for starting an application. For example, "Launch Microsoft Excel" means to start the Excel program.

link Web pages include links (also called hyperlinks) to other pages at that site or other sites entirely (see hyperlinks). Also, in OLE (Object Linking and Embedding), you can paste a linked copy of information from one document (the source document) into another (the target or destination document). When you update the original information, the linked copy updates as well, ensuring that the two files always contain identical information.

list box A list box in a dialog box lists a number of choices. You typically can scroll to display additional choices, and then click the choice you want to apply.

load After you start a program, your computer loads the program into memory. That is, the system transfers the program instructions from the hard disk to RAM. Web browser software also loads a Web page when it receives the page information and displays it on the screen after you click a link or specify a Web address to display.

log in or log on These terms describe the process of providing information to connect to a LAN (local area network) or an Internet connection. For example, to connect with an ISP, your system needs to send your username and password to verify that you have an Internet account. Most communications software make the log on process automatic.

log off When your computer logs off a network connection, it sends information to the server or ISP computer to terminate the connection.

M

M or MB These abbreviations stand for megabyte, a disk storage measurement. Each megabyte is 1,048,576 bytes of data. You also may see MB used to describe data throughput (data transfer) speed, in which case it stands for 1,000,000 bytes. Each M holds 1,024 K, equaling 1,024 x 1,024 bytes or characters of information.

macro Creating a macro in a program is essentially creating your own custom command. In many applications, you can record a series of commands and save them as a macro. Then, when you run the macro, the application performs the steps that you recorded.

mail merge The mail merge feature in a word processing program is used to create a mass mailing, including envelopes and mailing labels.

The mail merge inserts information from a database into specified locations (fields) in the word processor document, creating one personalized copy of a letter for each record in the database.

mail server The computer and/or software that routes and stores e-mail messages on a LAN or on the Internet. If you connect to the Internet via an ISP, the ISP's mail server sends outgoing e-mail messages and receives and stores incoming messages until you connect and retrieve them with your e-mail program.

margin The white space at the edge of the page around the contents of a printout forms the margin. A page with narrower margins can hold more information.

> Some printers limit the size of the margins you can use in a document. For example, some printers can't print within .25" of the edges of the page and will "cut off" information falling in the unprintable area.

maximize To return a file or application window to its full size.

Media Player The Windows accessory program that you can use to play music and video.

memory The term memory describes any chip in a PC that holds the values and instructions the system needs to run. A ROM (Read-Only Memory) chip holds a set of permanent instructions the system needs to start up. RAM (Random-Access Memory) serves as the working memory for your computer. RAM holds program instructions or information that you've entered into a file but haven't yet saved. Shutting down the computer clears everything out of RAM.

menu A menu lists commands in a program. Each menu groups commands for similar tasks. For example, the File menu lists commands for working with files and the Format menu lists commands for formatting either selected information or the whole file.

menu bar The menu bar lists each of the menus in an application and usually appears near the top of the application window under the window title bar. To open a menu, click its name on the menu bar.

To close a menu, click outside it or press ⎡Esc⎤ twice (to both close the menu and deselect the menu name).

message box A message box looks like a dialog box but appears for informational reasons only (rather than enabling you to choose command options, as does a dialog box). An application displays a message box to inform you when it has finished a particular operation, such as a spell check.

Microsoft Microsoft publishes many of the leading application programs used on PCs today, as well as the Windows operating systems. Microsoft's other products include Office (which, depending on the version of Office, may include Word, Excel, PowerPoint, Access, Publisher, and Outlook), FrontPage, Works, Encarta, Golf, and a number of other applications.

minimize To reduce a file or application window to its smallest size.

modem A modem (an abbreviation of MOdulator-DEModulator) converts digital computer information into an analog format and sends it over phone lines. A PC can use a modem to connect with the Internet or to an online service.

monitor The TV-like unit that displays computer information. The video card or display card in the PC draws screen images and then sends them to the monitor for display. Monitors come in different sizes and with other capabilities that determine the quality of the monitor image.

motherboard This circuit board holds the essential components of the PC, including the CPU, ROM, RAM, buses, and slots for adapters. The brand and model of motherboard determine what features it includes. For example, some motherboards today feature built-in (on board) networking or video. You can substantially upgrade a PC by replacing its motherboard, CPU, and RAM.

mouse A device that you roll on your desk to move a pointer on the screen.

mouse button A pressable mechanism on the mouse that you use to perform a computer action based on the on-screen mouse pointer location.

mouse pad A portable rubberized pad on which you move the mouse. The ball within the mouse has better traction on a mouse pad than on a slick desk surface, so a mouse pad allows the mouse to operate more smoothly. If you have an optical mouse, you don't need a mouse pad.

 Remember to clean your mouse pad occasionally. A lot of dirt can build up on the mouse ball, causing the mouse to work erratically.

MS-DOS Also called simply DOS, the Microsoft Disk Operating System (MS-DOS) was introduced for personal computers in 1981. MS-DOS controlled basic system operation and let the user give commands to the system.

multimedia Applications or presentations that integrate text, graphics, audio, video, and (often) interactive features.

multitasking This is when a computer executes commands from more than one program at a time.

My Computer The Window's icon or window that you can open to view the various drives and system folders on your computer. You can click Start | My Computer to display this window. If you have a desktop shortcut to My Computer, you can double-click this icon to display the contents of your computer (see Figure M.1).

Figure M.1. Open the My Computer window to see your disk drives and system folders.

My Documents A special Windows folder useful for storing the documents you create. You can click Start | My Documents to view the contents of this folder. Or if you have a desktop shortcut icon to this folder, you can double-click the icon to view the contents.

N

navigate To move around in a file or on the Web. In an application, navigation entails displaying another page, moving the insertion point, or selecting another cell. On the Web, navigating means moving from page to page on a Web site or displaying another site altogether.

netiquette A set of rules for behaving on the Internet. Netiquette helps Internet users treat each other with courtesy and use the Net's resources wisely.

network A group of connected computers that can exchange information. Computers connected to the network may also share central devices, such a file storage, a fast modem or Internet connection, or a printer. Generally, the networked computers are connected via cabling, and network operating software controls the network operation.

network adapter The network adapter card (also called a NIC or network interface card) installs in a PC so that you can connect the PC to a network. Connect one end of the cabling to the network adapter card and the other to a network connection such as a hub.

notebook computer These portable, compact size computers, also called laptops, transport easily and open like a notebook for use. A notebook weighs about 5-9 pounds.

number format In a spreadsheet program, applying a number format to selected cells controls how numbers appear in those cells. For example, if you apply a percent number format, the numbers display as percentages, including the % sign. Choosing a currency format adds a dollar sign and two decimal places.

numbered list In a word processor document, you can number each item in a list, as in a list of ordered steps. Top word processors can number a list automatically for you.

NumLock key On an enhanced keyboard, you press Num Lock to toggle the numeric keypad at the far right side between typing numbers and working as arrow (insertion point movement) keys.

O

object This term describes any non-text item you insert into a file. For example, a piece of clip art or other graphic is an object that you can select, format, and move.

Office Office, from Microsoft, is the best-selling software suite. The standard edition of office includes Word (word processor), Excel (spreadsheet), PowerPoint (presentation graphics), and Outlook (e-mail and scheduling). The professional edition adds Access (database) and Publisher (desktop publisher).

offline When a printer is offline it is not ready to receive data. Also, when not connected to the Internet or another online service, your system is offline.

OK button Most dialog boxes include an OK button. Click the OK button to apply your choices and close the dialog box.

OLE OLE (Object Linking and Embedding) technology enables applications to share information and tools. You can copy an object or information from one application (the source application), and insert it as a linked object in the destination (or target) application. Whenever you make changes to the original information in the source document, the destination document changes to match.

online When you are connected to the Internet, you are online. Also, your printer is online when it's ready to receive data; an indicator light on the top of the printer usually lights up when the printer is online and ready.

operating system The operating system is the software that runs the internal components of the computer, such as Windows, or the Macintosh operating system. The operating system software directs information from the keyboard into the system; between the CPU, RAM, and other system components; and from the system to devices like the monitor and the printer.

operators In a spreadsheet program, operators are the mathematical symbols in a formula that specify how the formula should calculate. For example, you can use the + (addition), * (multiplication), / (division), and < (less than) operators, among others.

optical mouse One of the newer types of mice. This pointing device uses a bouncing laser to point and move the mouse pointer. Because it doesn't have any moving parts, this mouse is less likely to develop problems, including dirt getting inside the mouse and affecting its tracking sensors.

option button Option buttons appear in groups in dialog boxes. Option buttons present mutually exclusive options. That is, you can click only one of the option buttons at a time.

orphan When the first line of a paragraph appears as the last line on a page, that line is an orphan. In some word processors, you can activate an option that prevents orphans by moving page breaks for you.

outbox The folder in your e-mail program where the e-mail program places messages to be sent.

Outlook and Outlook Express Microsoft publishes these information management programs. Outlook comes as part of the Office suite (or can be purchased separately), and includes e-mail, scheduling, an address book, a to-do list, and journal features.

overtype mode In a word processing program, overtype mode will type over any text to the right of the insertion point. Each character or space you type replaces an existing character or space.

P

page Each printed sheet of information from an application equals a page.

page break A page break in an application is a mark showing where one page ends and the next begins in a printout.

page layout The page layout consists of any settings you make in a file to control the appearance of the printout pages. Settings such as the margins, orientation, and page size affect the page layout.

 In many applications, you choose File | Page Setup to access the page setup settings.

page numbering A feature that tells a program to print a page number on each page of a printout. You usually can insert the page number in the header or footer, but many word processors enable you to insert page numbers in any area of the document.

paint program A paint program is used to create and edit bitmap graphics. Although you can drag to draw objects like rectangles in a paint program, you have to change individual pixels or dots to edit the image. Windows Paint is a paint program.

Paint Shop Pro This paint program from Jasc software has emerged as a popular and inexpensive alternative to professional programs. Paint Shop Pro offers a number of custom brushes and color effects. It enables you to import and save images in a variety of formats and even to create animated images for Web pages.

palette A palette presents color or pattern choices you can apply to selected text or objects in an application. Click the square for the color or pattern you want to apply to the selection.

pane In some applications, you can split a window into multiple areas called panes. Each pane shows a different part of the file or shows the file information using a different view.

password A secret code that you assign to a file, program, or Windows for security reasons. You must enter the password to open the file, program, or Windows.

paste When you copy or cut information, Windows places the information on the Clipboard. You can then insert that information into another location by pasting it from the Clipboard.

path Also called the path name, the path identifies the precise location of a file on a disk. The full path to a file might look like C:\My Documents\Memos\Memo.doc.

PC (personal computer) A complete computer system that can be used either as a stand-alone system or connected to a network. A PC includes all the key computer components, including the CPU, operating system, monitor, hard and floppy disk drives, input devices (mouse and keyboard), and a printer. Currently, PCs often come equipped with a modem and sound card and frequently include extra devices like a video camera.

.PDF The file name extension for Adobe Acrobat files, often found on the Web. Many types of files convert to the Acrobat format for reading and viewing with the Acrobat reader.

Pentium The name of the most popular computer processor, made by Intel. The most current version of the Pentium is Pentium 4.

PDAs *(personal digital assistants)*. A handheld computer used to store appointments, pictures, notes, contacts, and other information.

PhotoShop This paint program from Adobe enables you to create and work with images. PhotoShop offers professional features for retouching scanned photos and adding special-effects filters.

plug-in Plug-in programs help your Web browser software do something it can't do on its own. For example, the browser may need a plug-in program to play a certain type of video file. Some plug-ins download and install automatically when you need them. In other instances, you will need to download and install the plug-in manually.

pointer The on-screen symbol that moves when you move your mouse.

pointer speed The pointer speed refers to how far and fast the mouse pointer moves on the screen relative to the distance and speed with which you move the mouse.

port Devices plug into a receptacle, or port, on your computer. Most ports are part of an adapter card within the computer.

portrait orientation A tall page format that turns the page so the longer side runs along the side edge. Portrait orientation fits less information on each line or row of the document, but fits more lines of information per page.

power supply The computer's power supply device covers AC power from the wall socket to DC power for the computer's use.

power surge A power surge occurs when the power voltage increases substantially on the power lines coming into your home or within your home.

PowerPoint Microsoft sells the PowerPoint presentation graphics program both as an individual program and as part of the Microsoft Office suite. PowerPoint can import information from Word and Excel and offers a number of features for creating multimedia presentations.

print To send a file's information to the printer, which then creates some type of hard copy output. In most applications, you choose the File | Print command to print.

print buffer A temporary storage area that holds the print queue (information being sent to the printer) until the printer is ready to accept it.

print job When you choose File | Print, set printing options, and then click OK to send a file to the printer, you create a print job for the printer to handle.

Print Screen key When you press the Print Screen key in Windows, a graphical copy of the information shown on your screen is sent to the Clipboard. You can paste the image from the Clipboard into a graphics program to save it as a file.

print preview Many applications offer a print preview feature so that you can see how a file will appear when you print it. Print preview helps you ensure that pages break correctly.

printer A printer connected to your computer makes a hard copy of any file that you specify. The type of printer you connect and install for your system controls your printing options. For example, the type of printer determines the paper size you can use to print.

printer port A port through which you connect a printer to your PC. Most printers connect to a PC via a parallel port, but some can connect via a serial or USB port.

programming language A set of vocabulary, grammar, syntax (command structure rules), organization, style rules, and tools a programmer uses to create programs.

properties In Windows, you set properties to specify the performance of a particular feature. For example, the Display Properties dialog box will display wallpaper or a pattern on the desktop or control how many colors Windows displays.

protocol The rules and standards two devices must follow to communicate via modem, LAN connection, or Internet connection.

Publisher This inexpensive, entry-level page layout (desktop publishing) program from Microsoft allows you to create a variety of documents such as post cards, newsletters, and flyers. Publisher offers a number of wizards to lead beginners through the process of selecting and applying a document design.

pull-down menu This is another name for menus in Windows programs. Commands appear on a menu below the menu bar, as if you had pulled down the menu to open it.

Q

QuarkXPress This professional page layout (desktop publishing) program competes with Adobe PageMaker. Quark has long excelled in preparing documents for four-color printing, such as magazine layouts and ads.

query You perform a query in a database program to find and retrieve matching entries in the database. You enter criteria, and the database displays all the records that match.

quit To exit a program. In most programs, you choose the File | Exit command to exit the program.

R

range In a spreadsheet program, a range is a contiguous block of cells. For example, the block of cells that spans from cell C5 in the upper-left corner to cell G10 in the lower-right corner forms the range C5:G10. A range also may refer to a contiguous set of items in other applications, such as a range of pages to print from a word processing document or a range of records from a database.

read When a computer reads information, it retrieves the information from a disk into the system's RAM.

read-only When you mark a file as read-only, you are able to open the file but not change it.

Read Me file A program or software component typically comes with a Read Me file that contains necessary information from the software publisher. The Read Me file may be named *Readme.wri*, *Readme.txt*, or simply *Read.me*.

 You should always read the Read Me file for a new program, preferably before you install the program.

reboot To restart the computer, especially after you experience a problem with it or install a new piece of hardware or software.

record In a database program, a record represents one full entry. For example, if you create a database to list all your audio CDs, the full entry for each CD (including the *Title, Artist, Release Date,* and *Price* fields) forms a record. Also, recording is the process of using sound or video software to capture digital sound or video. For example, you can use Windows Sound Recorder to record your voice from a microphone.

Recycle Bin The Recycle Bin in Windows (Figure R.1) holds files that you've deleted from the hard disk. The files remain in the Recycle Bin in case you need to restore them.

 The Recycle Bin icon looks like an empty waste can when there are no files in the Recycle Bin folder. The icon changes to a waste can holding crumpled paper when it is holding some files.

Figure R.1. The Recycle Bin stores deleted files until you choose to delete them permanently.

refresh Most Web browsers offer a Refresh button. Click the Refresh button to reload a Web page that didn't display completely or correctly on your system.

removable disk Also called removable storage, a removable disk drive reads and writes information to a removable cartridge or disk holding a large quantity of information.

reply When you receive an e-mail message, you can click the Reply button in your e-mail program to write a message in response to the received message. If the message was sent to several people, you can click the Reply All button to reply to all the original recipients.

report In a database program, you create a report to view or print the data in a nicely-designed page format rather than in a plain table.

resolution The resolution for an image or computer screen indicates how large or detailed the image is or how detailed the on-screen display is.

restart Windows offers a command to restart the system. Choose Start | Turn Off Computer. Click Restart.

restore To reduce the size of a file or application window so that it doesn't fill the desktop or the working area within the application window. When you restore a window, you can resize the window or drag its title bar to move it.

restore point A point in time where all your system settings are saved. Windows periodically creates restore points. If something goes wrong with your computer (for instance, after you install a new device), you can go back to a previous restore point and undo the changes.

revision marks Revision marking in a word processing document (and now in some spreadsheet and presentation graphics programs) shows the changes made to a file using markings. The revision marking, or change tracking, feature uses a different color or style to identify changes made by each different colleague or editor with whom you share the file. You can then review each change and decide whether to accept or reject it.

Rich Text Format Files that contain not only the basic data but also basic formatting such as fonts and font sizes. Most word processors and some other types of programs can open .RTF files, allowing you to share information between programs more easily .

right align Aligning information against the right margin, the right side of the cell, or the right side of an object. Right alignment yields an uneven appearance at the left side of a block of text, called ragged left.

right-click To move the mouse pointer over an on-screen item and press and release the right mouse button once.

 You generally click using the left mouse button unless a program instruction tells you to do otherwise or you want to display a shortcut menu.

row A row in a table or spreadsheet consists of all the cells on one horizontal line across the table or spreadsheet.

 To select an entire row in a spreadsheet program, you generally can click the row number at the left side. Drag across multiple row numbers to select multiple rows.

run To start or load a program, or to execute a macro in a program.

sans serif A font lacking serifs (decorative cross strokes) on the letters, like **Arial**, **Gill Sans**, **Impact**, or **Helvetica**.

save To name and store a file in a folder on a disk. After making any changes in a file, you should save it again to include those changes in the stored version on file. In most applications, the File | Save command or a Save button on a toolbar will save the current file.

scanner A device that uses light to read an image from a hard copy, such as a photo, in order to convert it to a digital format that you can save on disk, edit, and print.

screen saver A screen saver displays an on-screen moving image after your computer has been idle for a specified period of time. Monitors originally needed screen savers to prevent images from "burning in" to the display material and leaving permanent ghost images. With improved monitors, screen savers are more of a way to personalize PCs.

scroll When you scroll a file, you change the portion of the file that's visible on the screen. For example, if you scroll down in a spreadsheet, you display the group of cells below the previously displayed cells. You also can scroll a list in a dialog box to display other options in the list. Note that scrolling does not move the insertion point or cell selector in a document.

scroll bar You use a scroll bar to scroll through a file. Each scroll bar appears as a long bar with an arrow at either end and a scroll box within the bar. You can click either arrow or drag the scroll box to scroll. An application window may offer a vertical scroll bar along the right side; use it to scroll up and down. The window might also offer a horizontal scroll bar along the bottom; use it to scroll left and right.

scroll box This box appears on a scroll bar. Click on either side of the scroll box to scroll through a screen of information. Drag the scroll box to scroll the document more quickly.

Scroll Lock key In some programs, pressing [Scroll Lock] will let you use the arrow keys to scroll through a document rather than to move the insertion point or cell selector.

SDRAM. Stands for Synchronous Dynamic RAM. One of the most popular types of RAM today and is found in most new systems.

search When you want to look for a particular word, phrase, or value in a word processor, spreadsheet, database, or presentation graphics program, you can perform a search, or a find, to identify matching instances of the word or value. When you're working on the Web, you can perform a search to find Web pages that mention the topic you specify. A Web search engine site will perform a Web search.

search and replace To find a match for a term that you specify and replace the match with other specified information. This feature, called search and replace, or find and replace (Figure S.1), helps save time when correcting a repeated mistake in a document.

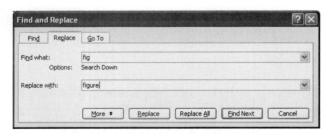

Figure S.1. Use the search and replace feature to replace information throughout a file.

search engine A Web site that performs a search of Web pages (and in some cases, newsgroups), to find pages with information concerning a specific topic. The search engine displays a listing of links to the pages covering the topic. Click a link to go to one of the listed pages. Each search engine keeps an index of pages registered by Web site operators and uses a slightly different method of matching terms.

 Most Web browsers include a Search button. Click this button to display the search bar and start a search. Many pages also include a search text box and button. You may be able to search just the site or the entire Web using the search features, depending on the page.

serif A decorative cross stroke that finishes off the ends of certain letters, such as the bottom of a lowercase "l" or "f." Serif fonts like **Bookman Old Style**, **Palatino**, and **Times New Roman** work well as body fonts.

server A server computer is the central control point on a LAN (local area network), and stores the networking software and central resources shared by other computers connected to the network. On the Internet, a server computer stores and manages a particular type of information. For example, a Web server stores and transmits Web pages.

setting A choice that you make to control how a program operates or how a command executes. For example, dialog boxes offer settings in programs.

setup Most applications come with a setup program (usually named *SETUP.EXE* or *INSTALL.EXE*) to install the application on your computer.

When you insert the CD for a new application, your system usually finds and runs the setup program automatically. If not, open My Computer, double-click the icon for the CD-ROM drive, then double-click the *SETUP.EXE* or *INSTALL.EXE* file icon.

shareware You can download shareware programs from the Internet and other online resources, or find them on sampler CDs that come with magazines and books. Shareware software operates on the honor system. If you decide you like the shareware and want to continue using it, you need to register it and pay a small fee to the shareware author.

Shift key Pressing [Shift] on the keyboard in conjunction with another key types a capital letter or a shifted character like @ or *. [Shift] may also be part of a shortcut key combination that performs a command or action.

Shift+arrow To select information in a word processor or other application, press and hold [Shift] while repeatedly pressing an arrow key.

Shift-click Press and hold [Shift] while clicking something on the screen. In a word processor, you can click at the beginning of a block of text to select, then Shift-click at the end of the block to finish the selection.

shortcut menu A shortcut menu, also called a context menu, offers commands that apply to the operation at hand. To display a shortcut menu (Figure S.2), right-click the item such as the desktop.

Figure S.2. Right-click to see a shortcut menu of commands.

shut down Before you turn off your PC, you should shut down Windows. Choose Start | Turn Off Windows.

small caps Words displayed in all capital letters using special smaller-sized capital letters, LIKE THIS. You apply small caps via a formatting selection within an application.

soft hyphen Also called an optional hyphen. You insert a soft hyphen into a word that appears near the end of the line. (In Word, press Ctrl + - to insert a soft hyphen.) If you make a change prior to the word with the soft hyphen that will cause it to wrap to the next line, the application will hyphenate the word at the soft hyphen location and only wrap part of it to the next line. Use soft hyphens to avoid short lines of text in a document.

 In the current version of Word, you can use the Tools | Language | Hyphenation command to have Word hyphenate a document automatically.

sort When you sort information, you place it in a new order. You can sort tables and lists in a word processor document, lists of entries in a spreadsheet, or records in a database. Choose a column or field of information by which to sort, as well as a particular sort order. For example, you could sort a list of names and address as in A–Z order by last name.

source An original file or selection that you're copying, or the location from which you copy or move a file or selection.

space character Enter a space character to separate words and sentences.

 You may have learned in typing class to enter two space characters after each sentence. That is no longer necessary because the font designs compress the space between letters within words, which makes a single space after a sentence a large enough break.

Spacebar Pressing the Spacebar key, the long key at the bottom of the keyboard, inserts a space character. Note that some keyboards have a divided Spacebar button, with the right half working like the traditional Spacebar key and the left half working like the backspace key.

spam Unsolicited email. Some email programs include features for blocking spam. You can also purchase programs specifically for blocking spam.

spelling checker A tool that can check the spelling of every word or entry in a file. The spelling checker compares each word to a dictionary and highlights any word that doesn't match an existing dictionary entry (Figure S.3). You can then decide whether or not the word needs correcting.

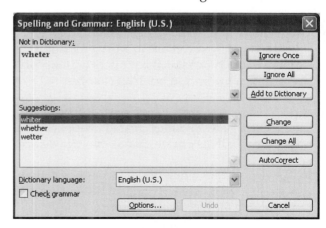

Figure S.3. A spelling checker highlights your spelling errors and suggests a replacement.

spinner buttons Spinner buttons, also called increment buttons, appear in a dialog box next to a text box holding a value. Clicking the up spinner button (it has an upward-pointing arrowhead) will increase the value in the text box. Clicking the down spinner button (it has a downward-pointing arrowhead) will decrease the value in the text box.

spreadsheet A spreadsheet program presents a grid of columns and rows that intersect to form cells. You can enter text (labels), a date, a value, or a formula in each cell. A spreadsheet formula includes mathematical operators to perform a calculation.

spyware Programs installed without your knowledge or consent that track where you go on the Internet. This information is then relayed to other companies. You can buy programs that check for and remove spyware programs.

Start menu In Windows, the Start menu serves as the main avenue for starting programs and accessing Windows features. To open the Start menu, click the Start button at the far left end of the taskbar.

start page The first page your Web browser loads when it connects to the World Wide Web. Also called the home page.

start up To boot up your computer. When you start the computer, it performs a number of steps, such as loading Windows, and displaying the desktop.

status bar The bottom of the application window in many programs has a status bar. The status bar often displays information about the open file, such as how many pages it has and the current page number. In some cases, the status bar includes tools you can use to work on the file. For example, the Word status bar offers buttons for recording a macro and tracking changes.

storage Storage is another name for disk space, the area where you store files created in applications. You may see a disk drive called a storage device.

style A style includes a number of formatting settings, such as the font, font size, and alignment. Instead of applying individual formatting settings to a selection, you can simply apply the style. Many word processors, presentation graphics programs, and spreadsheets offer predefined styles, or let you create your own styles.

subfolder A subfolder is any folder within another folder. Each subfolder is one level below the main folder, and appears indented in the tree. You can create subfolders within subfolders.

To create a new folder or subfolder, open the disk or folder you want to hold the new folder. Click File | New, and click Folder. Type a folder name for the folder that appears and press Enter.

submenu Some menu commands display a triangle (arrowhead) to the right of the command name. If you point the mouse pointer to such a command, a smaller menu, called a submenu, appears. You can then click a command in the submenu to select a command.

subscript Smaller-sized characters that appear dropped below the normally formatted text. This example illustrates normal and subscript text: Normal$_{subscript}$.

suite A software suite consists of a group of programs that, together, offer a full range of capabilities at a favorable price. At a minimum, a business software suite includes a word processor and spreadsheet. It also typically includes information management or scheduling software. Other types of suites offer applications for using the Internet or graphics applications.

superscript Smaller-sized characters that appear aligned above the normally formatted text. This example illustrates normal and superscript text: Normal^{superscript}.

support Support, or technical support, means help that you can get from the software publisher of a program that you've purchased or the hardware manufacturer of a piece of hardware that you've purchased. Usually, you can dial a toll-free number for a limited time after your purchase to get free help. Beyond the applicable timeframe, you can purchase additional telephone help by credit card. Most software and hardware manufacturers also offer a Web site that you can consult for technical support information.

surf To use Web browser software to move from page to page on the World Wide Web.

syntax Every type of command you use, formula you create, or query you develop follows rules called syntax. You must follow the correct syntax for the command, formula, or query to work correctly.

system requirements Every application has system requirements that spell out the features a PC needs to run the software efficiently. For example, the system requirements define what type of processor the system needs, how much RAM and hard disk space the program consumes, and any devices, like a modem or a sound card, that the software needs to perform its functions.

system tray The system tray appears at the right end of the taskbar in Windows. It displays the time and the volume control icon. It also may display icons for other items, like the power management features for a notebook. You can often right-click or double-click an icon in the system tray to work with the feature that it represents. For example, you can double-click the time to see a dialog box for resetting the system date and time.

system unit The system unit is the case or box holding the motherboard, CPU, power supply, internal disk drives, and other internal devices of a PC.

T

tab In the leading spreadsheet programs today, every file actually holds more than one spreadsheet, or worksheet. This structure lets each file hold more information and makes it easier to navigate. A tab like a manila folder tab identifies each separate spreadsheet in a file. To select a spreadsheet, click its tab. Dialog boxes with many options also have tabs; you can click the tab to display that set of options.

Tab key In many applications, you can press Tab to navigate. For example, you press Tab to move to the next cell in a spreadsheet or field in a database. In a word processor program, you press Tab to align text to the next tab stop. You can also press Tab to move between the different options in a dialog box.

tab stop A tab stop in a word-processing document is a location (or measurement) that you use to align text. For example, if you set a tab stop at one inch,

you can press the Tab to align text at that one inch tab stop.

table In an application, a table organizes information into cells formed by rows and columns that are divided by gridlines, much like a spreadsheet. You can insert tables into documents in many spreadsheet programs and onto slides or pages in many presentation graphics programs. Most databases use a table format in which you can enter data. In addition, Web pages can display data in a table format. In particular, catalog Web sites often display information in a table format. For example, if you search a Web-based catalog for a type of product, it may display items and prices in a table.

tag When using HTML and XML to create Web pages, you insert codes called tags to specify how particular information should display. For example, you use the <HEAD></HEAD> tags to identify the page header and the tags to center text. Web browsers read the tags to know how to display the Web page information.

tape backup drive You can connect a tape backup drive to a PC to back up information to cartridges holding magnetic tape. Tape works as a backup medium, but isn't as effective as a regular storage medium, because tape drives run more slowly and have to access data in the sequence in which it was recorded. In contrast, other disk drives can access information from any location on the disk.

target A target is a location to which you paste information previously copied or in which you insert an embedded OLE object. On a Web page, a target is a specific linked location. For example, if a page contains an alphabetical listing of information, you can click a letter at the top of the page to jump to the target link for that letter (the first item using that letter).

task A task is an application or operation on a computer. You can display the Task Manager to see applications and processes that are currently running. To do so, press Ctrl+Alt+Delete. A task also might mean a command or process that you complete within an application to alter a file.

task switching Every application opened in Windows is a separate Windows task. You can use the taskbar to switch between the open applications.

taskbar The taskbar is a bar with buttons and other features that appears below the desktop by default in Windows (Figure T.1). Each application that you launch in Windows appears as a button on the taskbar. To switch to another open application, click its button on the taskbar.

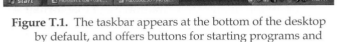

Figure T.1. The taskbar appears at the bottom of the desktop by default, and offers buttons for starting programs and switching among open applications.

telecommunications This term refers to using the telephone system to communicate. Telecommunication includes both voice and computer communications.

template You choose a template to make it the basis for a new file in an application. The template provides design elements, such as styles, page layout settings, and graphics. Some templates also provide basic information to help you create a finished document by "filling in the blanks."

text box A text box is a type of option in a dialog box, as in Figure T.2. The text box prompts you to enter information such as a file name when saving a file.

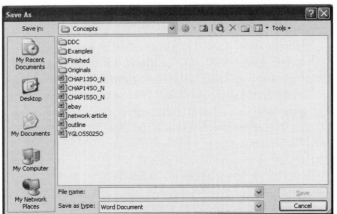

Figure T.2. Type information in a text box, like the File name in this dialog box.

text file A text file contains characters but no formatting. You can use the Windows Notepad applet to create text files, which use a .TXT file name extension. Choose Start | All Programs | Accessories | Notepad to start Notepad. Most applications can import plain text files.

thesaurus Leading word processors offer a thesaurus feature so that you can find a better substitute for a selected word. You may also find a stand-alone thesaurus program that you can use at any time.

.TIFF This file name extension, as well as the .TIF extension, identifies a graphic file in the Tagged Image File Format. .TIFF files are bitmap files. Scanners produce files using the .TIFF format, among others, because it handles color and shading gradations well.

tile To display open windows so that they do not overlap, but instead collectively fill the available working area. For example, if you tile four windows, each window fills a quarter of the screen. To tile open application windows, right-click the taskbar and choose Tile Windows Horizontally or Tile Windows Vertically.

title bar Every window and dialog box has a title bar. The title bar displays the application name, file name, or dialog box name. If the window isn't maximized, you can drag the window title bar to move the window to a new location.

toggle Some commands and dialog box options, such as check boxes, function as toggles, meaning they can be either on (selected) or off (not selected). When you toggle on a menu command, a check mark appears to the left of the command name.

toner The black or colored powder that a laser printer, plain paper fax machine, or photocopier uses to create images on paper.

toolbar A toolbar is a strip of buttons appearing in an application window (Figure T.3). You click a toolbar button to perform a command, apply formatting, or accomplish some other operation. Toolbars usually appear at the top of the application window under the menu bar, but they may also appear at the side or the bottom of the window, or even floating elsewhere in the window. You can often drag any toolbar to another on-screen location.

![toolbar]

Figure T.3. Click a button on a toolbar to perform a command.

toolbox A toolbox resembles a toolbar, but holds items such as drawing tools rather than buttons that perform commands.

trackball A trackball looks and works something like an upside-down mouse. Rather than moving the trackball around on your desk, you move the ball in the center of the trackball to control the mouse pointer.

TrueType font TrueType fonts offers two major benefits: both the computer screen and printer can use the TrueType font, eliminating the need for separately installed fonts and ensuring that the on-screen display exactly matches the printed result; secondly, TrueType fonts are scalable so you can change the size of the text. With older font technology, you had to install a separate font for each text size.

typeface A typeface is more specific than a font. A typeface is a complete set of characters using a particular font, style (bold or italic), and size.

U

underline You can underline selected text or numbers in an application. Many applications offer an underline button on a toolbar; click the button to apply or remove underlining.

underscore A keyboard character that appears to the right of the 0 key on the keyboard. (It's the hyphen's shifted character.) You can use underscore characters to create a line in a document. However, the underscore will not underline text.

undo This feature allows you to reverse a previous action. In some applications you can undo only the most recent action. In such a case, click an Undo button on a toolbar or choose the Edit | Undo command. In other applications you can undo multiple prior actions. In this case, you can click the Undo button multiple times or click the drop-down list arrow beside the undo button and use the list that appears to specify the number of actions to undo.

up arrow Pressing the ⬆ key on the keyboard moves the insertion point in a word processor document or presentation graphics page up one line, or moves the cell selector in a spreadsheet program up one row.

upgrade When you upgrade, you install a newer, and presumably better and faster, version of a software program or computer component. An upgrade may also consist of new or additional components for a system. For example, to upgrade a system's RAM, you add in more RAM rather than replacing all the existing RAM.

> When you buy new software, avoid buying the cheaper upgrade version unless you're sure that you have a previous version of the program (or an eligible substitute from another software publisher). An upgrade version won't install correctly unless you're legitimately upgrading from a prior program version.

upload To transfer a file from your computer to another computer, usually to an online service or the Internet. For example, a message you post to a newsgroup might include a file attachment. When you post the message, the attached file is uploaded to the news server.

uppercase Information presented in all CAPITAL LETTERS. Press ⇧Shift to type in uppercase.

USB A type of port on your computer. You can use this port to hook up components such as a digital camera, scanner, printer, or special USB drives.

USB Flash Memory drive A new type of portable storage device about the size of a car key. You can connect the device via a USB port and then use it to share data.

user interface The on-screen information that a computer system displays, enabling you to give commands, see the results from commands, and enter information.

user profile Descriptive information about yourself that you enter when you log on to online services, some Web sites, and chat rooms. Other users or the service administrator can look at the information to get an idea of who you are. Web sites and online services might use profile information to market services and products to you.

 If confidentiality is important to you, omit some user profile information. For example, you can give a handle rather than your real name, and leave out information, like your address or e-mail address, to prevent unwanted contact.

URL The acronym for Uniform Resource Locator, the address for a Web page (or other resource) on the Internet. The URL consists of several parts. The first is the content identifier: http:// or https:// for Web sites, or ftp:// for an FTP site, for example. The second part is the Web site, as in www.pearsoneducation.com. The final part is the location, or the path to a particular page, as in /html/order.html.

V

version A named or numbered edition of a product. Most older software used version numbers to represent different versions, with a full number increase representing a substantial product update and a decimal increase representing a minor update. Now, many software vendors use the year to distinguish different software versions.

virtual memory Windows creates virtual memory to expand a PC's memory capabilities. It uses space on the hard disk as extra memory.

virus A computer program that infects other files and programs. Viruses usually spread when you download files and programs or share files on disk. The virus can destroy files on your system to the point of deleting information or preventing the system from booting.

 Some newer types of viruses called macro viruses can infect files and templates in Word and Excel. Both Word and Excel offer a feature that will alert you if a file that you're opening includes macros and therefore, potentially, macro viruses.

voice recognition Software technology that enables a computer equipped with a sound card to recognize words and commands that you speak into a microphone.

volume The loudness of sound played or recorded by your system. Volume is also another name for a disk.

volume label A volume label is a name assigned to a disk. Windows displays the disk's volume label in the My Computer window, so you can tell at a glance what files a floppy or removable disk holds.

W

Web search To find information on a particular topic on the World Wide Web, you can perform a Web search to find links to applicable pages.

Web site A Web site is a collection of Web pages published by an individual, company, or other organization. The home page or start page for the site contains links to the other pages.

Webmaster The Webmaster is the individual (or group) responsible for maintaining a Web site.

Often, you can send an e-mail message to a site's Webmaster using an address in the format *webmaster@website.com*.

wildcard A wildcard character can represent unknown characters when you perform a file find or Web search.

window All versions of the Windows operating system present applications, programs, and files in rectangular boxes called windows. Dividing information into windows allows you to switch between applications and files.

Windows Explorer Windows Explorer is a file window with the Folders list displayed. The folders list displays a hierarchical view of all the drives and folders on your drive; you can drag files and folders from one pane to the next to move or copy files.

Windows NT A version of the Windows operating system used on networks. This version provides maintenance features and features facilitating Internet connections that are easy to use..

wireless Wireless devices share information without using wires. For example, if both your notebook and desktop PCs have infrared ports, you can send information between them without using a cable to connect them.

wizard A wizard helps you perform a particular operation, such as creating a new document or setting up an Internet connection. A wizard minimizes an operation into a series of easy choices.

Word The Microsoft Word word processor program anchors the Microsoft Office suite. Word offers a number of templates and wizards to help you create documents, perform a mail merge, or create a table in the document table.

word processor In a word-processing program, you can create documents such as memos, reports, and chapters. Word processors offer tools for entering, editing, organizing, and formatting text.

wordwrap The wordwrap feature automates the process of creating new lines in a word processor. When you enter enough text to fill the current line, the word processor starts a new line.

WordPerfect WordPerfect is the word-processing program that's part of the Corel WordPerfect Suite. WordPerfect offers many of the same capabilities as Word. It may be the best choice for users who have used previous versions of WordPerfect, or have many documents created using older versions of WordPerfect.

worksheet A worksheet is the same thing as a spreadsheet. Excel calls each spreadsheet in a file a worksheet, for example.

workstation A workstation is an individual computer (desktop or notebook) connected to a LAN. A workstation also may refer to an extremely powerful PC running software like CAD or UNIX.

World Wide Web (WWW) The World Wide Web is a network of Web server computers that store, organize, and deliver Web pages to users.

write-protect When you write-protect a disk (usually a 3 ½-inch floppy disk), you move a tab on the disk to prevent the drive from writing any new information to the disk.

WYSIWYG This acronym (pronounced *wissywig*) stands for "What You See Is What You Get." It applies to any display enhancements that ensure that the information displayed on the screen for a file exactly matches its printed output.

Y - Z

Zip drive A Zip drive is a type of removable disk drive that you can add to a PC. Each Zip disk holds much more information than a floppy drive. Iomega makes the Zip.

zoom To change a document's size on the screen. Zoom in (or increase the zoom percentage) to make the document look larger. Zoom out (or decrease the zoom percentage) to make the document look smaller.